Business Ethics After The Global Financial Crisis

T0298573

The global financial crisis (GFC) that began in 2007 concentrated attention on the morality of banking and financial activities. Just as mainstream businesses became increasingly defined by their financial performance, banks, it seemed, got themselves—and everyone else—into trouble through an over-emphasis on themselves as commercial enterprises that need pay little attention to traditional banking virtues or ethics. Although the GFC had many causes, criticism was legitimately levelled at banks over the ethics of mortgage creation, excessive securitisation, executive remuneration and high-pressure customer sales tactics, amongst other things. These criticisms mirror those that have been levelled at business more generally, particularly in the last decade, although the backdrop provided by the GFC is more dramatic and the outcomes of supposed wrongdoing more severe.

This book focuses on business ethics after the GFC, not on the crisis itself but how we should respond to it. The GFC has focused minds on the proper role of ethics in the understanding and conduct of business activity, but it is essential to look beyond the crisis to address the deeper challenges that it highlights.

The aim of this volume is to present examples of the latest philosophically informed thinking across a range of ethical issues that relate to business activity, using the banks and the GFC—the consequences of which continue to reverberate—as a point of departure. The book will be of great value to researchers, academics, practitioners and students interested in business, ethics in general, and business ethics in particular.

Christopher Cowton is Professor of Financial Ethics and former Dean at Huddersfield Business School, University of Huddersfield, UK.

James Dempsey was, from 2012 to 2015, Research Fellow on the UK Arts and Humanities Research Council major project FinCris on moral responsibilities in the financial crisis. He started his own business in 2016, which he endeavours to run ethically.

Tom Sorell is Professor of Politics and Philosophy at the University of Warwick, UK, where he leads the Interdisciplinary Ethics Research Group. He led the UK Arts and Humanities Research Council major project FinCris on responsibilities in the financial crisis (2013–2016).

Routledge Studies in Business Ethics

Originating from both normative and descriptive philosophical backgrounds, business ethics implicitly regulates areas of behaviour which influence decision making, judgment, behaviour and objectives of the leadership and employees of an organization. This series seeks to analyse current and leading edge issues in business ethics, and the titles within it examine and reflect on the philosophy of business, corporations and organizations pertaining to all aspects of business conduct. They are relevant to the conduct of both individuals and organizations as a whole.

Based in academic theory but relevant to current organizational policy, the series welcomes contributions addressing topics including: ethical strategy; sustainable policies and practices; finance and accountability; CSR; employee relations and workers' rights; law and regulation; economic and taxation systems.

For more information about this series please visit: www.routledge.com

Business Ethics After The Global Financial Crisis

Lessons From The Crash

Edited by Christopher Cowton, James Dempsey, and Tom Sorell

Routledge
Taylor & Francis Group

LONDON AND NEW YORK

First published 2019 by Routledge

2 Park Square, Milton Park, Abingdon, Oxon, OX14 4RN
605 Third Avenue, New York, NY 10017

Routledge is an imprint of the Taylor & Francis Group, an informa business

First issued in paperback 2020

Library of Congress Cataloging-in-Publication Data
A catalog record for this book has been requested

ISBN: 978-1-138-33050-4 (hbk)
ISBN: 978-0-367-78688-5 (pbk)

Typeset in Sabon
by Apex CoVantage, LLC

Contents

Contributors

Alexander Andersson is a PhD candidate in the Department of Philosophy, Linguistics and Theory of Science at the University of Gothenburg, Sweden.

Christopher Cowton is Professor of Financial Ethics and former Dean at Huddersfield Business School, University of Huddersfield, UK.

Boudewijn de Bruin is Professor of Financial Ethics in the Faculty of Philosophy at the University of Groningen, The Netherlands.

James Dempsey was, from 2012 to 2015, Research Fellow on the UK Arts and Humanities Research Council major project FinCris on moral responsibilities in the financial crisis. He started his own business in 2016, which he endeavours to run ethically.

Thomas Donaldson is Mark O. Winkelman Professor of Legal Studies & Business Ethics at the Wharton School of the University of Pennsylvania, Philadelphia, United States.

Ronald Duska, now deceased, was former Charles Lamont Post Chair of Ethics at The American College as well as an emeritus professor of Rosemont College, United States.

Richard Endörfer is a PhD candidate in the Department of Philosophy, Linguistics and Theory of Science at the University of Gothenburg, Sweden.

Ignacio Ferrero is Professor of Business Ethics and Dean of the School of Economics and Business at the University of Navarra, Pamplona, Spain.

Christopher Megone is Professor of Inter-Disciplinary Applied Ethics at the University of Leeds, UK.

Tara Radin is Teaching Assistant Professor of Strategic Management & Public Policy at George Washington University, Washington, DC, United States.

Joakim Sandberg is Associate Professor, Wallenberg Academy Fellow and Director of the Financial Ethics Research Group in the Department of Philosophy, Linguistics and Theory of Science at the University of Gothenburg, Sweden.

Alejo José G. Sison is Professor of Business Ethics at the University of Navarra, Pamplona, Spain.

Tom Sorell is Professor of Politics and Philosophy at the University of Warwick, UK, where he leads the Interdisciplinary Ethics Research Group. He led the UK Arts and Humanities Research Council major project FinCris on responsibilities in the financial crisis (2013–2016).

Adrian Walsh is Professor of Philosophy at the University of New England, Armidale, Australia.

Acknowledgements

The editors would like to acknowledge the support of the UK Arts and Humanities Research Council, Award AH/J001252/1.

1 Introduction

Christopher Cowton, James Dempsey and Tom Sorell

The global financial crisis (GFC) that began in 2007 concentrated attention on the morality of banking and financial activities in general. Just as mainstream businesses became increasingly defined by their financial performance, so banks, it seemed, had got themselves—and everyone else—into trouble through an over-emphasis on themselves as commercial enterprises. Such financialisation meant that little attention was paid to traditional banking virtues or ethics.

The GFC is not the first banking crisis in history, and almost certainly it will not be the last, but its scale and geographic spread were such that not only did it provide a profound shock to the system itself and cause a great deal of economic and social pain, but it also prompted an outpouring of critical explanation and commentary (e.g., Cable, 2009; Davies, 2010; Mason, 2009; Tett, 2010). It is no surprise that opinions about causes, consequences and cures abound, but one of the themes that came through in the commentary was a lack of ethics in the financial system and its principal institutions. The GFC demonstrated that finance could not be considered an amoral, purely technical, feature of modern life. Although the pursuit of profit is, and will continue to be, important, ethical responsibility needs to be part of the picture, not that bank profitability—despite its apparent prioritisation—has been impressive over the past couple of decades anyway once the GFC is taken into account.

Greed tends to figure prominently in criticisms of banks and bankers (e.g., Mason, 2009; Tett, 2010; cf. de Bruin, 2015), but as this volume shows, the ethical shortcomings involved in the GFC and the appropriate solutions for the future are more complex than a focus on eradicating or curtailing greed would imply. Ethical analysis of causes and criticism lead naturally to attributions of blame (e.g., Davies, 2010), but to be clear, this is a book primarily on business ethics *after* the GFC, not on the financial crisis itself. The GFC has focused minds on the proper role of ethics in the understanding and conduct of banking and other business activity. Several contributors to this volume give their own brief accounts of the GFC and its causes, where this is important for appreciating their subsequent analysis, but we must look beyond the crisis and its causes if we are to avoid simply reacting to a special set of circumstances that will not be repeated and instead address the deeper, more general challenges that it highlights. Attributions of blame for past actions can help point towards future solutions, but they can also blind us to other possibilities. What is needed is an imaginative and well-thought-through response, or set of responses, acknowledging that the banking sector is dynamic and unpredictable. The chapters in this volume pursue that agenda.

The assessment of ethical criticisms and the development of reasoned responses is the remit of business ethics as a normative enterprise. Yet it can be argued that, at the time the GFC 'storm' struck, there did not exist a well-developed body of knowledge about the ethics of banking or of financial ethics. Moreover, although there have been some promising policy developments (as well as some dubious ones), the debate around the GFC seems to us to betray, in the main, a lack of sophisticated thinking. The modern practice of banking is a highly sophisticated endeavour, yet beyond its important technical features, much of the discussion *about*—rather than *in*—banking can be surprisingly jejune. The full range of possible thought about banking does not spring directly from its practices (successful or otherwise), which means that other conceptual resources have to be sought and brought to bear. Philosophy provides one such set of resources. However, although some encouraging progress has been made in recent years (e.g., de Bruin, 2015; Dempsey and Sorell, 2018, to pick examples connected to this volume), the complexity and importance of the issues involved mean that there is still plenty of scope for further high-quality, philosophically informed writing that responds to the GFC and charts appropriate responses that might be helpful to those who work for, or have an interest in, the banks. We hope this volume makes a significant contribution.

In case it is thought that philosophy is a strange place to look for guidance or inspiration, it should be remembered that many of the terms that have been conspicuous in the aftermath of the GFC have long philosophical pedigrees. Several are to be found in this book, along with other terms that are probably less familiar. Even when a term seems familiar, in the hands of our authors, they can be used with a precision or for a purpose that goes beyond the familiar, everyday usage, thus providing new and deeper insights. Blame, restitution, responsibility, accountability, desert, exploitation, professional culture and virtue are just some of the terms that are put to work in the following chapters.

The range of concepts utilised in this volume means that a rich variety of insights is provided. Further variety is evident in the international institutional environments mentioned, although such details are provided essentially for illustrative purposes, as the authors explain their arguments. And although they tend not to focus on just one, there is variety, too, in the levels of analysis with which the authors are concerned.

The next five chapters might be seen to place emphasis primarily on system-level concerns. In Chapter 2, Sison and Ferrero examine the damage done by excessive financialisation, which loses its way because of the motivation that drives its agents. The authors show how financialisation displays the characteristic features of a vice from the perspectives of Aristotelian and MacIntyrean ethics as well as Catholic Social Teaching (CST). This characterisation of the problematic nature of banking in the lead-up to the GFC adds to the traditional criticisms from similar sources, which Walsh terms the 'exploitation' tradition. In Chapter 3, he explains how developments in banking mean that attention needs to be paid to the harms that can be done to the economic system itself, not just to individuals. He therefore outlines a conceptual framework for understanding the relationship between financial incentives and moral concerns, distinguishing amongst different kinds of profit motivational sets. Donaldson picks up a similar theme in Chapter 4. Identifying three troublesome ethical patterns that emerged in the context of the GFC, he argues that 'savvy', responsible banks should pursue broad strategies that he terms 'Pelican Gambits', by which is meant strategies that help manage risk not only to the firm but also to the industry and society.

Of course, the soundness of the banking sector and the quality of its contribution to the economy and society are supposed to be ensured by regulation, but it often fails or disappoints, for example, because of unanticipated consequences or subsequent regulatory capture. Nevertheless it has an important role to play and greater attention should be paid to what good regulation looks like. In Chapter 5, responding to Cicero's assessment 'more law, less justice', Duska and Radin propose a four-pronged test that laws and regulations should pass. Some of the regulations passed since the GFC have ostensibly been in the interests of consumers, but as de Bruin and Endörfer argue in Chapter 6, new regulations have sometimes prevented consumers from buying complex products, the availability of which would enhance their choice and freedom. However, freedom has been known to be taken advantage of, and so the authors address the issue of how the desired increase in the understanding of a complex product might be brought about, considering the regulation of information, epistemic virtues and interlucent communication.

Subsequent chapters then explore issues more at the level of the organisation and of the individual, often in interconnected ways.

Drawing on Aristotelian virtue ethics, Megone argues in Chapter 7 that more is needed of individuals than simply conforming to local culture or following rules, and banks (and other businesses) need to aspire to provide a culture that enables employees to live an examined life. Professionalism, at its best, also helps develop such employees. In Chapter 8, Cowton explains that professionalism entails both competence and ethics, both of which were in short supply in the GFC. He explores the potential for both banking and other professional bodies to engender a stronger sense of responsibility in the banking sector in the future and briefly examines the UK's Senior Managers Regime (SMR), which might either help or hinder such developments, depending on how it works in practice. With his particular interests, Dempsey sees considerable merit in the SMR. In Chapter 9 he offers a sophisticated account of how individual liability or blame might be derived via an understanding of the way values are carried by culture. However, as seen in the GFC, leaders of banks (and other businesses) have often been reluctant to take responsibility for harms associated with their organisations; apologies, when they come, appear to be half-hearted. One theory—Susan Wolf's—suggests that there is a failure in cases like these to exercise a 'nameless virtue' related to generosity. In Chapter 10, Sorell argues that in the few cases in which bankers have displayed the nameless virtue, its operation has sometimes obscured a failure to satisfy the requirements of justice. Sorell examines, in particular, the case of James Crosby who, like other senior bankers, was highly remunerated—an issue that has caused widespread criticism and resentment, given the damage wrought by the GFC. Some commentators have sought to characterise remuneration as a purely economic matter, but in Chapter 11 Andersson and Sandberg develop an argument regarding economic desert that explains and justifies the retention of moralising intuitions.

To conclude, the chapters in this book may be seen as attempts to explore and explain how ethics can be thought about and promoted in banking. We are not claiming that ethics is the only focus of attention that matters; regulation and competence, to mention just two, matter too—perhaps more so. However, good ethics 'on its own' would make a contribution to better banking. Moreover, all the other elements that might go towards providing a solution of how to do banking and business better than before the GFC are likely to be more effective with good ethics. For example, referring back to the two elements just mentioned, regulation that has a sound ethical basis possesses greater legitimacy, and the possession of competence can be seen as an ethical obligation.

We don't claim that this volume covers all the ethical issues and possible solutions (how could it?), but as it focuses more on the business ethics of banks than on more technical ethical issues with, say, particular financial products or practices, it should be of interest in connection with other businesses too. We offer this collection in the hope that it provides a set of useful perspectives that will stimulate better thinking (and hence practice) about banking and business ethics after the GFC. Each chapter can stand alone as a valuable contribution in its own right, but we believe that the volume is more than the sum of its parts. A few of the stimulating and productive links between the chapters have already been alluded to in the brief synopses of the chapters above, but we confidently hope that many more will become apparent as the reader reads on.

References

Cable, V. (2009). *The storm: The world economic crisis and what it means*. London: Atlantic Books.

Davies, H. (2010). *The financial crisis: Who is to blame?* London: Polity.

de Bruin, B. (2015). *Ethics and the global financial crisis: Why incompetence is worse than greed*. Cambridge: Cambridge University Press.

Dempsey, J., & Sorell, T. (Eds.). (2018). Moral responsibility and the financial crisis. *Midwest Studies in Philosophy, 42*(1).

Mason, P. (2009). *Meltdown: The end of the age of greed*. London: Verso.

Tett, G. (2010). *Fool's gold: How unrestrained greed corrupted a dream, shattered global markets and unleashed catastrophe*. London: Abacus.

2 Is Financialisation a Vice? Perspectives From Virtue Ethics and Catholic Social Teaching

Alejo José G. Sison and Ignacio Ferrero

Introduction: Financialisation and Its Enabling Conditions

Perhaps the simplest definition of 'financialisation' can be found in a Catholic Social Teaching (CST) document, which describes it as 'the shift in the capitalist economy from production to finance' (Pontifical Council for Justice and Peace, 2012, p. 9). Certainly, this does not refer so much to abandoning production for finance as in the greater weight now given to finance instead of production. However, earlier, more technical definitions can be gleaned from Epstein (2002, p. 3), 'the increasing importance of financial markets, financial motives, financial institutions and financial elites in the operation of the economy and its governing institutions, both at the national and international levels'; Stockhammer (2004, p. 720), 'the increased activity of non-financial businesses on financial markets'; Krippner (2005, p. 174), 'a pattern of accumulation in which profits accrue primarily through financial channels rather than through trade and commodity production'; and Palley (2007, p. 2), 'a process whereby financial markets, financial institutions and financial elites gain greater influence over economic policy and economic outcomes'. We gather from this that financialisation takes place only within the context of capitalism and that it refers primarily to the gains of finance in terms of importance, influence, activity and profits relative to the other sectors of the economy, such as production.

Despite being closely linked, it is helpful to distinguish the 'enabling conditions' from financialisation itself. The former are circumstances without which the latter would not occur; they are necessary, although insufficient by themselves to bring about financialisation as we understand it. To a large extent, the enabling conditions are identical to those of contemporary globalisation, such as the end of the ideological 'cold war' signalling the triumph of liberal democracy and capitalism over socialism and communism; the ascendancy of the Washington Consensus (the US government, the World Bank and the International Monetary Fund [IMF]) with its policies of deregulation, liberalisation and privatisation;

and last but not least, the development of 'net-technologies' in transport, communication and information whose utility increases almost exponentially with the addition of every unique user. (The internet is the best example: how useful is the internet if there is only one user? 0. If there are two people with access, we could represent its utility with the cardinal number 2. If we add a third user, its utility would be 6. For a fourth user, it would be 12, etc.) In finance, particularly, the combination of these factors made new entities (venture capital, private equity firms and hedge funds), regulatory institutions, products and services possible, significantly altering the nature of sectorial transactions.

Several indicators have been suggested to measure the degree of financialisation in an economy in accordance with the previous definitions. Stockhammer (2004) makes use of the 'rentier's income' (interests and dividends) of non-financial firms, and Krippner (2005), the portfolio income of non-financial firms and a comparison of their profits with those of financial firms. Freeman (2010) examines the financial sector's share of profits in the financial sector (financial intermediation, real estate, and renting and business activities), its ratio with respect to the wages and salaries of private-sector workers, and the proportion of financial assets divided by gross domestic product (GDP). In a study on the Organisation for Economic Co-operation and Development (OECD), Assa (2012) proposes two indicators: the value added in finance as a percentage of total value added and employment in finance as a percentage of total employment. However, probably the most widely used measure is that of Kedrosky and Stangler (2011), consisting of the size of the financial sector as a percentage of GDP.

The rest of the chapter continues as follows. After this brief introduction in which we cite several definitions of financialisation and identify its enabling conditions linked to those of globalisation, we proceed with our own characterisation in the next section. Our claim is that financialisation refers to a single class of activities, a 'continuum', which admits a full range of degrees with their corresponding impacts, both positive and negative, on the economy as a whole and on agents in particular. We distinguish between finance, the provision of resources for economic activities, and financialisation, when the financial sector increases its significance or weight in proportion to other sectors of the economy, mainly production. As a class of activities or continuum per se, financialisation is ethically neutral. However, there is a certain point past which financialisation turns into a vice. This is precisely the topic of the subsequent section, 'Where Did Financialisation Go Wrong? Responses From the Virtue Ethics Perspective'. We engage with this particular question making use of neo-Aristotelian and MacIntyrean virtue ethics frameworks. We explain the conditions in which what was initially an ethically neutral activity turns into an ethically (and, perhaps, also economically) deplorable one. An essential part of these conditions, however, cannot be determined by purely objective economic criteria as they require, above all, an ethical judgement of the activity and its circumstances. The final section concludes and suggests further avenues of research.

Financialisation: A Continuum in Its Range of Impacts

In theory, almost everyone agrees that financialisation can bring both advantages and disadvantages. Indeed, thanks to financialisation, a large segment of the population (including firms) has gained access to credit for production as well as consumption; new ways of leveraging capital have been invented, making it more productive; and risks have been spread more widely and thinly (or 'hedged') (Pontifical Council for Justice and Peace, 2012). Thanks to the ease in acquiring, processing and storing information, new financial intermediaries have lowered transaction costs for investing and provided greater liquidity to markets (Rajan, 2005), fostering growth, promoting entrepreneurship and favouring education (Zingales, 2015).

But in the wake of the Great Recession, the majority seems to believe that the harms of financialisation have far outweighed the benefits, particularly when private sector credit (Arcand et al., 2012; Cecchetti & Kharroubi, 2012; Schularick & Taylor, 2012; Zingales, 2015) or debt (Mian & Sufi, 2014) crosses the 'tipping point' of 80–100 per cent of GDP—the level at which the marginal effect of financial depth on output growth becomes negative (Arcand et al., 2012). It has been claimed that financialisation has resulted in tepid and slower economic growth for the European Union (EU) (Palley, 2007; Stockhammer, 2004), the OECD (Assa, 2012), and the global economy (Freeman, 2010). Purportedly, the financial system has become more fragile and volatile, as evidenced by the Asian Crisis; the dot-com bubble at the turn of the millennium; and more recently, the sub-prime mortgage meltdown in the United States that quickly spread to Europe and the rest of the world (Freeman, 2010; Palley, 2007). The twin spectres of debt deflation and prolonged recession now loom large (Palley, 2007). Disconnected from productivity growth, wages have stagnated and jobs have been lost in the West, causing greater income and wealth inequalities; further, most of the remaining employment is of poor quality (Freeman, 2010; Mishel et al., 2007). And to stabilise budgets after paying for expensive stimulus packages or bailouts, governments, traditionally the ultimate guarantors of social welfare, have found themselves obliged to cut drastically investments in public goods (Freeman, 2010).

We reject the widespread Manichean view of a 'good' versus a 'bad' financialisation, proposing instead an image of financialisation as a 'two-faced Janus', indicating a continuity in its range of effects and consequences. In place of two financialisations, one black and the other white, we suggest that we are confronted with a single entity, displaying the full range of shades of grey. We shall try to show this by making use of Nielsen's (2010) analysis of the four novel institutions representing what he calls—in a nod to Schumpeter—'high-leverage finance capitalism': high-leverage hedge funds, private equity-leveraged buyouts, sub-prime mortgage banking and high-leverage banking.

A practice dating back to the ancient Phoenicians and Greeks (Beaud, 2000; Ferguson, 2008), leveraging means borrowing more money than one's capital secures. Thanks to leverage, a family can buy a home while paying only 10 to 20 per cent of its price, and entrepreneurs can expand a business with only a similar fraction of its total costs, for instance. In Nielsen's (2010) account, each of the institutions representing high-leveraged capitalism have morphed from low to high leverage in a manner characteristic of financialisation, thus giving rise to all sorts of unwanted consequences. Although he mostly succeeds in indicating the major differences between the low- and high-leverage versions, nevertheless he is unable to say where the turning point lies for each particular institution.

Let's begin with high-leverage hedge funds. Initially, hedging comprises an investment strategy to reduce risk by dedicating part of the capital to a position opposite to the main investment. If a farmer were selling corn, for instance, he or she could agree to sell corn in the future at one price (main investment) upon planting, which would be relatively low, and at the same time invest in an option to sell at a higher price (hedge). Thus, he or she would be protected from selling corn at a lower price if, in the end, its actual market price after the harvest were to rise. High-leverage hedge funds, however, have been known to work with ratios higher than 1:50; that is, buying or selling $1 million worth of corn with only $20,000 of initial capital, to follow the previous example. Furthermore, high-leverage hedge funds have bought and sold these products (contracts on stocks, bonds, debt, etc.) without really getting involved in the investments. They borrowed enormous sums to invest, then invested in high-leverage debt products and hedged their own investments with even more highly leveraged insurance products—and all this without investors sufficiently understanding the risks they were taking. Everyone—sellers and buyers—was blinded by the higher potential returns offered by the leverage. Now, just at what leverage ratio should the high-leverage hedge funds have stopped?

As for the private equity firms, they originally involved long-term equity capital investments in new businesses, such as cutting-edge technology companies, for long-term (even beyond 15 years) returns (Nielsen, 2010). But now, private equity-leveraged buyout (PE-LBO) firms use highly leveraged debt and hardly any of their own money for an investment horizon of only two to five years. Moreover, a big chunk of this debt is used by the PE-LBO firm to pay itself immediately in cash dividends instead of investing it in business development. Typically, a company acquired by a PE-LBO firm is subjected to drastic restructuring and re-engineering, often accompanied by massive layoffs, before it is sold in pieces. That is why PE-LBOs are often accused of not really creating value but simply using borrowed money to raid a firm's coffers before chopping it up and selling it once more. But again, who is to decide how much debt and how much of one's own money should be used in buying a business and how long an investment horizon in a company should be? The same question arises for the proportion of debt to be used by the PE-LBO to pay itself, in cash dividends or any other form, as opposed to business development. Who is to determine this?

Consider sub-prime mortgages. Whereas in the early 1980s, clients had to give a down payment of 10 to 20 per cent of the value of the property to get a loan, in the run-up to 2008, a down payment of 5 per cent or less was sufficient for them to be able to borrow the rest. As an added sweetener, interest rates were often set below those of the market for an initial period of up to two years before they caught up to and even rose above prevailing rates. Everything went well as long as the value of the property kept rising as homeowners could sometimes get a second or even a third mortgage. Mortgage brokers did not care much about the buyers' ability to pay back as they already received huge fees and commissions for simply packaging and selling the loans (as structured investment vehicles and collateralised loan obligations), with the homes as collateral. In the end, if the market could bear—as it did—such percentages of down payments and interest rates on sub-prime mortgages, what was to stop firms offering them? Furthermore, although the business model and compensation scheme of the sub-prime mortgage brokers were detached from the quality of the loans, this wasn't illegal. Why should anybody else dictate the terms of the compensation package of the employees in one's own company?

Lastly, let's have a look at high-leverage banking. Traditionally, banks were meant to hold financial assets securely and grow them, offering depositors slightly higher than inflation interest rates while lending available funds at higher rates to individuals and firms for business development and consumption. High-leverage banks buy high-risk debts using a mix of their own capital, deposits and borrowed money. Next, they repackage these products and try to sell them on to other investors while charging hefty fees, commissions and bonuses. The contents of these high-risk debt products—regarded as off-balance-sheet items—were often very similar, with hardly any collateral to back them up. There was a lot of money to be made while the music played on. But once it stopped, streams of revenue dried up, loans could no longer be repaid, insurance companies discovered that they did not have sufficient collateral to make up for losses, and in consequence, the capital of banks was wiped out. Everything seems to be clear after the event. But while the party was going on, who could have determined what the right mix of deposits, loans and proprietary capital in making the investments was or the proper way of assembling the high-risk debt products and how long they should have been held on to? How were the banks to make money from the deals, whether from intermediation or from actually waiting for those loans to mature and be repaid? Furthermore, during all this time, they had the regulators' nod in keeping those investments off the balance sheets, so they weren't doing anything illegal.

As can be seen from these accounts, it is very difficult to tell when, if at all, substantive changes occurred in what the high-leverage financial institutions were doing, compared to the more traditional ways of conducting the banking business. The modifications that took place were, for the most part, in response to the evolving technological and regulatory environments, earlier referred to as the 'enabling conditions' of financialisation. To a considerable extent, the banks hardly had a choice, if they wanted to remain in business. When everyone else already communicates electronically, no company will last long if it insists on handwritten letters sent through the postal system. Something similar had occurred in banking. So when did financialisation, in itself an ethically neutral phenomenon, turn bad?

Only in retrospect do we realise that there were a lot of mis-steps, that limits were crossed, thereby triggering the crisis. But where exactly did those limits lie? Those established from the outside, coming in the form of laws and regulations, were clearly insufficient to prevent the collapse of the system. Perhaps, then, we would have to look somewhere else for the boundaries within which financialisation would be acceptable as a force for good. The transition point from an economically sustainable and ethically permissible financialisation to one that is neither cannot be determined on the basis of laws and regulations alone by a neutral, third-party observer, such as a utilitarian maximiser. As we shall soon see, one needs virtue, phronesis or practical wisdom to do this.

Where Did Financialisation Go Wrong? Responses From the Virtue Ethics Perspective

In the previous section we argued that instead of two financialisations, one good and another bad, there is, in truth, just one and the same process, which is morally neutral, albeit with a full range of degrees. We already know that this one and the same financialisation is a trend made possible by a host of technological and regulatory changes as enabling conditions. It's important to realise, however, that these conditions do not bring about financialisation by themselves. Human beings have to intervene to make the pertinent decisions and act on them. Instead of attributing the merits and faults of financialisation to these enabling conditions, therefore, it would be more appropriate to examine the human decisions that actually caused them to run astray. To do otherwise would be similar to blaming symptoms for the disease itself. This move brings us squarely into the realm of ethics.

From a forensic, utilitarian viewpoint, the evidence is apparently stacked against excessive financialisation, judging from the negative impacts of increased inequality, slower economic growth and greater unemployment (Assa, 2012). With the clarity that hindsight provides, one realises that these far outweigh the benefits, making society as a whole worse off. But how about from a virtue ethics perspective that focuses not so much on external outcomes or compliance with rules as on the internal results an activity produces in its agents? Granted that for virtue ethics, the reasons adduced by utilitarianism against financialisation aren't enough, what other motivations can it offer? How does financialisation fare in a virtue ethics analysis?

We think that past certain limits in the virtue ethics tradition, there is a degree of financialisation that could be characterised as a vice that affects both individuals and organisations. A vice is a morally harmful habit that arises from the repetition of flawed actions. An action may be considered ethically inappropriate on account of its object, the agent's intention, or the circumstances in which it is carried out (Arjoon, 2007). The object is what principally determines whether an action is good or evil. Certain actions are prohibited without exception because of their object. They are moral prohibitions for which 'we should [readily] suffer the most terrible consequences and accept death' (Aristotle, 1985, p. 1110a) rather than do them. Such 'intrinsically evil' actions simply should not be carried out. Where an action is *not* intrinsically evil, we have to consider the agent's intention. Intention indicates the end or purpose for which the agent carries out a deed, and the relevant circumstances correspond to external features or the non-psychological context of the action. Granted that financialisation admits of degrees, we believe it becomes morally problematic, not because of its object but because of the agent's intention and the circumstances or context of the action. The mere fact that finance-related activities represent a fairly high proportion of GDP is not in itself reprehensible. Financialisation becomes a vice when the actions that constitute this process are mainly motivated by greed, an excessive desire for wealth (intention), which leads the agent to ignore or underestimate looming dangers or risks (circumstances) in investments, throwing caution to the wind in a fit of unrealistic optimism. Closely related is the financial activity that consists of pure speculation or rent seeking often shielded from public scrutiny by a clubbish, plutocratic regime (Zingales, 2015). They both correspond to the abuse of 'non-natural chrematistics' according to Aristotelian categories and a 'corrupt practice' in MacIntyre's framework. Let us begin by explaining the first.

'Politics' in Aristotle refers primarily to a body of knowledge whose object is happiness (*eudaimonia*), the supreme human good and final end (Aristotle, 1985, p. 1094a–b). Bearing in mind that human nature is defined as that of a 'political animal' (Aristotle, 1990, p. 1253a), happiness is cast within the frame of a political community. For Aristotle, political communities—together with families and villages—are 'natural' societies in light of their end or purpose (1990, p. 1252b). Families may take care of the day-to-day needs and villages, those beyond the daily ones, but only political communities can provide all the means necessary for a full, flourishing life. That is why political communities are regarded as 'perfect' because they are 'self-sufficient' for the end that they seek, which is happiness (*eudaimonia*) (Aristotle, 1990, p. 1253a).

To achieve happiness, we need both material (external and bodily goods) and non-material (internal goods of the soul, excellences, or virtues) resources (Aristotle, 1990, p. 1324a). Material resources belong to the class of goods pursued not in themselves but for the sake of others; and their purpose is to allow us to perform virtuous actions and acquire the goods of the soul (Aristotle, 1990, p. 1323b). Each class of goods is the object of a different discipline. These are economy (*oikonomia*), related to external, bodily goods and ethics (*ethike*), related to internal goods of the soul or virtues, respectively.

Crucial to Aristotle's understanding of economy is the distinction between the art of wealth usage (economy proper) and the art of wealth acquisition or chrematistics (1990, p. 1253b). In both, he acknowledges the difference between a natural and a non-natural form. First let us refer to the art of acquiring and producing wealth or chrematistics. Natural chrematistics pertains to the provision of 'such things necessary to life, and useful for the community of the family or state, as can be stored' (Aristotle, 1990, p. 1256b); non-natural chrematistics is the supply of 'riches and property [which] have no limit' (Aristotle, 1990, p. 1267a). Natural chrematistics is premised on the knowledge that the kind and amount of property needed for a happy life has boundaries or limits. Beyond these, the accumulation of material things becomes more of a hindrance than a help. Non-natural chrematistics, on the other hand, presupposes that 'more is always better'; hence, it acknowledges no end in the quest to amass wealth and possessions. In Aristotle's primitive economy he provides the example of retail trade as 'non-natural chrematistics' because it allows one to multiply riches in the form of money or coins. He argues,

> coined money is a mere sham, a thing not natural, but conventional only, because, if users substitute another commodity for it, it is worthless, and because it is not useful as a means to any of the necessities of life, and, indeed, he who is rich in coin may often be in want of necessary food. But how can that be wealth of which a man may have great abundance and yet perish with hunger?
>
> (1990, p. 1257b)

Non-natural chrematistics develops when families grow and society becomes more complex, making the widespread use of money inevitable as a medium of exchange and a store of value: 'when the inhabitants of one country became more dependent on those of another, and they imported what they needed, and exported what they had too much of, money necessarily came into use' (Aristotle, 1990, p. 1257a). Together with these new activities comes the need to create larger organisations, first as extensions of the family and later on as 'economic friendships' (Aristotle, 1990, p. 1280b). These are the forerunners of our modern-day firms.

Insofar as business organisations participate in the production of goods and services for the benefit of society, they operate within the realm of chrematistics. In particular, firms are meant to help or complement families in providing the material resources they need but cannot by nature produce for themselves. Thus, business activity falls under the category of non-natural chrematistics as it goes beyond the production limits of families for their own consumption. In this sense, businesses are called upon to fulfil a very important, yet nonetheless subordinate, role in economy, which 'attends more to men than to the acquisition of inanimate things, and to human excellence more than to the excellence of property which we call wealth, and to the excellence of freemen more than to the excellence of slaves' (Aristotle, 1990, p. 1259b). For, as we have seen, according to Aristotle, the main purpose of economy is to facilitate the development of human excellence and the virtues by creating favourable material conditions. Only by the hand of the virtues will the material resources provided by economy help people attain their ultimate objective of happiness and full flourishing.

Let us now consider the second art of wealth usage or economy proper. Aristotle teaches that wealth usage is superior to chrematistics because the acquisition or production of wealth ought to be carried out only with a view to its use and enjoyment. Without resources, there would be nothing for the economy to administer. Hence, the importance of chrematistics, concerned with the production and provision of material means. Yet, chrematistics is only a secondary function for the economic manager, whose main duty is 'to order the things which nature supplies' (Aristotle, 1990, p. 1258a). Economy, therefore, deals more directly with the use of material resources and property than with their procurement and production. The latter activities Aristotle entrusts more to nature: 'the means of life must be provided beforehand by nature; for the business of nature is to furnish food to that which is born' (1990, p. 1258a).

Aristotle goes on to offer examples of natural and non-natural forms of wealth usage or economy proper. In the first case, he speaks of shoes: if worn, they are used properly, but if used for exchange, that is an improper use, 'for a shoe is not made to be an object of barter' (1990, p. 1257a). The proper use of material possession recognises limits within which it is honourable; whereas an improper use is void of limit and, as such, censurable. To illustrate the unnatural use of wealth, again within the bounds of a primitive economy, Aristotle turns to 'usury, which makes a gain out of money itself [. . .] For money was intended to be used in exchange, but not to increase at interest' (1990, p. 1258b).

It is important to realise that the difference between the natural and the non-natural in both the acquisition and the use of wealth depends on the interior dispositions of human beings, not on any characteristic of the material things themselves (Aristotle, 1990, pp. 1257b–1258a). Unbridled desires for wealth lead human beings to engage in non-natural forms of acquiring and using material possessions. Thus, their efforts to attain happiness become self-defeating. However, such failure is not the fault of the material things but of the individual's untutored desires or vices in their acquisition and use.

Financialisation beyond limits exemplifies the Aristotelian vice of non-natural chrematistics on several counts: firstly, because it refers to production (chrematistics) rather than use or enjoyment (economy proper) of material resources; secondly, because it produces its object—money—in a limitless or boundless way, as if the need for it were infinite, without regard or reference to the actual amount necessary for human flourishing (non-natural chrematistics). It is very difficult, almost impossible, for finance people to know what 'enough' means with respect to profits. If there is no such thing as 'enough', there is no limit or boundary. In other words, it has mistaken the true nature of money, which is that of a 'means' or 'instrument', a 'good sought for the sake of another', for that of an 'end', a 'good sought for itself' (Aristotle, 1985, p. 1096b). In some respect, what money was then is different from what money is now (plastic, bitcoin, etc.). But Aristotle's point is not so much on the form money takes but on its nature as a means or instrument for procuring other goods. In this regard, both securities and money are the same. Mistaking money as an end in itself is obviously a confusion, for what would we want money for, if there was nothing to buy with it? Therefore, it is rational to desire money only as a means and never as an end in itself. Implicit in this discussion is the question of the limit. Where is it found? Who determines it?

Objectively, the limit comes from flourishing (*eudaimonia*), the good that all human beings ultimately seek, which in turn depends on the use and enjoyment of a finite amount of material resources (economy proper) that first need to be produced or acquired (chrematistics). Yet it would be wrong to simply try to come up with a formula that yields an absolute, cardinal number in this calculation. As we have seen in the analysis of financial institutions, the evolution of enabling conditions provides a sliding scale, such that it would be impossible to identify this exact amount beforehand. We therefore need to complement our search with a subjective standard that comes not from outside the actors (economy) but from within them (ethics). In particular, we need the subjective standard of human excellence or the virtue of 'practical wisdom' (*phronesis*). The prudent person alone is able to tell the precise amount of material resources necessary in each situation for flourishing. That is because he alone has mastery or dominion over his wishes and desires, such that they are under rational control for purposes of production and consumption of external, material goods.

A couple of emendations have to be introduced to Aristotle's original teaching, nonetheless, to account for our far more developed and complex financial sector and market economy. Firstly, no longer is all interest on loans usurious, bearing in mind the foregone 'opportunity costs' of lenders for their financial resources. Interest would only be usurious if it far exceeded those opportunity costs, which furthermore can be determined only on a case-by-case basis. The reference to the simple lending of money as an example of the non-natural use of material goods, therefore, is no longer appropriate. Secondly, although all firms are engaged in 'non-natural chrematistics' or production because they go beyond the subsistence needs of a family, from the viewpoint of the political community, their activities could be considered 'natural' because they supply the needs of the political community as a whole. (In this case, an instance of non-natural chrematistics would be a dairy factory that produced more milk than its market required and actually received state subsidies to get rid of its surplus.) The pertinent limit here is not established by the needs of the family but those of the whole political community in its quest for happiness or flourishing. Insofar as the productive activity of firms recognises this limit, it could be considered 'natural' or 'virtuous'.

Financialisation could also be analysed through more updated MacIntyrean lenses by bringing to bear his ideas regarding 'goods of excellence' and 'goods of effectiveness', on the one hand, and 'practices' and 'institutions', on the other. 'Goods of excellence' correspond to what Aristotle calls 'goods choiceworthy in themselves' (1985, p. 1096b); these are goods internal to the agent, examples of which are happiness (*eudaimonia*), knowledge and the virtues. 'Goods of effectiveness', for their part, pertain to what Aristotle characterises as 'goods pursued for the sake of another' (1985, p. 1096b); these are goods external to the agent, of which money is paradigmatic. Goods of excellence are obtained from the exercise of what we could call an 'autotelic practice', an activity whose end or purpose is none other than its own fulfilment in the best possible way. Thus, we could think of loving relationships, seeking knowledge or making and listening to music, which come about from the exercise of virtues and skills; they are goods internal to a practice (MacIntyre, 1985). A practice is a social and cooperative human activity that produces internal goods in trying to achieve appropriate standards of excellence. Goods of effectiveness refer to external means, instruments or resources without which practices cannot be carried out sustainably. Without money, competitions, rewards and prizes, for instance, it would be very difficult to maintain and develop artists and musicians who make an invaluable contribution to the good of society. Institutions are concerned with the production of these external goods of effectiveness (MacIntyre, 1985).

In an ideal situation, therefore, adequate external goods of effectiveness will be produced by institutions to sustain and develop the higher-order internal goods of excellence that result from practices. But it can happen, and is often the case in business organisations or firms, that this order is subverted: external goods of effectiveness (e.g., profits) take precedence over internal goods of excellence (e.g., integral human development through the acquisition of skills and virtues in collaborative work), and institutions corrupt practices instead of supporting them (Moore, 2002). This describes precisely what occurs when financialisation loses its way; there is an inversion of means and ends. Financial institutions seek profit growth above all, independently of how such profits are made and these profits, in turn, are invested in purely speculative activities that create no real value. In consequence, financial practice and the internal goods of excellence it seeks are corrupted. Stable, long-term relationships with customers are replaced by largely anonymous communication and opportunistic deal-making. Prudent asset management and time-honoured professional skills (goods of excellence) are passed over for salesmanship and financial cunning (goods of effectiveness).

A healthy or virtuous financial system takes care of four major functions: it promotes household and corporate savings; it allocates these funds to their most productive use; it manages and distributes risks amongst agents; and it facilitates a reliable payment system (Greenwood & Scharfstein, 2012). Financialisation becomes a vice when the financial sector becomes inordinately bigger than the real economy motivated by an excessive desire for wealth; when resources, profits, power and influence accumulate in the financial sector to such an extent that there is little left for producing or manufacturing goods (food, machinery) and offering services (education, healthcare) that people really need. Instead of flowing out to serve of the rest of the economy, most of the financial resources are concentrated in activities which consist of pure speculation or rent seeking, resulting in harmful bubbles, spurious investments, speculative profits and massive job losses. This degree of financialisation does not promote savings but debt spending; it does not direct funds to other, more productive uses but only to its own speculative activities; it conceals risks and increases them, ultimately passing them on to unwary and gullible actors through different forms of 'duping' (Zingales, 2015); and it destroys confidence, thereby destabilising not only the system of payments but the whole economy also.

Lastly, in characterising the vice of financialisation, CST focuses on two features, namely, the 'commoditisation of business' and 'short-termism' (Pontifical Council for Justice and Peace, 2012, p. 9). Through commoditisation, the complex human social enterprise of business is reduced to the market value of its financial assets or resources. Workers are almost entirely neglected, if not equally 'commodified' in a manner offensive to their dignity. This lends support to the mistaken notion that the purpose of business lies exclusively in the relentless maximisation of value for shareholders instead of contributing to the common good of stakeholders and society as a whole (Sison & Fontrodona, 2012). Profits, regardless of how they are earned, become the only standard by which the value of a firm is measured.

'Short-termism' is closely related to this, inasmuch as it indicates a fixation on immediate success gauged solely by profits instead of strategic, long-term investments that are sometimes even more necessary for a prosperous economy and a thriving society. But huge, short-term profits in finance can be obtained only by assuming enormous risks, often beyond the limits that prudence dictates. Hence, a predominantly short-term mentality amongst financial managers makes them prey to taking more risks than they could truly bear. They easily fall in to the temptation of engaging in dubious and reckless behaviour just to achieve humungous gains quickly for their firm and, not the least, also for themselves. Greed, the upward spiral of desire for greater wealth, causes them to be blind to dangers and the chances of failure in their endeavours.

Together, 'commoditisation' and 'short-termism' constitute the core of Benedict XVI's warning:

> Without doubt, one of the greatest risks for businesses is that they are almost exclusively answerable to their investors, thereby limiting their social value [. . .] It is becoming increasingly rare for business enterprises to be in the hands of a stable director who feels responsible in the long-term, not just the short-term, for the life and results of the company.
>
> (Caritas in veritate, p. 40)

Conclusions and Further Research

The US Financial Crisis Inquiry Commission (FCIC) establishes amongst its conclusions that 'the crisis was the result of human action and inaction, not of Mother Nature or computer models gone haywire'; in other words, 'the fault lies not in the stars, but in us' (FCIC, 2011, p. xvii). It then proceeds to enumerate the different human failures that, put together, contributed to the near collapse of the financial sector and the economy as a whole: inadequate supervision by regulatory bodies; lapses of corporate governance and poor risk management by systemically important financial institutions; and overly complacent credit-rating agencies. These led to a toxic combination of excessive borrowing and overly risky investments shrouded, if not by fraud, by a cavalier lack of transparency.

Having said all this, the report goes on to state that 'to pin this crisis on mortal flaws like greed and hubris would be simplistic' (FCIC, 2011, pp. xxii–xxiii). But this seems to us to be incredibly strange: character flaws such as greed and hubris are precisely the factors that explain human actions that, in turn, brought about the resulting crisis. Without greed and hubris, there would be no vice of financialisation to speak of. At most, we would have only certain technological and regulatory conditions that facilitate the financialisation of the economy. More importantly, without such human inclinations and tendencies, it would be impossible to tell where financialisation goes wrong because, as we have seen, financialisation loses its way primarily because of the motivation that drives its agents, not the external, objective conditions in which it takes place. Unfortunately, there seems to be some self-select mechanism in play, such that individuals with marked exploitative and dishonest tendencies tend to congregate in jobs in the economic and financial sectors: immoral behaviour would be for them a simple error in calculating costs and benefits (Zingales, 2015).

A certain degree of financialisation can be characterised as a vice in Aristotelian terms as an instance of 'non-natural chrematistics'. This refers to the production or acquisition of means or instrumental goods—in particular, financial resources—for the mere sake of accumulating such means or instrumental goods themselves, without considering their end or purpose—human flourishing (*eudaimonia*)—which acts as an objective limit. The desire for financial resources, therefore, ought to be tempered subjectively by the virtues (*aretai*) of moderation and prudence or practical wisdom. These help the agent decide what amount of financial resources would be sufficient for his or her needs and circumstances, effectively balancing risks and possible gains.

From a MacIntyrean perspective, a certain degree of financialisation can also be described as the 'corruption of a practice'. That's because the 'internal goods' or 'goods of excellence' proper to the practice, such as prudent risk management, perseverance in hard work, a firm commitment to fiduciary duties, and stable, long-term client relationships, for instance, are all overshadowed by the 'external goods' or 'goods of effectiveness' consisting primarily of quick and enormous profits. This signifies a reversal of the proper order in which the 'external goods' or 'goods of effectiveness' sought by an institution should be placed at the service of the 'internal goods' or 'goods of excellence' generated by a practice.

CST likewise provides valuable insights to the understanding of the vice of financialisation through its allied mindsets of 'commoditisation' and 'short-termism'. Indeed, the vice of financialisation contributes to a reductionist view of business from a complex, human social enterprise or cooperative activity to a commodity valued exclusively through its market price. Shareholder wealth maximisation then becomes the sole purpose of business without regard for the good of other stakeholders such as workers, who become mere instruments to attain this goal. Because of the 'short-term' mentality, financial managers are pressured to assume exorbitant risks to achieve huge, immediate gains. They become blind in their judgement to anything else apart from profit and thus become unable to seek higher-order goods in the practice of their profession.

In closing, we believe that our analysis of a certain degree of financialisation as a vice through the lens of Aristotle, MacIntyre and CST will also be useful in understanding the issues surrounding executive compensation as another major factor that contributed to the Great Recession. But that, of course, will have to be the topic of a different chapter from this one.

References

Arcand, J. L., Berkes, E., & Panizza, U. (2012). *Too much finance?* (Working Paper WP/12/161). Washington, DC: International Monetary Fund. www.imf.org/external/pubs/ft/wp/2012/wp12161.pdf, accessed 25 January 2015.

Aristotle. (1985). *Nicomachean ethics* (T. Irwin, trans.). Indianapolis, IN: Hackett Publishing.

Aristotle. (1990). *The politics* (S. Everson, Ed.). Cambridge: Cambridge University Press.

Arjoon, S. (2007). Ethical decision-making: A case for the triple font theory. *Journal of Business Ethics*, 71(4), 395–410.

Assa, J. (2012). Financialization and its consequences: The OECD experience. *Finance Research*, 1(1), 35–39.

Beaud, M. (2000). *A history of capitalism: 1500–2000.* New York: Monthly Review Press.

Caritas in veritate. (2009). (Encyclical Letter of Benedict XVI.) Vatican City: Libreria Editrice Vaticana. http://w2.vatican.va/content/benedict-xvi/en/encyclicals/documents/hf_ben-xvi_enc_20051225_deus-caritas-est.html, accessed 15 January 2015.

Cecchetti, S. G., & Kharroubi, E. (2012). *Reassessing the impact of finance on growth* (BIS Working Paper 381). Basel: Bank for International Settlements. www.bis.org/publ/work381.pdf, accessed 17 January 2015.

Epstein, G. (2002). *Financialization, rentier interests, and central bank policy* (version June 2002). Amherst, MA: University of Massachusetts, Department of Economics and Political Economy Research Institute (PERI).

FCIC (Financial Crisis Inquiry Commission). (2011). *Final report of the National Commission on the causes of the financial and economic crisis in the United States.* www.gpo.gov/fdsys/pkg/GPO-FCIC/pdf/GPO-FCIC.pdf, accessed 27 January 2015.

Ferguson, N. (2008). *The ascent of money: A financial history of the world.* New York: The Penguin Press.

Freeman, R. (2010). It's financialization! *International Labor Review*, 149(2), 163–183.

Greenwood, R., & Scharfstein, D. (2012). How to make finance work. *Harvard Business Review*, March, 104–110.

Kedrosky, P., & Stangler, D. (2011). *Financialization and its entrepreneurial consequences.* Kauffman Foundation Research Series: Firm Formation and Economic Growth. www.kauffman.org/~/media/kauffman_org/research%20reports%20and%20covers/2011/03/financialization_report_32311.pdf, accessed 30 January 2015.

Krippner, G. (2005). The financialization of the American economy. *Socio-Economic Review*, *3*(2), 173–208.

MacIntyre, A. (1985). *After virtue* (2nd ed.). London: Duckworth.

Mian, A., & Sufi, A. (2014). *House of debt*. Chicago, IL: University of Chicago Press.

Mishel, L., Bernstein, J., & Allegreto, S. (2007). *The state of working America 2006/2007*. Ithaca, NY: Cornell University Press.

Moore, G. (2002). On the implications of the practice-institution distinction: MacIntyre and the application of modern virtue ethics to business. *Business Ethics Quarterly*, *12*(1), 19–32.

Nielsen, R. (2010). High-leverage finance capitalism, the economic crisis, structurally related ethics issues, and potential reforms. *Business Ethics Quarterly*, *20*(2), 299–330.

Palley, T. (2007). *Financialization: What it is and why it matters* (The Levy Economics Institute of Bard College, Working Paper 525). www.peri.umass.edu/fileadmin/pdf/working_papers/working_papers_151-200/WP153.pdf, accessed 17 January 2015.

Pontifical Council for Justice and Peace. (2012). *Vocation of the business leader: A reflection*. Rome/St. Paul, MN: Pontifical Council for Justice and Peace and John A. Ryan Institute for Catholic Social Thought of the Center for Catholic Studies at the University of St. Thomas, MN, USA.

Rajan, R. (2005). *Has financial development made the world riskier?* (NBER Working Paper 11728). www.nber.org/papers/w11728.pdf, accessed 7 November 2014.

Schularick, M., & Taylor, A. M. (2012). Credit booms gone bust: Monetary policy, leverage cycles, and financial crises, 1870–2008. *American Economic Review*, *102*(2), 1029–1061.

Sison, A. J. G., & Fontrodona, J. (2012). The common good of the firm in the Aristotelian-Thomistic tradition. *Business Ethics Quarterly*, *22*(2), 211–246.

Stockhammer, E. (2004). Financialization and the slowdown of accumulation. *Cambridge Journal of Economics*, *28*(5), 719–741.

Zingales, L. (2015). *Does finance benefit society?* (NBER Working Paper 20894). www.nber.org/papers/w20894, accessed 2 February 2015.

3 On the Morality of Banking, the Exploitation Tradition and the New Challenges of the Global Financial Crisis

Adrian Walsh

Introduction

The global financial crisis (GFC) of 2008 was a crisis of both governance and morality. The crisis demonstrated unequivocally the need within the financial sector not only for proper regulatory oversight by governments and statutory bodies but also the need for greater attention to the morality of banking (see Herzog, 2017, for an overview of the arguments as to why greater regulation is required). Of course, many of those working in finance have been explicitly opposed to the very idea of a morality of banking due in no small part to their commitments to the related ideas that finance is a 'morality-free zone' and that unfettered markets generate social benefits. In so doing they ignore a long tradition of philosophical thought undertaken by business ethicists and political philosophers on the morality of banking. However, there are genuine questions about how well that exploitation tradition, focused largely on the evils associated with exploitative and coercive financial loans undertaken by those in desperate circumstances, could have directed those in the modern finance sector to avoid the harms associated with the GFC. Much of the difficulty in 2008 and beyond arose from relatively recent financial practices in which debt is treated as a financial product and in which bad loans were sold off to third parties.

Moreover, the harms that arose in the aftermath of 2008 did not so much involve individuals being exploited or forced into debt bondage on which many public critics have focused as it involved threats to the financial system as a whole. Merely focusing on individual contracts is clearly not enough. I shall argue herein that the morality of banking needs to be *extended* beyond the *exploitation tradition* to encompass new practices in the banking sector, such as the resale of bad debts, and needs to focus on the collective nature of the harms caused by immoral financial practices. Whereas the concept of desperate exchange must remain an element of any proper morality of banking and finance, it cannot cover all that is required. Equally, the tradition of *moral rearmament* that solely focuses on inculcating moral attitudes is also inadequate, not merely because of its excessively optimistic view of the role of moral exhortation but also because of the failure to conceptualise adequately the relationship between morality and the profit motive. Herein, I develop what I take to be a plausible theoretical account of the relationship between profit seeking and morality that provides an overarching framework within which any moral claims about acceptable and unacceptable financial practices could and should be embedded. Let us now consider briefly the salient details of the crisis.

The Background to the GFC and Claims of Moral Deficit

The GFC occurred at a time in the Western world when free market views were in the ascendency. Two related ideas were of most significance here. The first was the idea that government regulation was unnecessary for the economy generally, and more specifically in the banking sector, because of the Invisible Hand that operates in markets in such a way that market agents will punish socially detrimental practices.[1] The second idea was the related claim that morality itself is not required on the part of individual market agents because individuals pursuing their own self-interest will always generate the best possible overall social outcomes. This is, in essence, the philosophical claim that Bernard de Mandeville (1957) develops in his notorious *Fable of the Bees*—captured by his pithy slogan that 'private vice generates public benefits'.[2] Influential policy-makers in countries such as the United States held these ideas with an almost religious fervour. However, that faith was misplaced. When one examines what transpired in 2008, and the role that unregulated greed played in almost bringing the financial system down, one can readily understand the despondency of the former chair of the Federal Reserve of the United States, Al Greenspan, at the clear evidence that individual greed did not always, and in every instance, give rise to the best overall economic outcomes and, further, that there might be cases where a morality of finance is required.[3]

Before exploring the moral and political significance of this in some detail, let us firstly consider very briefly what happened in 2008 in the United States and how those events represent a failure of both: (i) the regulatory regimes in place at the time and (ii) the moral 'compasses', as it were, of a great many of those working in the finance sector.[4] There were three pivotal events that led to the crisis. Firstly, the US government subsidised a massive credit expansion in the country's housing market largely through two government-sponsored enterprises (GSEs), Fannie Mae and Freddie Mac. As Baradaran (2015, pp. 20–21) notes, these entities purchased almost every mortgage in the United States at the time and then sold them on to investors. The loans enabled by the GSEs grew massively in the years prior to the crash: indeed, to highlight the point, their markets grew from \$367 billion in 1986 to \$4.46 trillion in 2007 (Dobos et al., 2011, p. 9). More significantly, a great number of the loans sponsored by these GSEs were issued to borrowers with few financial resources at their disposal and, as a result, had very low equity in their homes. Many also had poor credit histories.[5] These mortgages are the so-called sub-prime loans that were at the centre of the crisis, and there was a substantial growth in these in the years prior to the crash.[6] Such lending practices were highly irresponsible not only because of the poor credit histories of many of the mortgagees but also because the low levels of equity meant they were extremely vulnerable to any potential downturn in the housing market.[7] Secondly, the US Federal Reserve, to sustain what governments regarded as desirable economic growth, lowered interest rates, and this inevitably gave rise to a housing bubble that meant that many of those with sub-prime loans bought their houses when prices were exorbitantly high and well above what might be regarded as their true or real market value. Thirdly, to disguise the risk involved in the sub-prime sector, large numbers of the mortgages were bundled together, and these bundled mortgages were used to back securities known as collaterised debt obligations (CDOs); these were given the seal of approval by ratings agencies, ignoring the obvious risks (Graafland & Van de Ven, 2011).

When the downturn in the housing market inevitably came and mortgagees found themselves in negative equity, many forfeited on their loans. Subsequently when they forfeited, many of those who had bought the CDOs, despite their endorsement by the ratings agencies, discovered they were worthless. In September 2008 Lehman Brothers Holdings filed for bankruptcy, the largest bankruptcy ever filed in US history, and thereby caused a crisis right across the banking sector with a series of high-profile bankruptcies (Dobos, 2011, p. 10). As a consequence, the subsequent loss of trust in the banking sector led to an unwillingness right across the economy to lend that had further dire consequences for the economy (Herzog, 2017, p. 10). The crisis spread quickly to Europe, where long years of growth and economic stability had encouraged complacency. Consequently, many of the regulatory regimes in Europe were far less strict than they might and should have been. Significantly, the Basel Committee on Banking Supervision, which oversees the banking systems of the Group of Ten, failed to establish any mechanisms for ensuring that if an international bank failed, others would not follow (Dobos, 2011, p. 11). Indeed, at points in 2008 and 2009 it looked as if the banking sector and indeed the Western economy as a whole would collapse. The recession the crisis caused was global (Turner, 2016, p. 17).

It is worth noting at this point some more general changes to the banking sector in the years leading up to the GFC. In the first place, those years witnessed the growth of what some observers refer to as 'financialisation' (Beverungen et al., 2013). This involves, as Epstein (2005, p. 3) notes, 'the increasing role of financial motives, financial markets, financial actors and financial institutions in the operation of the domestic and international economies'. As a result, finance and financial thinking become more deeply integrated into our everyday thinking about social life (Beverungen et al., 2013, p. 16). Unsurprisingly, as part of this more general focus on finance and financial reasoning, debt itself became a financial product to be bought and sold. This is significant because it was the buying and selling of sub-prime loans that was at the heart of the GFC. This latter feature of the modern world of finance is one that the German social theorist Georg Simmel would have appreciated. Simmel, in his seminal work *The Philosophy of Money* written in the early 20th century (Simmel, 1990), argued that the abstractions involved with the world of money developed our capacity for abstract thinking.[8] For Simmel, the buying and selling of debt would have undoubtedly represented a force fostering such abstraction.

Secondly, the years prior to the GFC saw the emergence of a relatively new form of capitalism that involved highly leveraged risk taking (see Nielsen, 2010). During this period there was a remarkable increase in the tolerance of risk. Years of growth had led many to believe that financial markets were entirely immune to failure. Those years were also marked by the systematic *encouragement* of delinquency. The system of selling financial products that is part of financialisation and also the system of incentives to those in charge provide an incentive to delinquency or, at the very least, little reason to prevent it. An assumption of earlier systems had been that those lending and running banks had no incentives to encourage delinquency because it was not in their self-interest to do so, and this view fits nicely with the laissez-faire view that market agents left to their own devices will give rise to optimal social outcomes. As it transpired, those in charge of lending did have powerful incentives for encouraging debt and for not being concerned whatsoever with delinquency.

These events did not occur in a social and political vacuum. They reflected changes in attitudes to finance, markets and government regulation that had occurred right across the Western world over the previous 40 years. Since the 1970s there had been a remarkable deregulation of the economy, and this deregulation created a competitive environment that placed pressure in a real sense on financial institutions to make riskier decisions. The lack of regulative oversight freed bankers to take riskier decisions—the obvious case before us being sub-prime loans. Additionally, competition amongst lenders meant that those who were more cautious might well not be able to survive when competing with those who were willing to throw caution to the wind.

The changes in financial practice were also encouraged by the rise of neo-liberalism, which provided much of the intellectual justification for deregulation. Neo-liberalism, as the term is understood here, is essentially the view that state intervention in the economy should be kept to an absolute minimum because it simply interferes with the natural pro-clivities of human beings to produce, trade, and thus flourish.[9] Ideally, according to this line of reasoning, government would not be required at all because of the workings of the Invisible Hand operating in the market, which ensures human needs will be met through the actions of commercial agents. Adair Turner, the former head of the UK's Financial Services Authority, notes that during this period, finance academics and regulators had an overly optimistic view of the role of markets left to their own devices in the creation of beneficial outcomes. Turner writes that this reflected the assumption that

> free competition was bound to result in useful rather than harmful activity and that increased financial activity, by making more markets complete and efficient, must be improving capital allocation across the economy.
>
> (Turner, 2016, p. 28)

One also finds reluctance on the part of agents within the financial sector to admit the necessity of *other-regarding* moral motives. Sometimes this reluctance is justified by calling on the so-called Invisible Hand—if the pursuit of self-interest gives rise to social benefits, then why would we require financial actors to be morally motivated? However, often the reluctance to admit other-regarding motives as relevant is simply a consequence of the cutthroat world in which most financial actors are enculturated.

The GFC demonstrated the need for greater *regulative oversight* of the financial sector, not simply because of the many people who were harmed—including those who lost their livelihoods or savings and those who were defrauded into believing that they were buying genuinely valu-able stocks—but also because the system as a whole was threatened. This conclusion flies in the face of much of the free market message of neo-liberalism. If markets in financial services are left to their own devices, then they might seriously damage what Ann Pettifor (2016, p. 155) describes as the public good of banking. Free market solutions do not work: indeed, it is clear that such solutions nearly brought down the whole system. Unsur-prisingly, given the nature and extent of the crisis, in the years since the GFC, there has been considerable discussion in the literature of the kinds of regulative reform that is required. The remedies have included greater levels of transparency, restrictions upon leverage levels, and controls over the amounts of compensation to be derived from leverage.[10]

However, the possible regulative solutions and their respective merits will not be my concern herein; rather it will be with the moral failings of those who worked in the sector and, in particular, those involved in the packaging of sub-prime loans, which I take to be a significant causal factor in the GFC. These moral failings included amongst other things serious deception, a lack of transparency and a willingness to engage in excessively risky financial practices with little or no concern for the potential social consequences. It will be assumed that in addition to regulative oversight, there is a need in the finance sector for substantive moral commitments on the parts of those working in the sector. As Lisa Herzog (2017, p. 20) notes, although after the GFC the focus of reform has been on legal regulation, she doubts that this on its own is sufficient. She suggests that a change in ethos and culture of financial markets is also required. What is also clear is that finance itself has gone through a crisis of legitimacy, and this undermines its functionality. As Rosa M. Lastra and Alan H. Brener note: '[I]n order to exist and prosper, financial institutions and markets need to maintain their legitimacy in the eyes of those they affect' (Lastra & Brener, 2017, p. 39). They also remark that financial institutions and markets need to engage with the communities they affect to explain their rationale in creating wealth in the interests of society as a whole and not just the privileged few.

In summary, in addition to a commitment to more effective regulation, moral change is required if financial crises such as the GFC are to be avoided. The challenge will be to identify not only the sources of the moral deficit but also what the *solution* might be. How might we inculcate moral values into what is often regarded as the amoral world of finance? In the next two sections I shall consider two normative approaches that attempt to provide a moral account for dealing with finance. They provide theoretical frameworks for understanding the moral deficits of the GFC in terms of either the moral corruption of the financial system or of financiers.

The Exploitation Tradition

One common or garden response to the GFC, and to the damage to the world economic system that ensued, was that it was a result of the *exploitative nature* of financial practices. Here critics draw on a tradition according to which bankers in general engage in exploitative practices that involve taking advantage of those who borrow money because they find themselves in economic difficulty. When applied to the crisis of 2008, the claim is that financiers in the years leading up to the GFC exploited those who took out sub-prime loans and also those who bought the bundles of bad debts. According to this explanation of the crisis, banking is and always has been an exploitative practice that involves taking advantage of vulnerable people.[11]

This kind of analysis was common at the time of the crisis. Critics argued that greedy banks and other financial institutions always act deceptively and take advantage of borrowers' ignorance or need to exploit them. Typically, such critics assumed that there is something *intrinsically wrong* about the activity of banking. They regarded the failings of 2008 as symptomatic of the corruption of the banking system as a whole in all its manifestations. To avoid such undesirable outcomes, there is said to be a need either (i) to prohibit moneylending, or (ii) to place severe restrictions on the range of activities in which financial agents and institutions are permitted to engage. Although there are strong elements of truth in this critique—and governments should indeed act to prevent the exploitation of those in desperate circumstances—I suggest that such an analysis misidentifies both the harms and the causes of the harms that were *specific to* this crisis. This is because exploitation of those in need is *not the only* moral hazard associated with banking.[12]

The idea that banking (and indeed any related form of financial practice) is intrinsically wrong *because it is exploitative* draws on a number of long and highly influential historical traditions in political thought. (Notice that this tradition runs in a diametrically opposed direction to the neo-liberal dictum that all voluntary exchanges should make both parties better off.) One finds the claim being defended in the medieval critiques of so-called usury, according to which the lending of money at interest was thought to be sinful and hence should be outlawed (Walsh, 2004). Medieval thinkers identified a number of different normative reasons—some of which now appear incredibly fanciful—for rejecting the activities of moneylenders who were pejoratively referred to as 'usurers'. One commonly expressed objection to interest, which had its origins in the writings of Aristotle, was that it was unnatural. Money was thought to be barren and hence could not generate offspring. Moneylenders, however, 'make the barren breed' and in this way engage in an unnatural act.[13] In addition to these rather metaphysically strange objections, concerns were also raised about the potentially exploitative nature of the practice that the historian Odd Langholm (1998, p. 65) calls the 'argument from compulsion'. Many medieval critics believed that the usurer took advantage of the dire circumstances of those seeking funds. For instance, the medieval philosopher Gerald Odonis (c.1290–1348) claimed that the person who borrows from a moneylender is like the person who pays ransom money not to be killed.

This idea of the exploitative nature of moneylending was a theme taken up also by many 19th-century socialists. Although it is true that the usurer is not usually responsible for the circumstances in which the debtor finds him- or herself, the thought is that the banker or moneylender takes advantage of the borrower's desperation and establishes 'parasitic' relationships in which borrowers finds themselves caught in contractual relations out of which they cannot escape. It was argued by writers such as the French utopian Charles Fourier that bankers took advantage of those with little or no social resources. Fourier compares bankers to a 'swarm of birds of prey that ravages one by one the diverse regions where it comes to rest' (Beecher, 1986, p. 102). One might naturally include Marx in this group as well. However, his views on banking are slightly more complex. Marx believed that industrial capital would discipline the old usurious moneylending of pre-capitalist epochs, which Marx referred to as 'usury capital'. He would have no doubt been surprised by the persistence of practices involving compound interest, which charged fees beyond the ability to pay and which led to crises and foreclosures of property.[14] However, even here in his criticisms his focus is primarily on the counterproductive economic consequences of usury capitalism. To find typical views one needs to focus on utopian socialists such as Fourier.

In the 20th century many on the Left criticised the exploitative lending practices that occurred in the developing world by Western companies and development organisations. These financial arrangements often deepened the poverty of citizens in the developing world. Writers such as Susan George have focused on the effects, in human terms, in the developing world of servicing unreasonable and unmanageable debt. In *A Fate Worse Than Debt*, George (1988) argues that IMF policies of adjustment, which enable developing nations to repay their debts, simply increase the hunger and poverty of the poor (see also Wiarda, 1990). More recently, those interested in lending practices in the developing world have turned their attention to the phenomenon of microfinance, and many question whether such loans are exploitative, given the high rates of interest charged. As in all of the earlier discussions of exploitation and banking, the key determinant of the normative status of the loans revolves around the issue of whether or not they represent forms of desperate exchange.

How applicable is this exploitation analysis to the GFC? What role might concerns with desperate exchange play here? There are good reasons for holding that the exploitation tradition is, in fact, not particularly helpful with respect to the GFC, despite the ongoing political significance of the notion of desperate exchange, nor is it adequate if we wish to provide a *complete* analysis of the morality of banking as a whole. Firstly, the tradition fails to acknowledge that not all loans are zero-sum interactions. Both the debtor and the financial institution can benefit in cases where the loan is used for productive investment. To be sure, if the loan is purely undertaken for consumptive purposes and is used to cover basic survival needs, then presumably only the lender benefits in the long run.[15] But in cases in which the debtor uses the money for an investment that yields great profit, he or she might well make more money than the person or organisation that originally lent the money. Indeed, the exploitation tradition typically fails to acknowledge the productivity of borrowed capital. (Note that this is the kind of point that needs to be generally acknowledged by the public at large if the finance sector is to regain and maintain legitimacy.) Secondly—and this point follows directly from the first—not all loans are undertaken in desperate circumstances. Those wishing to take investment loans rarely do so because of straitened circumstances, and this was particularly true of those in the GFC who bought the bundles of bad debt. Thirdly, the tradition fails to acknowledge that banking itself is a public good. This is a theme Ann Pettifor (2016) explores in her book *The Production of Money*.[16] Finally, a focus on *exploitation alone* fails to capture the significant point that desperate exchange is not the only form of harm to which banking and financial speculation might give rise. The undertaking of risky, highly speculative loans might, if the loans are large enough or carried out by sufficient numbers of lenders, threaten the banking system and indeed the economic system as a whole and in so doing threaten the livelihoods of countless numbers of people. For these reasons a focus on desperate exchange cannot provide us with a complete analysis of the morality of banking.

Turning our attention to the GFC itself, it soon becomes apparent, in part because its targeted phenomena are not present, that the exploitation tradition does not provide the requisite explanatory insight. Firstly, one of the central causal factors of the 2008 crisis was the selling of bundles of debt. The exploitation tradition, however, is focused on more straightforward borrowing and lending between agents when the debtors are in desperate circumstances. Notice two salient features. Firstly, in the GFC the central cases involved the buying and selling of financial products, and furthermore, it is not the case that those who bought the debt were in desperate circumstances. Of course, deception is embedded in the bundles of debt themselves, but it is difficult to regard it as a form of exploitation, at least in the sense usually employed within the exploitation tradition. Secondly, despite the harm to individual debtors, the most significant and troubling harms in the GFC were to the banking system and subsequently to the economy itself. Further, the causes of those harms were the willingness on the part of financial agents to speculate and to undertake risky financial deals rather than there being a ready willingness to exploit the needy. Thus, in the case of the GFC, we need to focus on risk instead of exploitation.

The exploitation tradition, thus, fails to provide us with the relevant means of identifying the central morally salient features of the GFC. That said, it is important to remember that concerns with desperate exchange should always be a key element of the morality of banking in general because there are many situations in which the idea of desperate exchange accurately captures what is morally undesirable about many lending practices. Hence I am not rejecting the exploitation tradition *in toto*. To the contrary, instead I simply suggest that those insights about desperate exchange need to be incorporated into a broader moral framework that accepts that banking can be morally permissible because (i) not all loans are desperate, and (ii) there are many instances in which banking has beneficial social consequences.

What is required is a moral system that accepts the legitimacy and potential creativity of a great deal of lending and, furthermore, that profit can be a legitimate goal of agents. The desired account also needs to focus on the harms of financial products that involved the packaging of bad debts and the possible harm this might cause to the financial system (Herzog, 2017). Our primary concern in relation to the GFC is not with the exploitation of the vulnerable but the potential downfall of the system as a whole. Let us now consider a second approach to the morality of banking that accepts the legitimacy of banking practices.

Moral Rearmament

According to what I shall refer to (somewhat facetiously) as the 'moral rearmament' approach, failures such as the GFC reflect, or are caused by, the moral failings of both financial institutions and financial agents. It was common after 2008 to hear critics speak vehemently of the need for a revitalisation of the moral attitudes of all players in the financial sector (see, e.g., Gagnon & Chou, 2014). Here two main claims are made:

1. The harmful outcomes that arise in financial crises such as the GFC are entirely caused (or at least in large part caused) by the moral deficits of financial institutions and those who work in them;
2. To prevent such harmful outcomes we need to revivify the moral virtues and sense of moral responsibility of those who work in the financial sector.

There is considerable variety with regard to how vigorously these claims are pursued. Some writers defend stronger versions of the thesis than others. Some critics suggest that the moral deficit was merely *part* of the problem; whereas there are also those who lay the blame for the crisis almost entirely on the lack of ethics.[17] Equally, some argue that all that is required to change the moral cultures of the financial sector is a 'return to the core virtues', whereas others argue that such a change can occur only if it is supported by institutional changes that enable banks to put their values into practice.[18] Both camps are in agreement, however, that there is a desperate need for a renewed commitment on the part of those in the financial sector to adopt morally responsible business practice. The most compelling evidence in defence of this claim of moral deficit as a cause of the GFC is to be found in the morally dubious practices engaged in prior to the GFC including: (i) the deception and intentional lack of transparency in the bundling of bad debts; (ii) the willing pursuit of wildly risky financial transactions despite the potential cost to any individuals who might suffer if the transactions 'turn bad'; and (iii) the willing pursuit of those transactions despite the potential costs to the economic system as a whole.

Curiously, there are those who suggest that it was not so much a moral deficit that led to these behaviours but rather that the failure was one of ideological blindness or perhaps historical ignorance. On this approach the bankers involved in the GFC are far less morally complicit. If bankers believed that the rise in housing prices would necessarily continue into the indefinite future, then the recklessness might be regarded as a consequence of optimism rather than moral failings. As Graafland and Van de Ven (2011, p. 612) note: 'If it is indeed true that the brokers, like many economists, believed that there was no end to the steady increase in house prices, the sub-prime loans actually made good business sense'. There might be some truth in this, at least for a sizeable portion of those involved in the financial sector, but it is hard to believe that all were so willfully ignorant. Moreover, many of those involved in the packaging of debt were without doubt aware that they were selling bad products.

The proposed solution of this line of thinking is for there to be a moral 'rearmament' in the financial sector, for financial operatives to internalise the values embodied in their codes of ethics, and more significantly for them to take seriously their obligations towards the public at large. Could this work? Is this a plausible approach? Does the idea of a moral deficit provide us with genuine insight into the nature of the causes of the GFC? I shall argue that it does in part at least—so long as it is not treated as the whole of the morality of banking. There is a need for the financial sector to endorse and to adopt a morality of banking that acknowledges the long-term public dangers of financial risk when it goes wrong.

However, we must also grant potential pitfalls of this approach, at least as it is typically propounded. The first point that must be acknowledged is that moral rearmament cannot be, and must not be, regarded as a *stand-alone measure*. There remains a need for strong government regulation to provide oversight and ensure transparency and accountability in the sector. There is also a need for institutional reform that reinforces the ideals of responsible banking. Regulatory measures will not work without genuine uptake on the part of the financial sector—after all, prior to the crisis, these institutions had codes of ethics that warned against and indeed proscribed many of the practices that led to the GFC.

The second pitfall to avoid involves an issue regarding so-called desperate exchange, which was raised in the previous section. Those concerned with the morality of banking cannot ignore the problem of desperate exchange. Although much of the crisis was caused by a very cavalier attitude towards risk, it is also true that many of those debtors who took on sub-prime were in desperate circumstances. The circumstances that gave rise to the GFC are not the only kinds of circumstances with which the morality of banking should be concerned. There is always the threat of those in straitened circumstances agreeing to contracts that exploit them and place them in an even worse long-term financial situation. This is part of the permanent landscape of the morality of banking.

The third and final pitfall concerns the ways in which we conceptualise the relationship between profit and morality. We need to avoid characterisations of the relationship between morality and profit-seeking activity that frame the two as mutually exclusive. We should not employ moral discourses that frame the two as emanating from necessarily hostile camps, for doing so, in the context of the profit-oriented banking environments, ultimately leads to morality itself being treated dismissively. Our aim should instead be for those engaged in financial activity to regard moral considerations as significant elements in their all-things-considered judgements. To realise this aim, we need to reconceptualise what it means to act morally in a market context. The source of the conceptual problem here is the common tendency—to be found within folk morality and also within more philosophically sophisticated theoretical accounts of our social obligations—to regard profit seeking as antithetical to morality. The idea is that profit seeking is necessarily selfish and devoid of other-regarding content. This is the *avarice-only* conception of profit seeking, and it is mistaken because it ignores the real possibility of agents simultaneously having moral motives and financial ones.[19] To take a non-financial example, consider the case of a doctor who wishes to profit from the exercise of his or her medical skills. The mere fact that he or she does so does not mean the doctor is not concerned at all with patients or with the maintenance of a medical system that provides excellent services for the public at large. Indeed, it is simply not true that being concerned with financial gain means that one is concerned only with making a profit and that one's motives are entirely avaricious. Equally mistaken is the related claim that being motivated by moral ideals somehow rules out the possibility of pursuing self-interest—be it financial or otherwise—when acting morally. This is the *altruism-only* conception of moral action. Indeed, when assessing the moral status of the actions of others, it is all too common for critics to point to the presence of some form of self-interest and use that presence as grounds for denying the existence of any moral component whatsoever. However, the *mere presence* of self-interest in a course of action does not *necessarily* rule out the possibility that the agent or institution in question could also be motivated by other-regarding moral concerns. As the philosopher Antony Flew notes, '[N]o one [. . .] has any business simply to assume that the desire to make a (private) profit is always and necessarily selfish and discreditable' (Flew, 1976, p. 316). The previous example of the doctor motivated by a desire to heal patients would be a case in point. The mere fact that he or she also has financial motives does not negate the authenticity of the doctor's moral concerns for the patients. Oftentimes moralists have demanded far too much purity on the part of their ideal moral agents.

More needs to be said here. The conceptual mistake in both the avarice-only conception of the profit motive and the altruism-only conception of morality is the belief that financial self-interest and moral motivation are mutually exclusive, and hence, the mere presence of one necessarily rules out the possibility of the other.[20] This conceptual mistake is underpinned by a failure to recognise the fact that real-life agents regularly act upon multiple motives when deciding what it is that they should do. Their choices are regularly motivated by more than one single reason. Indeed, I would suggest that the presence of multiple and mixed motives is the norm rather than the exception, and this is just as true in the world of finance as it is anywhere else in the realm of human action. Furthermore, this conceptual mistake has real-world consequences for the morality of banking. If one regards morality and financial motives as essentially hostile, then one is forced to choose between the two. In the world of finance, where a priority is given to the pursuit of profit, any conceptual schema that treats morality as *necessarily* at odds with financial success will lead inexorably to a disregard for the demands of morality.

In summary, then, we need a moral system that accepts the legitimacy of pursuing profit yet, at the same time, provides guidance regarding how moral considerations might interact with those profit-seeking aims. It is unfortunate that some of those in the 'moral rearmament movement' are unrealistic in what they expect from business in terms of moral commitment, and indeed, such attempts at rearmament are likely to be counterproductive if morality is somehow framed as being antithetical to business. What is required then is a conceptual framework for our moral concern that recognises that morality and profit seeking are not always in conflict and attempts to distinguish between legitimate and illegitimate ways of pursuing profit. It is within this framework that moral claims about particular practices in finance should be assessed. In the final section I outline, in brief, such a system.

Focusing on Profit Motivational Sets

In the previous section I discussed ways in which a single action might be inspired simultaneously by a number of distinct motives. I also noted that concerns with financial gain are able to co-exist alongside other motives, including moral motives, within a single action. In this final section I defend the claim that it is misleading to talk of *the profit motive* as if actions directed towards profit always contain a single element, namely, the desire for profit. Instead it would be more productive to speak of *profit motivational sets*; these are sets of action in which the desire for financial gain is (often) one element amongst others of the motivational set that animates a single action or series of actions. Furthermore, we can distinguish amongst different kinds of profit motivational sets that vary depending on the role that different motivational elements play within the intentional set.

Let us begin by considering the different kinds of roles that moral concern for others and for desirable social goals can play within a person's motivational set. To bring greater precision to the analysis, it is helpful to begin with Robert Nozick's distinction between *goals* and *side constraints*. Nozick distinguishes between (i) the specific or primary goal of any action and (ii) those values or interests that might place limits or constraints on what we are prepared to do in pursuit of our goal (Nozick, 1975, pp. 28–33). If we conceive of moral aims using this formulation, then it follows that some moral concerns will be the primary goal of an action. Some will act as side constraints upon action, and in some cases they will not be present at all. Applying this Nozickian framework of side constraints and goals, it is possible to distinguish different ways in which commercial and philanthropic goals might be articulated in an agent's motivational set and, accordingly, give rise to distinct action types. Consider three distinct types of commercial activity, all of which involve profit seeking:

> *Lucrepathic Action*: here, seeking profit is the sole or dominant consideration in an agent's all-things-considered judgements.
>
> *Accumulative Action*: here, whilst the profit motive is a primary aim of action, its pursuit is moderated either by moral goals that have weight or by moral side constraints.
>
> *Stipendiary Action*: here, the profit motive is not a goal but rather functions as a side constraint on action directed by other non-commercial goals.[21]

What is morally objectionable—and I would suggest lies at the heart of much disquiet about the profit motive in the public's eye—is the first category, namely, the 'lucrepathic'. The general public is, on the whole, genuinely concerned with cases in which market agents place financial ends ahead of the morally significant needs of others or of the society as a whole. Moreover, if we reconsider the financial meltdown of 2008, it was the willingness of financial agents and institutions to pursue profit with little or no regard for the consequences of their actions for other people or for the economic system as a whole that gave rise to it.

Typically, we do not expect those working in the financial industry to be what are labelled stipendiary agents and to treat profit itself as a side constraint—indeed it would be highly unrealistic to require them to do so—but we do expect them to observe relevant moral side constraints. Hence, the standard that financial agents and organisations must not fall below is that of so-called accumulative action. The relevant side constraints in the case of finance concern injunctions against the morally dubious practices outlined in the previous section. Thus financial agents should recognise that their pursuit of profit should be constrained by injunctions against, for instance, pursuing highly risky investments or selling bad debts to unsuspecting investors.

This, then, is a model of profit seeking that explains how moral concerns and the desire for financial gain can co-exist. It is a model that does not imply that profit seeking always involves avarice, nor does it suggest that moral aims necessarily rule out self-interest. In reinforcing the need for financial agents to take seriously the demands of morality with respect to transparency, non-deceptive dealing, and the avoidance of excessive risk within a conceptual framework that clearly outlines the role of those concerns with commercial activity, one makes it less likely that the finance sector will treat those demands airily (Herzog, 2017). In highlighting the moral requirements, it is not the case that this model is unrealistic about the strong orientation of financial agents to make a profit. Here the moral concerns are simply part and parcel of the profit motivational set and, hence, cannot be dismissed as the other-worldly concerns of moral saints.

Observant readers will note that I have not specified the specific moral side constraints required within finance and within banking more generally. Instead of providing such content I have provided an account of how any such moral constraints should be integrated with the aims of commercial financial activity. Nonetheless, the discussion in the previous sections should indicate the kinds of moral constraints that I have in mind. For instance, with respect to the practices that led to the GFC, we should be concerned to ensure that in pursuing profit, financial agents do not engage in deception about the nature of the loans that they are selling, nor should they undertake excessive risks that would threaten the stability of the system as a whole. More generally, within banking it should also involve taking into account socio-political phenomena such as the desperate circumstances of some borrowers.

Conclusion

Numerous commentators have noted the direct challenge that the global financial crisis of 2008 presented for free market theorists who held that all markets (including financial markets) should be free from government regulation. The GFC clearly demonstrated the need in the financial sector for greater regulative supervision of finance and also for a deeper commitment to moral principles on the part of those working in the sector. What has been less commented upon is the intellectual challenges it provides to normative theorists who wish to realise such deeper commitment to moral theory. Although political theorists and business ethicists have long considered normative issues about banking, the GFC presented normative theorists with a new set of challenges. The first and most pressing of these is the advent of high-risk, highly leveraged loans that potentially threaten the system. Traditional normative theory has typically focused on the harm in terms of exploitation to individuals rather than risk to the economic system itself. The second challenge is a practical one and concerns how one might bring about a greater commitment on the part of financial agents and institutions to the good of the whole system.

Unfortunately, the moral traditions often employed to explain and provide solutions to what we might call the 'moral deficit of finance' fail to identify the nature of the problem and, accordingly, fail to provide adequate solutions. In developing what I take to be an adequate moral response to the problems raised by the GFC, I have made three distinct claims here. Firstly, I have argued that to respond to the moral deficit, we require a moral system that acknowledges the legitimacy and value of the financial system as a whole and thus accepts the moral legitimacy of financial incentives and yet, at the same time, acknowledges the political context. Secondly, I have argued that the key practices that led to the crisis did not involve loans in the straightforward ordinary sense of the term or at least as lending is ordinarily understood. The crisis was largely a consequence of processes of *financialisation* in which loans themselves were bought and sold. Thirdly, the most significant harms arising from the GFC were not straightforwardly to borrowers who were exploited or treated unfairly but rather involved the financial system as a whole.

In the final sections of the chapter I outlined a conceptual framework for understanding the relationship between financial incentives and moral concerns that I suggest is able to incorporate moral imperatives into business practices in a far more satisfactory manner. This account involves distinguishing amongst different kinds of profit motivational sets. Profit motives in the banking industry need to be constrained by both (i) other-regarding motives and (ii) an acknowledgement of the social context that leads many to agree to contractual agreements that they would refuse if they were not in straitened circumstances. The hope is that through the development and promulgation of a more sophisticated account of the relationship between commercial activity and the demands of morality, we might be better placed to ensure that those in the financial sector take the demands of morality seriously and subsequently make catastrophes such as the GFC of 2008 far less likely.

Notes

1. As Robert Nozick (1975, p. 19) notes, Invisible Hand explanations are explanations of institutional, or systemic, or collective outcomes, which 'explain what looks to be the product of someone's intentional design as not being brought about by anyone's intentions'. The term originates, of course, from the writings of Adam Smith. For an excellent analytic account of the idea of the Invisible Hand, see Ullmann-Margalit (1978).
2. For a comprehensive discussion of Mandeville's ideas, see Goldsmith (1985).
3. Greenspan, who had been an ardent advocate of the free market, admitted to a congressional committee in the US House of Representatives in late 2008 that he was distressed by the fact that the GFC exposed flaws in his economic philosophy. He conceded that his opposition to regulatory curbs on financial products was wrong. Most notably he acknowledged that he made a mistake in 'presuming that the self-interests of organizations, specifically banks and others, were such that they were best capable of protecting their own shareholders and their equity in the firms' (Clarke & Treanor, 2008).
4. For a very insightful historical overview of the events leading up to the GFC in the United States, see Baradaran (2015).

5. See Baradaran (2015, p. 149) for a discussion of the ways in which those with poor credit histories were encouraged by financial institutions to undertake loans.
6. In 1994 in the United States sub-prime mortgages counted for only 5% of the banking market with a total value of $36 million. Twelve years later, they made up 20% of the market with more than $600 billion worth being issued in that year (Dobos et al., 2011, p. 8).
7. This does not mean that we should regard those who took on sub-prime loans as entirely responsible for the crash. Baradaran spends a great deal of time demolishing the myth that it was government policy that forced banks to make bad loans to 'uncreditworthy borrowers' that caused the crisis. She notes that this simply feeds the 'narrative that the poor are irresponsible', while the banks are thereby relieved of any responsibility (Baradaran, 2015, p. 147).
8. Simmel regarded the shift to paper money, in which the monetary token no longer embodied the value it represented but was instead symbolic, as a significant element in the development of our powers of abstraction.
9. For a discussion of the connection between neo-liberalism and policies in the financial sector, see Dobos (2011).
10. These are briefly discussed in Nielsen (2010, p. 325). For a more detailed discussion of the regulative options, see Admanti and Hellwig (2013).
11. For a helpful review of philosophical discussions of how we should understand the meaning and nature of exploitation, see Herzog (2016).
12. For a useful discussion of the idea of moral hazard in finance, see Claassen (2015).
13. Other medieval critics argued that the usurer sells time, which properly belongs to God and, in this way, is selling something that does not belong to him or her. The idea was roughly that when one lends money at one point in time and then receives more money in return at a later point, then one is taking money for the difference in time and hence selling time.
14. See Hudson (2010), who notes that Marx expected capitalist economies to act in their long-term interest and in this way avoid 'over-exploitation, under-consumption and debt deflation' (p. 423).
15. It is worth noting that in the medieval period most loans were used to fund consumption, and hence, a great number of loans would have been undertaken in desperate circumstances.
16. Her question is how we can restore to our democracies the public good that is the modern banking system. Shiller (2012) makes similar points about the role finance has played in increasing general wellbeing and argues that after the pain of 2008, rather than being condemned, it needs to be reclaimed for the common good.
17. For a typical example of this approach, see Saha (2013).
18. See, for instance, Graafland and Van de Ven (2011), who argue that a renewed sense of responsibility on the part of financial agents can only occur if it is supported by relevant institutional changes.
19. For a discussion of the avarice-only version of profit and the altruism-only version of morality, see Lynch and Walsh (2003).
20. For a more detailed discussion of the relationship between the profit motive and morality, see Walsh and Lynch (2008, pp. 74–76).
21. For further discussion of this, see Walsh and Lynch (2008).

References

Admanti, A., & Hellwig, M. (2013). *The bankers' new clothes: What's wrong with banking and what to do about it*. Princeton, NJ: Princeton University Press.

Baradaran, M. (2015). *How the other half banks: Exclusion, exploitation and the threat to democracy*. Cambridge, MA: Harvard University Press.

Beecher, J. (1986). *Charles Fourier: The visionary and his world*. Berkeley, CA: University of California Press.

Beverungen, A., Dunne, S., & Hoedemaekers, C. (2013). The financialisation of business ethics. *Business Ethics: A European Review*, 22(1), 102–117.

Claassen, R. (2015). Financial crisis and the ethics of moral hazard. *Social Theory and Practice*, 41(3), 527–551.

Clarke, A., & Treanor, J. (2008). Greenspan-I was wrong about the economy. *Sort of the Guardian*, Friday 24th October. www.theguardian.com/business/2008/oct/24/economics-creditcrunch-federal-reserve-greenspan

de Mandeville, B. (1957). *The fable of the bees* (Vol. 1). Oxford: Clarendon Press.

Dobos, N. (2011). Neoliberalism: Is this the end? In N. Dobos, C. Barry, & T. Pogge (Eds.), *Global financial crisis: The ethical issues* (pp. 63–81). Basingstoke: Palgrave Macmillan.

Dobos, N., Barry, C., & Pogge, T. (2011). Introduction. In N. Dobos, C. Barry, & T. Pogge (Eds.), *Global financial crisis: The ethical issues* (pp. 1–23). Basingstoke: Palgrave Macmillan.

Epstein, G. A. (2005). Introduction: Financialization and the world economy. In G. A. Epstein (Ed.), *Financialization and the world economy* (pp. 3–16). Cheltenham: Edward Elgar.

Flew, A. (1976). The profit motive. *Ethics*, 86(4), 312–322.

Gagnon, J.-P., & Chou, M. (2014). Bringing the free market down to earth is a moral question. *The Conversation*, 1 October. https://theconversation.com/bringing-the-free-market-down-to-earth-is-a-moral-question-30727?sa=google&sq=2008+Financial+Crisis+moral&sr=3

George, S. (1988). *A fate worse than debt*. Harmondsworth: Penguin.

Goldsmith, M. M. (1985). *Private vices, public benefits: Bernard Mandeville's social and political thought*. Cambridge: Cambridge University Press.

Graafland, J., & Van de Ven, B. (2011). The credit crisis and the moral responsibility of professionals in finance. *Journal of Business Ethics*, 103(4), 605–619.

Herzog, L. (2016). Exploitation. In E. N. Zalta (Ed.), *Stanford encyclopedia of philosophy*. https://plato.stanford.edu/entries/exploitation/

Herzog, L. (2017). Introduction. In L. Herzog (Ed.), *Just financial markets? Finance in a just society* (pp. 1–38). Oxford: Oxford University Press.

Hudson, M. (2010). From Marx to Goldman Sachs: The fictions of fictitious capital and the financialization of industry. *Critique*, 38(3), 419–444.

Langholm, O. (1998). *The legacy of scholasticism: Antecedents of choice and power*. Cambridge: Cambridge University Press.

Lastra, R. M., & Brener, A. H. (2017). Justice, financial markets and human rights. In L. Herzog (Ed.), *Just financial markets? Finance in a just society* (pp. 39–55). Oxford: Oxford University Press.

Lynch, T., & Walsh, A. (2003). The Mandevillean conceit and the profit motive. *Philosophy*, 78(303), 43–62.

Nielsen, R. (2010). High-leverage finance capitalism, the economic crisis, structurally related ethics issues, and potential reforms. *Business Ethics Quarterly*, 20(2), 299–330.

Nozick, R. (1975). *Anarchy, state, and utopia*. New York: Basic Books.

Pettifor, A. (2016). *The production of money*. London: Verso.

Saha, M. (2013). The ethical dimensions of financial crisis in the world of globalized finance. *Munich Personal RePEc Archive*. https://mpra.ub.uni-muenchen.de/45565/

Shiller, R. J. (2012). *Finance and the good society*. Princeton, NJ: Princeton University Press.

Simmel, G. (1990). *The philosophy of money* (2nd enlarged ed.) (D. Frisby, Ed.). London: Routledge.

Turner, A. (2016). *Between debt and the devil: Money, credit and fixing global finance*. Princeton, NJ: Princeton University Press.

Ullmann-Margalit, E. (1978). Invisible hand explanations. *Synthese*, *39*(2), 263–292.

Walsh, A. (2004). The morality of the market and the medieval Schoolmen. *Politics, Philosophy and Economics*, *3*(2), 241–259.

Walsh, A., & Lynch, T. (2008). *The morality of money: An exploration in analytic philosophy*. London: Palgrave Macmillan.

Wiarda, H. J. (1990). The politics of Third World debt. *Political Science and Politics*, *23*(3), 411–418.

4 How Competition Harmed Banking

The Need for a Pelican Gambit

Thomas Donaldson

Introduction

The global financial crisis (GFC) and the Great Recession seemed to strike *ex nihilo*. The forecasting was feeble, and the warnings were few. Years later we can slowly apprehend the long length of the recession's shadow. Even as late as 2015, GDP levels were far below what pre-recession trends predicted. Lawrence Paul of John Hopkins University estimates that the aggregate GDP loss from the Great Recession for the Eurozone was 8.4% (Ball, 2014). Years of industrial growth were sacrificed.

In confronting the question of whether bad ethics played a significant role in igniting the GFC, we should move beyond the simple distinction between intentional and unintentional behaviour. Poor ethical behaviour may not fit the simple model of 'I knew I could cheat, and I did'. Negligence, omissions, incremental lapses of attention and the decay of corporate culture are less salient but equally important factors in fuelling ethical misbehaviour. With this in mind, three troublesome ethical patterns emerge in the context of the financial crisis: (i) the normalisation of questionable behaviour; (ii) tech-shock; and (iii) paying for peril (Donaldson, 2012a).

Heeding all three lessons requires managerial attention not only to factors of individual firm success, but to ones of industry patterns and finally, societal welfare. The GFC taught us three painful lessons: first, that individual firms must be alert to industry-level normalisation of questionable behaviour that might damage both firms and society; second, that firms must be alert to tech-shock consequences that damage both firms and society; and finally, that firms must align incentives to avoid pay-for-peril practices that damage both firms and society. Heeding these lessons is especially difficult. Business schools use models that make attending to issues of ethics difficult. The popular models fail at the most basic of levels; namely, they fail directly to reference societal welfare. Calculations of optimisation under conditions of scarcity, or strategic calculations of firm success, are powerful tools for managers to use in achieving efficient outcomes, both with respect to the uses of capital broadly and achieving firm financial goals. But these calculations are not designed to unravel situations in which social welfare issues such as the integrity of the global financial system are at stake. The solution is not simply better government policy and more regulation. As I will explain, the tools in use are feebler than most imagine.

Jim Walsh and I have argued that the roots of the problem of inadequate models can be traced back to a form of the composition fallacy, one committed en masse by most of us teaching in business schools (Donaldson & Walsh, 2015). We all concede that the purpose of business has something to do with the creation of 'value'. But current academic attitudes are bedevilled by a blurred double image of the concept value. The image of what counts as value for a single firm is laid atop an image of what counts as value for business in general. These two images cannot match. The conceptual error that results is a classic instance of the composition fallacy, that of presuming that what is characteristic of the parts is characteristic of the whole. Any theory of business (to be distinguished from any theory of the firm) must reference values that have objective authority for achieving social welfare. 'Business', properly understood, is a form of cooperation involving the production, exchange and distribution of goods and services for the purpose of achieving collective value (Donaldson & Walsh, 2015). The implications for firms are massive.

I will explain why savvy, responsible firms should change course by pursuing broad strategies that do three things: block industry-level 'normalisation', mitigate 'tech-shock' and avoid 'pay-for-peril'. These are 'Pelican Gambit' strategies that help manage risk to the firm, the industry and society (Donaldson & Schoemaker, 2013).

Three Ethical Roots of the Financial Crisis

Did bad ethics play a significant role in the GFC? Or was the crisis fuelled mainly by ignorance, innocence and exogenous forces? In hindsight we can spot indisputable ethical lapses. Careless homebuyers overreached their financial capacity to purchase expensive homes beyond their means. Mortgage companies rushed mortgage applications up the line for the loans to be tranched and collateralised. With sharply conflicting interests, rating agencies such as Standard & Poor's carelessly green-lighted dubious financial products.

But the darker, more serious allegations of bad ethics are harder to justify. Was Wall Street greed the simplest and truest explanation for the crisis? Did bankers knowingly sell misleading and effective financial products? Did they brazenly flout warnings of systemic risk that they knew threatened to tear down global financial markets? Here, snap conclusions are perilous. Consider the ubiquitous allegations of Wall Street greed. No doubt many Wall Street bankers are greedy, but so too are millions of business persons off Wall Street and so too, for that matter, are millions of ordinary citizens. No serious study has demonstrated that greed is higher in financial services than other industries, and the attempt to measure the level of ethics in different industries is notoriously difficult. In the studies undertaken, the financial services industry does not rank consistently lower than other industries, for example, real estate, retail clothing, advertising or petroleum. Greed no doubt rose to new heights in certain parts of the financial services industry in the run-up to the crisis, but measuring the extent to which it did is virtually impossible. We would do well to remind ourselves that greed is a common concomitant of human behaviour.

Whenever greed metastases to harmful behaviour we find self-interested opportunities and rationalisation existing side by side. This is where the more subtle and important part of the ethical story of the GFC begins. The ethical detective work here involves moving beyond the simple distinction between intentional and unintentional behaviour to discover more subtle patterns. As I have written elsewhere (Donaldson, 2012a), three troublesome ethical patterns emerge in the context of the financial crisis: (i) the normalisation of questionable behaviour, (ii) tech-shock and (iii) paying for peril.

Normalisation of Questionable Behaviour

Psychologists speak of the 'normalisation of danger', a phenomenon in which people become accustomed to a context fraught with danger and, in turn, interpret it as 'normal'. The 'new normal' becomes a standard, despite the continuing presence of threats. In business ethics a corollary phenomenon, the 'normalisation of questionable behaviour', marks the worst of corporate malfeasance. A glance at the most notorious of the so-called corporate Watergates of the last 50 years, that is, of Enron, of WorldCom, of LIBOR fraud and more recently of Volkswagen, shows the 'normalisation of questionable behaviour' phenomenon in abundance. Enron slowly accumulated toxic accounting practices; WorldCom incrementally and relentlessly pursued financial deceit; banks involved in the LIBOR scandal slowly adopted interlocking routines with other players in the industry; and Volkswagen fell slowly into a pattern of deceit so pernicious that after five years, its engineers took the fraud for granted.

Where, we might ask, were the bosses who should have stopped the sub-prime gambles that wrecked the financial markets? Some were blindsided themselves. They became numb to the 'normalised' questionable behaviour. The bad practices were institutionalised, and initial queasiness gave way to industry-wide acceptance. For any given firm to abandon the rewards promised by securitised, sub-prime mortgages could have placed it at a large, short-term disadvantage with competitors in the financial services industry. As Chuck Prince remarked, 'As long as the music is playing, you've got to get up and dance'. Such creeping accumulation of precedent is common. When, in the late 1990s, accounting firms discovered novel, legally suspicious tax shelters for clients, most of the big accounting firms eventually embraced them—at heavy long-term cost. And when in the early 1990s investment banks first confronted research showing that investment bank analysts tended to give higher ratings to client companies' stocks, they continued to reward analysts partly with an eye to client involvement—until the government finally blew the whistle. Industries often permit and finally accept a practice that enriches the short term only at the expense of the long term. The financial crisis offers a sobering lesson about the importance of vigilance against the normalisation of questionable behaviour.

Tech-Shock

Markets evolve, technology improves and the world transforms itself. The transformed world throws novel challenges at participants, but oddly, old habits persist. The results can be disastrous. Thomas Dunfee and I discussed the concrescence of norms and habits in economic communities under the heading of 'microsocial contracts' (Donaldson & Dunfee, 1999). Microsocial contracts are agreements, explicit and implicit, about norms of behaviour for economic participants. Examples of microsocial contracts include routines of corporate culture, rules governing informal auctions and agreed-upon ways of dealing with rogue industry practices. When a set of industry practices morphs significantly and confounds existing microsocial contracts, the results are unpredictable and often deadly. New microsocial contracts evolve slowly, and in the meantime people apply, often clumsily, broad, basic ethical principles (Donaldson, 2009). This pattern of obfuscation and slow evolution happens not only in economic contexts. Consider advances in medical technology. New medical technologies routinely spawn ethical confusion, and only later, after slow and painful adjustment, does society invent and apply practices that better fit the innovation. Consider the slow but steady introduction of medical technology that extended the duration of life. These technologies are simple in comparison to more complex, recent biotech innovations but followed a similar pattern of obfuscation. The invention of feeding tubes, respirators, oxygen therapy and antibiotics pushed medicine to corners of human experience previously unknown. For the first time, technology could extend a patient's life beyond the point of cognisance. This created dramatic ethical challenges for patients, families and doctors. In the beginning professionals reverted to basic ethical principles that for centuries had guided medicine: in particular, in the Hippocratic Oath, whose maxim is 'do no harm'. But the maxim, 'do no harm', proved impotent in the face of pressing questions about whether to unplug or maintain life-saving devices when the brain was dead and the body alive. It remained for the slow process of microsocial contract evolution to accommodate the challenges beget by medical technology. It remained for the evolution of ex-ante 'living wills', documents that specify more precisely what an individual wants at the end of life; for the institutionalisation of hospital ethics committees; and for new, agreed-upon definitions of 'death' that depended more on brain activity and less on physical respiration. Finally, it depended on systems of code designations for critically ill patients that allowed hospital staff to deal effectively with treatment options for the dying. Similar tech-shock has occurred regularly in the healthcare industry. Inventions such as in vitro fertilisation, cloning and stem cell therapies all provoked moral confusion at the outset but later submitted slowly to the evolution of new principles and practices. Using the language of Integrative Social Contracts Theory (ISCT) people confront technological disruption first with basic moral principles or 'hypernorms' but later manage the disruption by developing microsocial contracts.

The phenomenon of the securitisation of mortgage debt during the financial crisis clearly exhibits analogous tech-shock. To be sure, the novel and ingenious financial techniques used to create liquidity and distribute ownership of mortgage debt were not tangible pieces of physics or chemistry. But they constituted a new 'technology' nonetheless and were disruptive in ways comparable to disruption in the healthcare industry. Many of the creators of the highly leveraged synthetic derivative products found them so complex that they, themselves, were unable to price their products. Bundles of mortgages were sliced into different tranches, each of which carried a different level of creditworthiness. The bundled products proved notoriously hard to value, and this was true even prior to the time when markets for the products nearly vanished in 2008. There was little uniformity in pricing and often no true market price.

The final aftermath of tech-shock's rattling of the financial markets will be unknown for decades. But if the course of events follows a customary trajectory, the evolution of microsocial contracts in the banking industry will include not only explicit legal strictures such as Dodd-Frank regulations but also informal and semi-formal industry arrangements that regularise the creation, buying and selling of highly leveraged mortgage derivatives. One lesson of the GFC, then, is that industries need to be alert to the potential of tech-shock and to make sure that institutions are in place that can start the slow process of microsocial contracts construction.

Pay-for-Peril

'Paying for peril' refers to the practice of rewarding short and risking long. Bankers who make bets with their institutions' or clients' money confront both long- and short-term risks. These risks affect themselves and their respective firms. In the run-up to the GFC, banks rewarded short-term successes with annual bonuses that constituted significant percentages of bankers' annual compensation. But clever bankers can fake good performance in the short run. A 'Taleb distribution' offers high chance of a handsome gain in any period with a corresponding low chance of a massive loss. A Taleb pattern can easily tempt a manager to gamble on, say, a 10 per cent annual risk of disaster to reap a huge bonus in the current year. He or she is well aware that he or she is gambling with other people's money and that if the one-in-10 chance occurs, he or she may be sacked. But the odds are in his or her favour (10–1), and after all, it's not his or her money. If the gamble fails, he or she gets to keep whatever bonuses have accumulated to date—all in all, not a bad bet. If the one-in-10 chance occurs, however, then the firm and/or the client will suffer massively.

This ploy, repeated tens of thousands of times, contributed to the financial crisis. It is perhaps the most widely recognised and addressed ethical foible that contributed to the Great Recession. By 2018 it remained unclear whether government-sponsored initiatives, such as the Eurozone attempts at controlling bonuses and instituting claw-back regimes, will be effective. But even without government intervention, firms in the financial services industry have taken steps to limit pay-for-peril risk taking. As a general rule, industry-led responses have had higher success rates than government-imposed schemes when managing executive compensation. A lesson from the historical record of pay-for-peril practices is that industries' pay incentives should be aligned with the *long-term* objectives of the firm and of society, whether those incentive systems are government led or firm/industry led.

The Wrong Model of Business

The wrong model of business is part of the problem. As we saw when examining the three ethical roots of the GFC, three lessons emerge. Firstly, from our analysis of the normalisation of questionable behaviour, it became clear that firms and industries must be vigilant to avoid ethical normalisation. Secondly, from our analysis of the phenomenon of tech-shock, it became clear that that industries need to be alert to the potential of tech-shock with its ensuing ethical confusion and to ensure, in turn, that institutions are in place that are capable of instigating the slow process of microsocial contract evolution. Thirdly, and finally, from our analysis of the practice of pay-for-peril, it became clear that pay incentives within firms and industries must be aligned with long-term welfare both of the firm and of society, whether those incentive systems be government initiated or firm/industry initiated. These lessons should be heeded, but *can* they by today's bankers? The prospects appear dim, and here is the rub. Business schools teach models of firm decision-making that fail to acknowledge societal welfare directly. Calculations of optimisation under conditions of scarcity are powerful tools for financial managers to use in achieving efficient outcomes, both with respect to the uses of capital broadly and achieving firm financial goals. But such calculations are not designed to confront situations in which the very integrity of the global financial system is at stake.

In 2013 I spoke with the Department Chair of the Finance Department of one of the world's leading business schools. He mused about how often he had been asked why Wall Street bankers used financial models that relied on uncertain assumptions in the run-up to the GFC. His face darkened. 'I'll tell you why they used those models', he said. 'Because those are the models we taught!' His observation highlights a broader point: what business schools teach is what students practise. Hence, when analysing the causes of the GFC, we should attend to a disturbing fact: the models commonly taught in business schools struggle with social welfare objectives.

Professor James Walsh (of the University of Michigan) and I have asked both colleagues and students to fill in the blank of the following statement:

> Law is to justice, as medicine is to health, as business is to _____
> (Donaldson & Walsh, 2015)

The first reaction is one of embarrassed silence, followed by a ragtag collection of volunteered answers, including 'innovation', 'prosperity', 'profit' and 'global wealth'. What becomes clear quickly is that business academics have no settled answer to the question of the purpose of business. Interestingly enough, however, the same question when asked about the purpose of the business *firm* (in contrast to asking about 'business' in general) receives sophisticated and nearly unanimous answers. Those answers coalesce around economic models such as Agency Theory and Transaction Cost Economics that are deeply integrated with traditional microeconomic concepts such as optimisation and exchange (Jensen & Meckling, 1976; Williamson, 1985).

Professor Walsh and I have argued that the deeper problem can be traced to how those of us in schools of business commit a version of the composition fallacy en masse. Most theorists concede that the purpose of business involves the creation of 'value'. But current academic attitudes are bedevilled by a blurred double image of value. The image of what counts as value for a single firm is laid atop an image of what counts as value for business in general. These two images are out of step. The conceptual error that results is a classic composition fallacy, that of presuming that because something is characteristic of the parts, it is also characteristic of the whole. From the fact that Jim, Akin and Suja are each good researchers, we cannot deduce that the three together will make a good research team.

Disputes about the purpose of the business firm have raged since the 1970s and have included the question of whether that purpose includes societal welfare (Blair & Stout, 1999; Donaldson, 2012b; Donaldson & Preston, 1995; Freeman, 1984; Jensen, 2002; Jones & Felps, 2013a,

2013b; Jones & Wicks, 1999; Margolis & Walsh, 2003). Without question, the dominant model of the firm referenced and taught in schools of business today is the so-called economic model that derives from neoclassical economics (Gibbons, 2005, 2010), two of the most popular instances of which are Agency Theory (Jensen & Meckling, 1976) and Transaction Cost Economics (Williamson, 1985). These models are indirectly connected to welfare but only through the back door, for example, through notions of Pareto Optimality.

But whether talking about the dominant 'economic' model of the firm or even more progressive 'stakeholder' or 'citizenship' or 'CSR' or 'team production' models, the problem of the fallacy of composition remains. We cannot answer the question 'What is the purpose of business?' by simply extrapolating from a particular model of the individual firm. Economic models, for example, have focused on value returned to owners and have been helpful in advancing efficiency in the practical governance of firms. But it does not follow that one can interpret the purpose of business in society through simply the concept of efficiency or of value contribution to owners. Even the quickest reflection reveals a broader purpose for the firm: businesses exist in part to satisfy consumer wants and needs. And when questions arise about the behaviour of business in a context such as the GFC and systemic risk, management calculations must reference factors beyond simple financial returns for owners.

The current neoclassically inspired bundle of theories of the firm constitutes what Walsh and I have called 'a beleaguered strawman' (Donaldson & Walsh, 2015). This strawman has been battered by critics for decades (Davis, 2005; Ghoshal & Moran, 1995, 1996; Granovetter, 1985; Perrow, 1986) but persists for reasons of usefulness and parsimony. It stands beleaguered not for its own failings but for the outsized expectations foisted upon it. It was never designed to address questions of broad, intrinsic social values such as financial integrity and environmental sustainability. As Alfred North Whitehead once noted, 'The field of a special science is confined to one genus of facts, in the sense that no statements are made respecting facts which lie outside that genus' (Whitehead, 1929, p. 9).

As Professor Walsh and I have also argued, any theory of business—in contrast to any theory of the firm—must reference values that hold objective authority for society (Donaldson & Walsh, 2015). Taking a page from moral philosophy, those values may be identified as 'intrinsic' ones, that is, values that are non-derivative from other values (Zimmerman, 2010). The chain of reasons offered to justify human action must end somewhere, and that somewhere constitutes an 'intrinsic value'. My reason for going to the store may be to buy broccoli, but the action is open to a second-order query: 'Why do you want broccoli?' I may well respond to this by saying, 'Broccoli is good for health!' But then a third-order query can be made, 'Why do you want health?' Here the answers must stop. Here, the best answer is likely one that references an 'intrinsic' value, namely, health. A person may reasonably respond: 'I don't want to be healthy only for some *other* reason'; rather, 'I place intrinsic worth on health'.

A theory of business, in contrast to a theory of the firm, hence, should include the agglomeration of both intrinsic and non-intrinsic values. The working definition we have advanced for a reformed theory of business is: 'Business: a form of cooperation involving the production, exchange and distribution of goods and services for the purpose of achieving collective value'. Collective value, in turn, is defined in terms of the agglomeration of business participants' benefits, and those benefits, in turn, are defined as contributions made by business to the satisfaction of business participants' intrinsic values (Donaldson & Walsh, 2015). I cannot here lay out the entire argument on behalf of these definitions, but the relevant point is that business decision-making exists against the backdrop both of theories of the firm and of a broader theory of business that references intrinsic values. This is especially relevant when confronting systemic threats to the global economy or to the environment.

In this sense each firm has both a 'focal' and a 'contextual' purpose. The focal purpose is familiar to any business student; it can and does vary widely. It may be a very traditional purpose, for example, optimising return on investment for corporate shareholders. Or it may be a hybrid social purpose. We live in an age of experimentation with the corporate form, and a firm may be created as a 'social impact' firm or a so-called B-Corp (i.e., a 'benefit corporation'). The day-to-day thoughts of managers may properly be consumed almost entirely by the satisfaction of the goals specifically designed for their corporation, say, the maximisation of profit. But the relevance of a 'theory of business' is that managers can never entirely neglect the need for outcomes that are at least compatible with 'collective value'.

Consider a litmus test for whether a manager properly incorporates a theory of business along with his or her obligations to achieve firm-specific objectives. Imagine a young investment banker in the year 2005 constructing a leveraged derivative financial product for a Greek municipality. Suppose for the sake of argument our young investment banker is aware that systemic risks could roil the Euro banking zone with pernicious impact on both the Greeks and the Euro economy. Traditional economic theories of the firm provide little advice other than inside-out, backdoor prudence. To the extent that the bank's future reputation or finances might be affected, traditional theories counsel caution. But the deeper questions about intrinsic values at stake in the possibility of an economic thunderstorm striking Greece and Europe require reference to a broader theory of business—one that acknowledges the intrinsic worth of values put at risk by a massive recession, such as employment, health, self-respect, education and fairness.

Beyond Regulation and Beyond Individual Firm Control: Pelican Gambits

How then, can society be guided by intrinsic values to navigate the shoals of social and financial risk? The answer no doubt lies in a massive and multifaceted global transition, one involving altered approaches to firm management, improved governmental regulation, revised corporate governance structures, increased international cooperation and changed curricula in business education. I want for the present, however, to focus on a small but overlooked aspect of the bigger solution, one dealing with 'systemic risks' to society. Systemic risks arising from underlying interdependencies can create havoc at an industry level and are by definition too formidable for any single firm to manage (Donaldson & Schoemaker, 2013). In most instances they also exceed the reach and capacity of regulatory authority. They are industry-level (and sometimes even supra-industry-level) challenges that pose risks to firms, industries and society. Systemic issues, moreover, transcended national borders. Because of the social component of the risk, intrinsic values relevant to society such as stability, fairness and human dignity must play a role in guiding any solution to such systemic risks. The GFC itself is an example of such a systemic risk—badly managed.

Three Examples of Industry-Level, Systemic Risk Failure

An improved 'theory of business' such as the one described previously holds important clues for addressing systemic, industry-level challenges in banking. Before spelling them out it, let us illustrate specific examples of systemic risk outside the banking industry. Non-banking industries have struggled with and sometimes been upended by systemic, industry-level risk; in turn, their stories hold important lessons for financial services. Paul Shoemaker and I have examined three such industries: accounting, pharmaceuticals and petroleum. We found that these three industries were often victims of self-inflicted wounds stemming from failures to manage systemic risk (Donaldson & Schoemaker, 2013). Consider the accounting industry. Decades ago audit firms discovered that they could augment their auditing services to clients by offering consulting services. This transformation jolted the industry. It netted giant revenue streams for the accounting firms yet generated systemic risk because of inherent conflicts of interest existing between auditing and consulting. Because the risk was systemic, no single firm could control it while remaining competitive. The Enron era scandals and the attendant death of Arthur Andersen, one of the 'Big Five', represented the final explosion of these systemic risks, with painful consequences for both the industry and society. The US accounting industry shrank to the current 'Big Four'; CEOs and countless employees lost their jobs; and public trust was pummelled. Had the accounting industry recognised and dealt effectively with the systemic risks reflected in the consulting/auditing intersection, both it and society would have benefited.

The pharmaceutical industry confronted similar systemic challenges as it morphed its policies for testing and for disseminating new drug information. The ticking clock of patent protection and diminishing returns in new drug exploration tempted firms into lax testing and approval practices. These eventually became the industry norm. Selective reporting of data, erasure of inconvenient outlier results and the failure to communicate results from some studies constituted practices that eventually metastasised. Plaintiffs' attorneys, often working in parallel purpose to the FDA, savaged Weyth's Fen-Phen, Merck's Vioxx, and GlaxoSmith-Kline's Avandia and Paxil, amongst others. Billions of dollars of fines were eventually imposed, and billions more were paid to settle legal suits. Had the pharmaceutical industry been able to recognise and deal effectively with the systemic risk reflected by lax patterns of testing and data management, both it and society would have benefited.

Finally, the petroleum industry confronted systemic challenges in the opening decade of the 21st century relating to the evolution of new technology. New deep-water drilling techniques allowed oil companies to extract oil far beneath the ocean's surface, more than 26,000 feet (5 miles) underwater. Much of this technology could not be tested properly until *after* wells were drilled. Most people nowadays are fully familiar with the nightmare of the BP oil spill in the Gulf of Mexico. Millions around the world watched TV as crude oil gushed from the sea floor of the Gulf of Mexico. Yet although BP has become the poster child for tragedy in deep-water drilling, and the firm may (or may not) have been especially negligent in its management of the Macondo Well, it is worth remembering that all major petroleum companies, and not only BP, undertook significant risks as they applied a neophyte deep-water drilling technology to novel projects. This risk was systemic and industry wide. Had the petroleum industry been able to recognise and deal effectively with the systemic risk reflected in the unprecedented novelty of complex, deep-water drilling techniques, both it and society would have benefited.

The Need to Adapt Corporate Thinking to Industry-Level Risks

Our discussion about a 'new theory of business' can now be connected to the failed risk management instances in the industries of accounting, pharmaceuticals and petroleum. In each instance, as we saw, cooperative efforts within the industry, ones aimed at recognising and dealing with the systemic risks involved, might have avoided a tragedy. In each instance, single firms were powerless to address the risk. This was true in part because of competitive pressures that limited single firm control of industry practice.

Government regulators were also impotent. The failure of regulators to understand and successfully control events within an industry should not surprise us. Those inside an industry often know far more about shared practices and the creeping normalisation of bad practices than regulators on the outside. The emerging technology of deep-water drilling, much of it involving proprietary intellectual property, was known best to experts *within* the industry. After the Macondo deep-water disaster in the Gulf of Mexico, regulators were forced to play catch-up.

The solution to such industry-level, systemic risk, then, must lie in some form of industry-level cooperation. But existing theories of the firm and contemporary models of business strategy pay exclusive attention to competition, not cooperation. Agency Theory (Jensen & Meckling, 1976), Transaction Cost Economics (Williamson, 1985), Resource Dependency strategy (Barney, 1991), and the Five Forces model of strategy made famous by Michael Porter (Porter, 1985) all betray an eerie silence in response to the question of how and when a firm should cooperate in the face of systemic risks that threaten both industry and society. The absence of answers amounts to a practical edict: 'Compete to create competitive advantage; don't cooperate'. This is the edict that is implied in much of business school education. The silence of traditional business theories can be contrasted to the insistence of the new 'theory of business', advanced here, that interprets the success of the overall business system in terms of the optimisation of collective value and in which collective value is driven by the satisfaction of intrinsic values. From the standpoint of optimised collective value, then, any individual firm has both a 'focal' and a 'contextual' purpose. Its focal purpose is expressed in traditional terms, that is, efficiency, shareholder value and remaining in conformity with legal requirements. Its contextual purpose, however, obliges it to sometimes—in special circumstances—adjust its activities to at least be compatible with the pursuit of optimised collective value (Donaldson & Walsh, 2015, p. 18). Optimised collective value must be tethered to intrinsic values such as environmental integrity (e.g., the Gulf oil spill), health (pharmaceutical practices) and financial integrity (accounting conflicts of interest).

Key intrinsic values were obviously at risk in the GFC. Three of these were financial security, fairness and meaningful jobs. The GFC damaged financial security for most global citizens; it created unfair distributions of harms both for individual persons and nations; and it decimated meaningful employment around the world. Such intrinsic values, again, cannot play active roles in traditional theories of management and governance. They are missing terms. Nonetheless, these values must sometimes be heeded by firms and industries as they embrace a more complete conception of the purpose of 'business'.

Pelican Gambits

Insofar as banks and other financial institutions are obliged to attend to the values of financial security, fairness and meaningful employment in the broader financial system, they should ensure their own activities do not directly clash with the satisfaction of those values. As we saw earlier, this implies initiative at an industry level. Paul Shoemaker and I have labelled industry-level initiatives when undertaken by individual firms 'Pelican Gambits'. The term, 'Pelican Gambit', connotes a similarity between certain industry initiatives and a phenomenon biologists and zoologists call 'reciprocal altruism'. Pelicans, blackbirds, lions and many other species engage in 'reciprocal altruism' wherein individuals of these species appear to sacrifice in the short run only to succeed in the long run. A 'gambit' in chess, similarly, is a move that appears to sacrifice an advantage only to recoup a win later on. These acts of reciprocal altruism may be viewed as 'gambits' structured to serve the long-term protection of a certain strategic group or the survival of a species (Donaldson & Schoemaker, 2013, p. 30). Remarkably, even fiercely competitive male pelicans will sometimes share nesting material with a rival male (Anderson, 1991; Cook & Schreiber, 1974). In this way, the protection of the species' genetic legacy is enhanced. Industry leaders, in turn, might learn from the phenomenon of reciprocal altruism in the animal kingdom. Indeed, the satisfaction of values such as financial security, fairness and meaningful employment may well ultimately depend on industry cooperation to counter systemic issues that elude government and individual firm management. Paul Shoemaker and I define 'Pelican Gambits' as strategic, industry-level moves towards cooperation in highly competitive environments for the purpose of limiting risk to one's firm, the industry and society (Donaldson & Schoemaker, 2013, p. 24).

One successful Pelican Gambit may be found in the initiative launched decades ago by the Canadian chemical industry. Following a train derailment and tragic railcar explosion in 1979 that spread poisonous toluene and chlorine into the surrounding area, a few key leaders in the Canadian industry gathered together in an attempt to bring other members into an organised reaction to the crisis. By 1985 their efforts had led other Canadian companies into a collective project that was eventually labelled the Responsible Care Initiative. This initiative turned out to be prescient in foreshadowing the infamous Bhopal, India, Union Carbide disaster that happened only nine months later in which poisonous gas from the Union Carbide plant in Bhopal killed more than 12,000 people. The Responsible Care Initiative had not yet spread fully beyond Canada's borders at the time the Bhopal tragedy occurred, but the deaths galvanised cooperation in the chemical industry on a global level. Today the Responsible Care Initiative helps manage chemical operations risk in more than 52 countries and has been the recipient of numerous awards, including one from the United Nations (Belanger et al., 2009; King & Lenox, 2000).

The Responsible Care Initiative stands as an intriguing example that the financial services industry might emulate as it moves forward. It has had its own share of systemic issues. Although not on the scale of the GFC, the scandals from 2012 to 2016 involving the manipulation of LIBOR rates and also the abuse of foreign exchange transactions displayed industry-level characteristics that defied single-firm control (Donaldson, 2014). Moreover, in both instances government regulators seemed incapable of matching the sophistication of the insider knowledge of traders and banking executives. Future banking crises will no doubt share this industry-level feature.

Hence, one clear ethical lesson from the financial crisis is that collective action at an industry level often constitutes the only effective means to manage risk both to the industry and to society. In the fall of 2008 as the GFC was metastasising, U.S. Treasury Secretary Hank Paulson arranged an unprecedented meeting of the heads of major Wall Street firms at the Federal Reserve Building in Manhattan. His plea was for united action, a cooperative solution to address the Lehman Brothers meltdown and its implications: the slow unravelling of the global economy. At the meeting, he appealed to the members' sense of broader responsibility and especially their sense of duty to protect the financial stability of society. Paulson's plea arguably was too little, too late, but its underlying conception was precisely right. His conception appealed to a sense of responsibility that extended beyond traditional notions of strategic firm competition to reflect the critical intrinsic values that were at stake in the unfolding financial crisis. This attention to critical intrinsic values, then, is perhaps the most obvious ethical lesson of the GFC.

References

Anderson, J. G. T. (1991). Foraging behavior of the American white pelican (Pelecanus erythrorhyncos) in Western Nevada. *Colonial Waterbirds, 14*(2), 166–172.

Ball, L. M. (2014). *Long-term damage from the Great Recession in OECD Countries* (NBER Working Paper 20185). Cambridge, MA: National Bureau of Economic Research.

Barney, J. B. (1991). Firm resources and sustained competitive advantage. *Journal of Management, 17*(1), 99–120.

Belanger, J., Topalovic, P., & Krantzberg, G. (2009). *Responsible care: History and development.* Hamilton: McMaster University. http://msep.mcmaster.ca/epp/publications/RC_Final_IUPAC_2009-April-23.pdf

Blair, M., & Stout, L. (1999). A team production theory of corporate law. *Journal of Corporation Law, 24*(4), 751–806.

Cook, J. J., & Schreiber, R. W. (1974). *Wonders of the pelican world.* New York: Dodd, Mead & Co.

Davis, G. F. (2005). New directions in corporate governance. *Annual Review of Sociology, 31*(1), 143–162.

Donaldson, T. (2009). Compass and dead reckoning: The dynamic implications of ISCT. *Journal of Business Ethics, 88*(4), 659–664.

Donaldson, T. (2012a). Three ethical roots of the economic crisis. *Journal of Business Ethics, 106*(1), 5–8.

Donaldson, T. (2012b). The epistemic fault line in corporate governance. *Academy of Management Review, 37*(2), 256–271.

Donaldson, T. (2014). The deep Libor lesson. *Ethisphere Magazine.* https://insights.ethisphere.com/the-deep-libor-lesson/

Donaldson, T., & Dunfee, T. (1999). *Ties that bind: A social contracts approach to business ethics.* Boston, MA: Harvard Business School Press.

Donaldson, T., & Preston, L. E. (1995). The stakeholder theory of the corporation: Concepts, evidence, and implications. *Academy of Management Review, 20*(1), 65–91.

Donaldson, T., & Schoemaker, P. J. H. (2013). Self-inflicted industry wounds: Early warning signals and pelican gambits. *California Management Review, 55*(2), 24–45.

Donaldson, T., & Walsh, J. P. (2015). Toward a theory of business. *Research in Organizational Behavior, 35*, 181–207.

Freeman, R. E. (1984). *Strategic management: A stakeholder approach.* Boston, MA: Pitman.

Ghoshal, S., & Moran, P. (1995). Bad for practice: A critique of the transaction cost theory. *Academy of Management Annual Meeting Proceedings*, 12–16.

Ghoshal, S., & Moran, P. (1996). Bad for practice: A critique of the transaction cost theory. *Academy of Management Review, 21*(1), 13–47.

Gibbons, R. (2005). Four formal(izable) theories of the firm? *Journal of Economic Behavior & Organization, 58*(2), 200–245.

Gibbons, R. (2010). Transaction-cost economics: Past, present, and future? *Scandinavian Journal of Economics, 112*(2), 263–288.

Granovetter, M. (1985). Economic action and social structure: The problem of embeddedness. *American Journal of Sociology, 91*(3), 481–510.

Jensen, M. C. (2002). Value maximization, stakeholder theory, and the corporate objective function. *Business Ethics Quarterly, 12*(2), 235–247.

Jensen, M. C., & Meckling, W. H. (1976). Theory of the firm: Managerial behavior, agency costs and ownership structure. *Journal of Financial Economics, 3*(4), 305–360.

Jones, T. M., & Felps, W. (2013a). Shareholder wealth maximization and social welfare: A utilitarian critique. *Business Ethics Quarterly, 23*(2), 207–238.

Jones, T. M., & Felps, W. (2013b). Stakeholder happiness enhancement: A neo-utilitarian objective for the modern corporation. *Business Ethics Quarterly, 23*(3), 349–379.

Jones, T. M., & Wicks, A. C. (1999). Convergent stakeholder theory. *Academy of Management Review, 24*(2), 206–221.

King, A. A., & Lenox, M. J. (2000). Industry self-regulation without sanctions: The chemical industry's Responsible Care Program. *Academy of Management Journal, 43*(4), 698–716.

Margolis, J. D., & Walsh, J. P. (2003). Misery loves companies: Rethinking social initiatives by business. *Administrative Science Quarterly, 48*(2), 268–305.

Perrow, C. (1986). *Complex organizations: A critical essay* (3rd ed.). New York: Random House.

Porter, M. E. (1985). *Competitive advantage: Creating and sustaining superior performance.* New York: Free Press.

Whitehead, A. N. (1929). *Process and reality, an essay in cosmology.* Cambridge: Cambridge University Press.

Williamson, O. E. (1985). *The economic institutions of capitalism: Firms, markets, relational contracting.* New York: Free Press.

Zimmerman, M. J. (2010). Intrinsic vs. extrinsic value. In E. N. Zalta (Ed.), *Stanford encyclopedia of philosophy*, Winter 2010 Edition. http://plato.stanford.edu/entries/value-intrinsic-extrinsic/

5 Contemporary Laws and Regulation

An Argument for Less Law, More Justice

Ronald Duska[†] and Tara Radin

Introduction

When societal problems occur, too often the tendency is to reach for a regulatory response. Perhaps, nowhere is this more evident than with the global financial crisis (GFC). The response in the United States was the Dodd-Frank Wall Street Reform and Consumer Protection Act (Dodd-Frank), signed into federal law in 2010. Although such a solution might satisfy the political demand for an immediate response, it does not necessarily improve banking or business. In fact, critics argue that Dodd-Frank has ended up creating new problems.

Dodd-Frank was initially greeted by a fanfare of positive attention. In the years that have followed, though, it has met with considerable criticism; large portions have now been repealed and/or undone. It is widely recognised that the legislation is overly cumbersome and unnecessarily complicated such that any guidance offered was largely obscured. Such a law seems to serve anything but justice. It is instead unfortunately symptomatic of a larger, more general societal problem: an increase in legislation resulting in an almost certain decrease in justice.

This chapter examines the relationship between law and justice. According to Cicero, justice is the goal of laws. Simply put, laws do not exist for their own sake but for the goal of serving social justice. In other words, laws should promote justice within society. Justice relates both to how principles or policies or laws are designed and to how they are implemented. In other words, it has both procedural and substantive components. It translates into helping society operate more effectively and responsibly.

When discussing 'law', we will refer not only to laws but also to rules and regulations (such as those implementing laws and/or those passed by government agencies). This chapter argues for a critical reexamination of contemporary laws and their relationship to justice. As Cicero warns, 'more law, less justice'; too much law can obscure justice and, at the same time, overcomplicate and interfere with business. We argue that this is what is happening today; that is, increasing laws (often counterproductive

† Ronald Duska died on December 25, 2018.

laws) are decreasing justice. Although this theme is global, we rely on Dodd-Frank as an example. We propose a four-pronged test based on Aquinas's definition of law to determine if a law is just; Dodd-Frank fails. We therefore argue for our criteria to be applied to laws before they are passed to ensure that the laws that govern society promote justice. Such criteria should be applied not just to official laws but also to regulations, such as those passed to implement laws or those made by government bodies, including banking regulators. Regulations are not the same as laws, but they do act similarly and need to meet the same criteria in promoting justice.

We begin with a four-pronged test to determine if a law is just. We illustrate how Dodd-Frank fails that test. We then examine a further example from the financial services industry, the so-called Merrill Rule. We recommend that such criteria be used not simply by scholars but by legislators and regulators, ideally before laws are passed. If the goal is a just society, and a just society is governed by just laws, laws must be just.

Purpose of Law Versus Purposes of Laws

Before examining specific legislation, we reiterate the importance of determining the purpose of law. Cicero is often acknowledged as having established the purpose of law. Even the American founding fathers, such as John Adams and Thomas Jefferson, credited Cicero for being 'an unknowing architect of constitutions that still govern our lives' (Everitt, 2002, p. vii).

According to Cicero, laws promote justice by protecting the public good. According to Miller (2016), both justice and the public good (or common good) share similar basic requirements having to do with fundamental rights and freedoms. The public or common good refers to the common or shared good of society (what tends to benefit people in a particular community), taking into account fundamental rights and freedoms. This definition departs from the pure utilitarian view that the public good is linked to maximising utility, without regard to fundamental rights or freedoms; justice is how the public good is served. In addition, justice, according to Cicero, increases responsible liberty. He said that liberty is the ability of a person to choose how he or she lives. Clear laws (transparency) enable people to know the bounds of their freedom so that they can maximise freedom within those bounds. 'We are in bondage to the law', said Cicero, 'so that we might be free'.

Laws should exist to help promote justice and serve the public good by ensuring that individuals have access to what they deserve. If a law or rule does not meet the criterion of serving the public good, the law can be considered unjust. The mere presence of laws on the books does not ensure justice, however. The laws themselves must be just. Cicero asserted, 'The foundations of justice are that no one should suffer wrong; then, that the public good be promoted' (Cicero, 1913, I. 10). Each law, therefore, must be tested to determine its purpose and efficacy in promoting the public good.

Cicero expressed concern about laws that exist to serve ends other than the public good. Some unscrupulous lawyers today at times applaud the passage of new laws because they provide more work for the lawyers to help clients manoeuvre their ways around laws. Most lawyers make money through billable hours; the more regulations, the more hours lawyers can bill to clients in ensuring that they adhere to the regulations. Cicero would be appalled by such an attitude; he spoke out explicitly against people using the presence of laws for personal gain:

> Through such interpretation also a great deal of wrong is committed in transactions between state and state; thus, when a truce had been made with the enemy for thirty days, a famous general went to ravaging their fields by night, because, he said, the truce stipulated 'days,' not nights. Not even our own countryman's action is to be commended, if what is told of Quintus Fabius Labeo is true—or whoever it was (for I have no authority but hearsay): appointed by the Senate to arbitrate a boundary dispute between Nola and Naples, he took up the case and interviewed both parties separately, asking them not to proceed in a covetous or grasping spirit, but to make some concession rather than claim some accession. When each party had agreed to this, there was a considerable strip of territory left between them. And so he set the boundary of each city as each had severally agreed; and the tract in between he awarded to the Roman People. Now that is swindling, not arbitration. And therefore such sharp practice is under all circumstances to be avoided.
>
> (Cicero, 1913, I. 34)

Cicero was rightly sceptical of laws that could be used to promote personal gain. What's more, he argues that the presence of too many laws can defeat justice. The more complex the laws or legal system, the more vulnerable a society is to misapplication, misunderstanding, and misuse of laws. Cicero warned:

> Injustice often arises [. . .] through chicanery, that is, through an oversubtle and even fraudulent construction of the law. This it is that gave rise to the now familiar saw, 'More law, less justice'.
>
> (Cicero, 1913, I. 33)

The Four-Pronged Test

We propose a four-pronged test to determine if a law is just. We base this test on the writings of Thomas Aquinas, a 13th-century scholastic philosopher. Aquinas provided the classic definition of a law as 'an ordinance of reason promulgated by one in authority for the common good' (Aquinas, n.d., Prima Secundae, Question 90, article 4). From this simple statement comes the test we propose: (i) Is the authority legitimate? (ii) Is the law rational? (iii) Has the law been promulgated effectively? (iv) Is the law productive of the common good? The ordering does not reflect the importance; an affirmative answer must exist to each of these four questions for a law to be considered just. Although we will discuss all four, our primary focus will lie on the rationality and promulgatability criteria.

Is the Authority Legitimate?

The first question has to do with the entity passing a law. Answering this question for Dodd-Frank is relatively straightforward: the legislation was passed by the U.S. Congress, and Congress is the entity in the United States authorised to pass federal legislation. Although critics periodically argue with how Congress behaves, its legitimacy is not necessarily attacked. It is worth noting, however, that passage by a country's legislative body does not necessarily render a law legitimate or just. There are countries where laws or regulations are passed by entities that do not look out or provide for the good of the people. This prong therefore enquires into the legitimacy of the entity passing the law, which would include determining if the law or regulation falls within the scope of an entity's authority.

Without getting into deeper arguments about the nature of Congress in the United States, it can be said that Dodd-Frank passes the first prong of the test. It is not necessarily popular, but it is legitimate. Although it can be argued that the legislative process in the United States, and perhaps elsewhere, is politicised, that is not the point of this prong of the test. This prong asks simply if a law (or rule or regulation) has been passed by a legitimate authority.[1] In the United States, for example, orders by the executive branch of the government are sometimes challenged on the basis of the argument that the chief executive has acted outside the scope of his or her authority.

Is the Law Rational?

Rationality, as part of the four-pronged test, refers to the reasonableness of a law. It questions the suitability of a law for its prescribed purpose(s) and the ability of the law to do what it intends. The first part of rationality has to do with the designated purpose of a law. Does the purpose fall within the scope of the legislature's authority? The second part has to do with feasibility. Can the law as presented achieve its purpose? The third part involves internal consistency. Are there internal contradictions?

Dodd-Frank embraced an important societal issue. Passed in response to the 2008 GFC, it endeavoured to improve financial stability and consumer protection. Congress is charged with responsibility for such issues; in other words, the legislation rightfully claims a rational purpose.

An important element of rationality is linked to viability. A law that contains inherent conflicts or contradictions cannot be considered rational or just. Karen Petrou, managing partner of a firm that analyses bank regulations, was quoted in a *New York Times* column by Joe Nocera: 'If we don't understand the cross-cutting effects and inherent contradictions in all of the stringent standards now being written into final form [of Dodd-Frank], we risk doing real damage to the sound, stable and—yes— profitable financial industry' (Nocera, 2012).

Rationality is also linked to tenability. Can a law be considered tenable if excessively lengthy? Dodd-Frank spanned approximately 2,300 pages when passed and included implementation of more than 400 new rules and mandates. Although this piece of legislation encompassed a noble goal, the very size of the associated legislative text would seem to prevent it from being considered rational according to this prong of the test.

Why does size matter? If a piece of legislation is too lengthy and complex, it becomes untenable. Laypeople then do not understand it, and even jurists find it challenging to apply consistently. Business stakeholders get lost in lack of clarity and are not necessarily sure how the law is directing behaviour. In addition, lawyers can find persuasive arguments to make for their clients, no matter how they behave, but they do not even understand what the law is saying.

Has the Law Been Promulgated Effectively?

Promulgation is an essential part of ensuring that laws are just. Laws do not simply exist; they must be promulgated or announced so that people affected by a law are aware of its specific demands. To 'promulgate' means 'to promote or make widely known'. 'Promulgation' requires that a law be conveyed in such a way that it is sufficiently understandable by the people who affect or are affected by it.

Jeremy Bentham provided insight into when promulgation is effective. For him, obeying a law requires knowing what the law demands and from whom:

> [T]o promulgate a law, it is not only necessary that it should be published with the sound of trumpet in the streets; not only that it should be read to the people; not only even that it should be printed: all these means may be good, but they may be all employed without accomplishing the essential object. They may possess more of the appearance than the reality of promulgation. To promulgate a law, *is to present it to the minds of those who are to be governed by it in such manner as that they may have it habitually in their memories, and*

*may possess every facility for consulting it, if they have any doubts
respecting what it prescribes* [emphasis added].

(Bentham, 1843, Section I)

According to Bentham, for a law to be legitimate, it must be known and
understood. For Bentham, such a requirement is simply common sense.

When we apply the criterion of promulgatability to Dodd-Frank, it
seems clearly unreachable because of its sheer size in addition to everything else. Its mere publication does not make it understandable or its
application straightforward.

Is the Law Productive of the Common Good?

The fourth and final requirement of the four-pronged test for a just law
requires examination of the effectiveness of the law in bringing about the
common good. The second test, the rationality test, examines the purpose
itself; this requirement considers if the purpose is served. This requirement
is sufficiently broad to capture diverse types of purposes (i.e., deterrence,
efficiency, restitution, etc.). It involves a simple question: Does the law
serve its purpose, whatever it is, effectively?

Quite simply, Dodd-Frank does not serve its purpose effectively. The
past decade's rampant criticism of the legislation demonstrates its failure
to meet this prong of the test. Dodd-Frank is a sprawling piece of legislation that contains 17 separate sections and governs everything from
car loans to CEO pay to Congolese conflict minerals. 'The statute itself
declared that it would "end too big to fail" and "promote financial stability" ', stated Jeb Hensarling. 'None of that has come to pass. Too-big-to-
fail institutions have not disappeared. Big banks are bigger, small banks
are fewer, and the financial system is less stable. Meanwhile, the economy
remains in the doldrums' (Hensarling, 2015).

The issue is not that this law does not make everyone happy; it satisfies
virtually no one. Even advocates acknowledge its flaws; they simply prefer
Dodd-Frank to nothing. That, though, is not a rational basis for allowing
an unjust law to remain in force.

Application of Four-Pronged Test to Dodd-Frank

Dodd-Frank contributes to the kind of 'more law, less justice' scenario of
which Cicero warned. This conclusion is not to impugn the motives of
the lawmakers but to evaluate their product. An article in the *Economist*
that compares Dodd-Frank to prior laws governing the financial industry
highlights the problematic nature of the law:

> The law that set up America's banking system in 1864 ran to
> 29 pages; the Federal Reserve Act of 1913 went to 32 pages; the Banking

Act that transformed American finance after the Wall Street Crash, commonly known as the Glass-Steagall act, spread out to 37 pages. Dodd-Frank is 848 pages long. Voracious Chinese officials, who pay close attention to regulatory developments elsewhere, have remarked that the mammoth law, let alone its appended rules, seems to have been fully read by no one outside Beijing. [. . .] And the size is only the beginning. The scope and structure of Dodd-Frank are fundamentally different to those of its precursor laws, notes Jonathan Macey of Yale Law School: 'Laws classically provide people with rules. Dodd-Frank is not directed at people. It is an outline directed at bureaucrats and it instructs them to make still more regulations and to create more bureaucracies'. Like the Hydra of Greek myth, Dodd-Frank can grow new heads as needed.

Take the transformation of 11 pages of Dodd-Frank into the so-called 'Volcker rule', which is intended to reduce banks' ability to take excessive risks by restricting proprietary trading and investments in hedge funds and private equity (Paul Volcker, a former chairman of the Federal Reserve, has argued that such activity contributed to the crisis). In November four of the five federal agencies charged with enacting this rule jointly put forward a 298-page proposal which is, in the words of a banker publicly supportive of Dodd-Frank, 'unintelligible any way you read it'. It includes 383 explicit questions for firms which, if read closely, break down into 1,420 sub questions, according to Davis Polk, a law firm. The interactive Volcker 'rule map' Davis Polk has produced for its clients has 355 distinct steps.

(Economist, 2012)

Dodd-Frank is long, complicated, and over-reaching. It endeavours to cover so much territory in such detail that it fails to provide efficient or effective direction. It contains internal contradictions that render it inherently irrational.

Financial Services Industry Example: The Merrill Rule

A somewhat recent brouhaha in the financial services industry illustrates how the public good can get lost in the presence of an unjust law, rule, or regulation. Several years ago, the Securities and Exchange Commission (SEC) proposed an exemption for brokers/dealers who provide non-discretionary advice. As long as that advice was incidental to their brokerage services, they did not have to register as investment advisors, even if they were compensated for that advice. This proposal created the so-called Merrill Lynch Rule or Merrill Rule. The regulation allowed brokers to charge asset-based fees in brokerage accounts without being subject to regulations (and standards) governing investment advisors. The effect of the rule (why it was controversial) was to lower the standard of care to which clients were entitled by brokers providing investment advice deemed incidental to other services. Investment advisors are subject to fiduciary duty, whereas brokers according to the Merrill Rule were required only to meet suitability.

The presence of such a rule echoes the concerns raised by Cicero, Aquinas, and Bentham that ground our four-pronged test. We assert that the Merrill Rule fails all four prongs of the test. The 2007 decision by the U.S. Circuit Court of Appeals for the DC Circuit to vacate the rule supports our conclusion.

The Financial Planning Association (FPA) is the organisation in the United States that leads and advocates for financial services professionals. The FPA filed suit against the SEC in 2004 on the grounds that the SEC overreached its authority under the Investment Advisors Act of 1940 in crafting that new exception (failure of prong 1). The FPA argued that brokerage houses, particularly those that advertise as full-service brokers, present themselves to the public as advisors and ought to be held to the same standard of accountability as other investment advisors.

A careful review of the debate surrounding this rule reveals that the two standards—'fiduciary' and 'suitability'—have become hopelessly muddled. How and why is suitability a lesser standard than fiduciary? Why have the requirements for fiduciary responsibility become so complex? Why is it the case that if an advisor is a fiduciary, he or she needs to meet suitability standards, but meeting suitability standards does not imply he or she is a fiduciary?

'Financial and suitability are the two standards of care in the financial services industry. The fiduciary standard requires that an advisor put the client's interests first; the suitability standard requires only that an advisor provide advice that is suitable for the client's needs. The suitability standard does not require that advice be consistent with a client's best interests. The Merrill Rule allows for advisors to meet only the suitability requirement. It remains unclear, however, exactly where that standard begins and ends (failure of prong 2).

Lack of clarity remains a challenge. An unclear rule, regulation, or law can be seen as failing the requirement that it be reasonable or rational. If lawyers and financial services professionals debate the meaning of terms like suitability and fiduciary, how can laypeople be expected to discern the difference? Clients simply expect to receive the advice they request. When the advice concerns their investment options, they implicitly expect their best interests to be taken into account. After all, the commonsense meaning of advisor is someone who tries to discern and recommends a course of action in the interests of the recipient of the advice, the advisee. This expectation is not based on what the law says but on simple morality and common sense.

Getting back to Cicero and Aquinas, shouldn't the law protect morality and common sense? Although it is true that a lot of finance and banking are inherently complicated, at the very least, people affected by a rule, regulation, or law should be able to discern from that rule, regulation, or law how they are expected to behave. In this instance, it is the rule, the Merrill Rule, that is complicating finance, not the other way around.

In addition, although the rule was technically published, it is not clear that clients affected by the rule were reasonably made aware of its existence of significance (failure of prong 3). Even though this rule was technically published, it is not clear how the true spirit of promulgation has been satisfied. The essence of promulgation requires more than a mere announcement of a rule, regulation, or law. For a rule, regulation, or law to be 'promulgated' in the truest sense of the term, it needs to be accompanied by some sort of education, explanation, or meaningful implementation.

What a client implicitly expects is that financial advice will meet the fiduciary standard. Although treatises and law journals complicate its meaning, the meaning of 'fiduciary' seems fairly clear in its dictionary definition, which is where laypeople go to find out what words mean. *Webster's Third New International Dictionary* defines 'fiduciary' as 'of, having to do with, or involving a confidence or trust'. A 'fiduciary relation', also according to Webster, is

> the relation existing when one person justifiably reposes confidence, faith and reliance in another whose aid, advice or protection is sought in some matter: the relation existing when good conscience requires one to act at all times for the sole benefit and interests of another with loyalty to those interests: the relation by law existing between certain classes of persons (as confidential advisor and the one advised).

Those definitions are simple and clear-cut to apply. If a person trusts another person to give financial advice, he or she pays that person to give financial advice, and if he or she willingly agrees to that relationship, then he or she is obligated to act for the payer's benefit with loyalty to his or her interests.

The problem arises because, in the world of financial services, there are two distinct types of services that can be offered, although it is not always clear where one ends and the other begins. The first involves brokering, that is, the act of selling on behalf of someone else or making financial products available; the second involves giving advice about which of these complicated products best fits the client's needs. A broker/advisor does not have to do both. Clients can engage brokerage services simply to facilitate sales transactions. In such a situation, the financial services professional literally 'brokers' a product in the primary sense of the word 'broker'; he or she acts as a mediator between a buyer and seller. This view is clearly the view that the SEC has of brokerage services because, according to the Merrill Rule, advice could be 'incidental' to such service. In relying on a broker, the client is engaged in a transaction that resembles a purchase at a retail store where someone simply comes in off the street to buy a product. The broker's role is that of middleman, and the autonomous buyer takes responsibility for his or her own choice.

Here is where the rule failed the 'public good' requirement (prong 4). The Merrill Rule allowed clients to receive different levels of advice, often without their realising that that was what was happening. The 'public good' is not served if clients are receiving advice different from what they reasonably expect. It is not uncommon for investors to ask for opinions from brokers. It is natural for such a conversation to slip into recommendations for specific products, even if unintentionally. In the financial services industry, although some people are clearly advisors and others just transactional brokers, there are situations in which the distinction is not nearly as clear; in such situations, a broker can slide into an advisory role. In short, there is a continuum of possible relationships that can be established between financial services professionals and clients, and it is not always easy to draw the sort of bright lines people would like.

Consider three different types of transactions: buying a computer at Costco, buying a computer from Dell, and hiring an IT consultant to buy a computer. If a person buys a computer at Costco, he or she buys at his or her own risk with little purchasing guidance. Dell, on the other hand, is expected to offer some degree of guidance in helping a customer pick a particular model computer that will meet his or her needs. Dell thereby enters into an implicit advisory relationship with the purchaser. This relationship requires that Dell do more than just sell what the purchaser is willing to buy. How much more, however, remains unclear. The purchaser remains the ultimate decision maker. The third type of transaction, which includes hiring an IT consultant, creates an explicit relationship. The IT consultant is not only responsible for helping the purchaser select the best computer to fit his or her needs but also for helping him or her determine and articulate what those needs are and how they should be prioritised.

The continuum seems clear within the context of a computer purchase. At Costco, the purchaser is responsible for determining his or her own needs and selecting the computer that best meets those needs. At a specialty store, the purchaser is responsible for determining his or her needs, but he or she also has a reasonable expectation of informed input to be provided from the sales representative. In the third kind of situation, a trained professional is responsible for determining the purchaser's needs and identifying an appropriate product to meet those needs. The computer purchaser typically hires an independent IT consultant. If the consultant recommends a Dell product, that recommendation is viewed as independent. If the purchaser were to hire an IT consultant from Dell, he or she would expect the consultant to be biased towards Dell products. Because the IT consultant is not from Dell, the purchaser reasonably expects that the advice will be based on the purchaser's best interests.

A similar continuum exists in financial services. Investors can control their own investment decisions through options like E*TRADE, an online brokerage that directs its services to retail investors who do not want guidance. Its very fee structure implicitly rewards clients who do not seek advice. A similarly situated retail client can also make the same investment choices through an account at Morgan Stanley. Morgan Stanley charges a fee for holding particular products, but the investor controls all the choices. That same investor, though, can also go to Morgan Stanley for explicit investment advice.

This continuum in financial services creates not only a potential but a reasonable likelihood of investor confusion as the line blurs between the two roles played by Morgan Stanley. The investor's personal stake in investment choices is not always transparent. For example, a commission might be higher in products considered riskier. If Morgan Stanley is acting only as a broker, the lack of transparency is possibly irrelevant; it is the investor's choice to take on the risk. Once the broker begins answering questions and providing anything like advice, the absence of transparency could be viewed as relevant, particularly if the investor is wavering and the broker tips the balance in swaying the investor towards the risky product. A regulation that implicitly permits brokers to influence investment decisions that might run counter to the best interests of investors can clearly not be construed as consistent with the 'public good'.

Although brokerage houses are not necessarily intentionally deceptive, the deception that resulted was foreseeable. To compete, brokerages present themselves as friendly, being 'on your side' and 'looking out for you'. They call themselves 'full-service' companies, and their advertisements and websites proclaim that they are in business to help their clients. That is the value added they promote to help them compete with purely transactional brokers like E*TRADE. Because the value added of the financial advisor is the advice (of a fiduciary), the FPA was rightly concerned about even 'incidental' advice offered in the context of a trade, particularly by an entity that bills itself as 'full-service'. The computer purchaser does not have to follow the advice of the IT consultant, but he or she has a right to the type of advice he or she 'purchased', that is, advice consistent with the purchaser's interests. The investor does not even entirely know the type of advice he or she is 'purchasing'.

The SEC was created to restore investor confidence in capital markets by providing more reliable information and clear rules for honest dealing. Because the SEC's raison d'être is to look out for the welfare of the investor, the Commission's position on Rule 202(a)(11)-1 is somewhat puzzling. It seems to protect brokers more than investors. Not only that, but the formulation of the rule is logically troubling. Removing the qualifying descriptors, 'non discretionary' and 'solely incidental to their brokerage services', results in a rule that '[b]rokers who provide [. . .] advice are exempt from registering as advisors'. If a law calls for advisors to register, those who advise, even though that advice is 'non-discretionary' or 'incidental', are still advising. Either there is value to this 'non-discretionary' and 'incidental' advice or there is not; and if there is value, it is advice of an advisor.

The Merrill Rule, then, fails the four-pronged test. Regulations such as the Merrill Rule illustrate why such a test should exist.

Conclusion

Although Cicero, Aquinas, and Bentham might seem strange bedfellows, they share a common interest in law that spans centuries, and their insights, together, contribute to a test that should be applied by legislators and legislatures, ideally before laws are passed or regulations are promoted. If not, then, at least in their application, authorised bodies should consider how their laws fare in terms of authority, promulgation, rationality, and the public good. Law has traditionally been seen as the answer to the question of how to guide proper behaviour. Our answer is not more general law (lengthy, complex laws) or more specific laws. We simply need just laws, regardless of whether that means more or fewer laws.

What we call for is special attention to the elements of the four-pronged test. Our laws should represent reasonable attempts to address specific goals in a feasible way. And our laws should be announced, promulgated, not simply on paper but to the affected audience in a way that they can reasonably understand. Mere words on paper are not enough.

Laws too cumbersome to be read or understood will fail the test of a just law; and justice, according to Cicero and others, is the goal of law. Laws that involve inherent contradictions and are not truly promulgatable (more than on paper) are not laws or are 'unjust laws'. The presence—and proliferation—of such laws leads to a breakdown of law in general and to arbitrary enforcement. Instead of allowing more law, less justice, it is time that we demand more justice, even if that means less law.

Note

1. The vulnerability of that authority to politics is a different issue not tackled here.

References

Aquinas, Thomas. (n.d.). Treatise on law. In *Summa theologica*. https://www.ccel. org/a/aquinas/summa/FS.html

Bentham, J. (1843). Section 1, Of Promulgation of the laws and promulgation of the reasons thereof. In *The works of Jeremy Bentham* (Bowring ed., Vol. I). Edinburgh: William Tait.

Cicero. (1913). *De officiis* (W. Miller, Trans.). Cambridge, MA: Harvard University Press.

Economist. (2012). The Dodd-Frank Act: Too big not to fail. *Economist*, 18th February, 22–24.

Everitt, A. (2002). *Cicero: The life and times of Rome's greatest politician*. New York: Random House.

Hensarling, J. (2015). After five years, Dodd-Frank is a failure. *Wall Street Journal*, 19th July.

Miller, D. (2016). Justice. In E. N. Zalta (Ed.), *Stanford encyclopedia of philosophy*. https://plato.stanford.edu/entries/justice/

Nocera, J. (2012). Keep it simple. *New York Times*, 16th January.

6 Freedom in Finance

The Importance of Epistemic Virtues and Interlucent Communication

Boudewijn de Bruin and Richard Endörfer

Introduction

The global financial crisis (GFC) that started in 2007 has made us aware of the vulnerabilities of sellers and buyers of mortgages; for whereas economists have over the years uncovered many larger causal factors of the crisis, there is little doubt that most contemporaneous commentators thought the crisis had started with the 'subprime mortgage meltdown'. Sub-prime mortgages, the story went, were borrowed by people who couldn't really afford them from lenders who didn't care because they knew that they could easily get rid of the risks by selling the mortgages on to structured finance firms that would 'repackage' them into the notorious mortgage-backed securities—a supply chain of misinformation, moral hazard, and myopia.

There is little doubt that something else would have started the recession if the sub-prime mortgage bubble had not burst, but mortgage regulation is nonetheless central in many policy responses to the crisis. In the United States, the Dodd-Frank Act aimed, amongst other things, at providing consumer protection in mortgage markets by setting compensation standards for loan originators, minimum standards for mortgages, and minimal underwriting standards, and it capped fees for borrowers of high-cost mortgages. EU Mortgage Credit Directive 2014/17/EU introduced information requirements. These helped borrowers make better mortgage decisions and aimed to protect borrowers from over-indebtedness through a set of conditions on their mortgages' loan-to-income and loan-to-value ratios. Such measures were motivated by observations concerning the informational challenges that certain consumers face. Elderly and less educated consumers use most financial services significantly less than well-educated and younger consumers and have less trust in consumer protection in mortgage markets (Clifton, 2017).

There is certainly merit in the idea of introducing regulation that ensures the industry creates 'products that consumers actually want—and actually understand', as former U.S. president Barack Obama (White House, 2009) once phrased it. But that only takes us so far. There are two ways in which you can make sure that a given consumer understands a product: you can decrease the complexity of the product until the desired understanding is reached; or you can increase the understanding of consumers until they grasp the complexity of the product. Most regulators seem to have taken the first route. Indeed, this is often a very sensible route, but not always, because it may stifle innovation that we badly need.

We first swiftly marshal evidence for two preliminary claims: firstly, that consumers have an interest in fostering what we call *known freedom* (consumers will be said to have known freedom about mortgages whenever they have sufficiently detailed and justified information about relevant mortgage options); and secondly, that consumers have an interest in being able to buy complex products. (Vulnerable consumers in particular may need complex products to deal with life's adversities.) These claims are meant to establish that complexity must be increased in certain cases. We then consider a case that has received significant attention in the finance literature: the Continuous Workout Mortgage. Finally, we address the issue of how the desired increase in understanding of a complex product might be brought about, considering the regulation of information, epistemic virtues, and interlucent communication.

Known Freedom

Why would consumers assign value to freedom? We are fairly neutral here with respect to the precise definition of freedom: all we assume is that typically your freedom grows if your choice set grows, and your freedom shrinks if your choice set shrinks. We are here loosely inspired by Carter's (1999) and Kramer's (2003) work on (pure) negative freedom. One argument is that freedom boosts *desire satisfaction*. If desire satisfaction is valuable, and if in addition to that it is true that if your freedom increases, your desire satisfaction increases, it follows that freedom is valuable. This is a fairly standard observation based on the assumption that the likelihood with which your desires are satisfied increases with the number of actions available to you. A more deontological argument could be put in terms of *responsibility*: if you assign value to personal responsibility, and if, in addition, you hold onto the view that your personal responsibility increases if your freedom increases, then freedom is again of value to you. The idea is that if you make a choice, you not only decide in favour of some action but also *against* the other available actions, and thus, the argument goes, you bear responsibility for choosing one thing and for excluding the other things (Hurka, 1987).

These are not just two arbitrary arguments for the value of freedom. As Brown (2009) has argued persuasively, it is these two arguments (taken together as implying that there is value to assuming personal responsibility for satisfying your own desires) that informed the Reagan and Thatcher administrations to move the responsibilities for, amongst other things, healthcare, housing, and financial planning from the state to the individual. So these arguments were essential to provide ideological backing for deregulation (which increases freedom of business and, as a result, may increase freedom of choice for consumers) that is often alleged to have caused so much trouble.

One might doubt whether these arguments are still very appealing after a financial crisis. We believe they are; but only if we realise that we need to insert an additional premise that seems to have been ignored in many cases of deregulation—namely, that genuinely to use your freedom to assume personal responsibility for your desire satisfaction, you need to *know* what your freedom amounts to. You need what we call *known freedom*.

To exemplify the concept of known freedom, we will first give a more precise picture of a person's choice situation. Firstly, there is a set of available actions from which you can choose: your choice set. Secondly, each of these available actions has numerous consequences arising with objective probabilities. A person discussing mortgages with an adviser, for instance, may face a choice between various mortgages involving different down payments, interest rates, maturities, and so forth. These options naturally have different characteristics. They have different possible consequences, and even if two options have identical possible consequences, the probability with which they arise may not be the same. We will say that you possess *known freedom* in a choice situation if you know, firstly, which actions are available and which ones are not; secondly, what the possible consequences of these actions are; and thirdly, what the probabilities are with which these consequences arise. To be sure, full known freedom is practically impossible to attain. But much value can be gained from approximating the ideal.

Our claims now follow easily: if we assume that the larger your known freedom, the greater is your desire satisfaction (or personal responsibility, respectively), then known freedom has value for you; for if freedom increases desire satisfaction and responsibility, known freedom increases these things to an even larger (or at least not smaller) extent because none of the actions available to you are curtailed if you exhibit known freedom.

You may have ample freedom, but as long as you lack information about the particular actions you can select, you won't use these actions to satisfy your desires or to assume personal responsibility for those that you are unaware of and don't select. Furthermore, even if you have ample freedom, if you are not aware of the actions available to you, your capacity to be responsible for choosing or omitting a particular course of action is impaired.

When policy-makers or the financial industry maintain that innovative, complex financial products and services help people to satisfy their desires, the implicit assumption is that these people are sufficiently well informed about these products and services to be able to make a responsible choice. If this assumption does not hold, consumers do not have known freedom.

Complex Innovation

Although many commentators have accused financial innovation as being one of the major contributing factors to the crisis, Nobel-prize winning economist Robert Shiller has been an outspoken advocate of innovation. In *Finance and the Good Society*, Shiller (2012) outlines how innovation in financial capitalism may enable consumers to secure and safeguard a wide array of long-term interests that, he believes, are morally relevant. Shiller shows that contrary to what it is popular to think today, financial instruments are not there just to please Wall Street; rather, well-designed products mitigate risks that have adverse effects on the satisfaction of essential needs and interests of consumers (e.g., access to food and clothing, adequate housing and education, etc.). In capitalist societies, the degree to which individuals can secure such long-term needs and interests depends to a significant degree on budget constraints determined by income, assets, access to credit, and so on. Consumers find a host of threats on their way to achieving these goals, including things such as health problems, crime, natural catastrophes, wars, and macroeconomic shocks. Such events may severely contract consumers' budgets and thereby decrease their chances of securing their long-term interests. These risks are, in Dworkin's well-known terminology, cases of 'brute' luck: They have negative effects on your budget constraints, but you don't take on these risks in a 'deliberate and calculated' manner (Dworkin, 1981, p. 293).

As Dworkin argues, insurance effectively transforms brute luck into option luck, by which he means a risk that is calculable and can be assumed deliberately. Although insurance has been with us since the Italian Renaissance, there is still a wide range of brute luck events not addressed by off-the-peg insurance policies. One reason why insurance may be hard to come by has to do with moral hazard. *Moral hazard* is the risk that policyholders behave less carefully than they would without insurance (e.g., with insurance against bike theft, you might be less likely to use an additional bike lock). Shiller proposes that more sophisticated insurance contracts could be designed whose coverage and efficiency go beyond standardly offered policies.

Here is a stylised example (Shiller, 2012). Because crops depend heavily on weather conditions, it would help farmers if they could buy insurance against excessive rainfall, droughts, and so on. If the policy covers crop failure itself, moral hazard is likely to be a problem as farmers may shirk their responsibilities or engage in downright fraud. Meteorological information technology has advanced to such a degree, however, that the actual insurance contracts can refer to third-party data about local weather conditions rather than to crop failure data deriving from the policy-holders themselves. Shiller observes, however, that because such policies are more complex than traditional crop insurance, uptake amongst farmers in developing countries is poor. A policy that refers to statistical models provided by some meteorological organisation may just be very difficult for them to understand. At the same time, however, they would clearly benefit from such insurance.

Better Mortgages?

Crop insurance may not be the most straightforward concern for most people. But mortgages probably are. We will now consider the example of the CWM, as proposed by Robert Shiller (Shiller et al., 2017), to illustrate how a complex product consisting of a fairly standard mortgage contract and an innovative, index-based insurance product benefits consumers.

Consider first a fixed-rate mortgage (FRM). FRMs are debt contracts for the purchase of real estate with two components: the principal, that is, the amount of money borrowed from the lender that has to be fully repaid; and the interest the borrower has to pay. Typically, each month the borrower pays some interest and repays some part of the loan until the loan has been fully repaid after, say, 30 years (maturity). FRMs are fully amortised, which means in this case that if borrowers make the scheduled monthly payments, they will have repaid the entire loan after 30 years. With a fixed interest rate, monthly payments are constant over time, but the portion of interest decreases, while the portion of repayment increases. The consequence of this is that equity in the house grows at a lower rate in the first years of the loan than in the last years. For instance, if you borrow £100,000 at a rate of 5% with a maturity of 30 years, your interest in the first month is £417 and repayment is £120, whereas in the last month your interest is £2 and your repayment is £535. The interest rate is fixed, so the monthly payments are constant at £537. After 15 years, you haven't even repaid a third of the total loan (£32,116, to be precise).

FRMs have two advantages. Constant payments decrease the risk that a borrower's income will be insufficient to cover the monthly payment at some point in time. This contrasts with adjustable-rate mortgages that, even though they may fully amortise, may lead to ups and downs in the monthly payments. And this contrasts, too, with interest-only mortgages that do not amortise and which require the borrower to pay off the total principal at maturity.

Although a fully amortised FRM is a little more complex mathematically than an interest-only mortgage, it has emerged as the popular standard mortgage contract after the Great Depression of the 1930s. But brute luck may kick in. Take an extreme case first: for whatever exogenous reason, the house becomes worthless after 15 years. With an FRM you still have to keep on repaying £100,000—£32,116 = £67,884 for a house that is worthless on the market. Unsurprisingly, such cases of 'negative equity' often lead to repossession of the house by the lender. U.S. households exposed to negative equity have historically been twice as likely to default (negative equity is often considered a necessary condition for default) or involved in serious mortgage-related delinquencies (Haughwout & Okah, 2009).

CWMs were created to counteract the effects of negative equity; they do this by insuring borrowers against decreases in house prices. The repayment schedule of a CWM differs from that of an FRM: it adjusts to regional house prices because it is linked to a regional house price index such as the Shiller-Case Index (Case & Shiller, 1989), such that monthly payments decrease if the index drops. At the origination of a CWM, a maximum annual repayment is specified, which is determined by the value of the regional house price index at the time of origination. If at some point in time the index exceeds this initial value, the borrower has to repay the maximum. But if the index is lower than the initial value, the repayment is going to be lower as well. So if a house loses market value (as measured by the index), the borrowers' payments decrease and in the extreme case described they would have to repay nothing, not even interest.

A result of this is that *lenders* cannot know what they will earn. If house prices decline and CWM repayments are reduced due to this, it is the lenders that have to absorb these losses. So one should expect them to want to be compensated. The compensation they request is a risk premium that CWM borrowers pay. This risk premium is the difference between the initial maximum repayment negotiated at the origination of the CWM contract and the (slightly lower) repayment for an equivalent FRM. In good times, when the house price index is high, CWM payments will be slightly higher than FRM payments; but in bad times, CWM payments will be substantially lower than FRM payments.

Unfortunately, despite their potential to safeguard consumers from negative equity, CWMs have remained rather unpopular amongst mortgage borrowers. A particularly plausible reason is that whereas consumers are not prohibited from access to CWMs, they refrain from choosing these loans because of a failure to grasp the contract sufficiently well. We make several quick observations in this connection. First, risk-adverse consumers have no strong incentive to experiment with non-standard mortgages outside times of crisis or times in which crisis are relatively recent. As we hinted earlier, FRMs emerged as the popular standard in the United States only after the experiences of the Great Depression when it became clear that short-term 'balloon' loans became virtually impossible to refinance due to limited bank lending, which caused a wave of foreclosures (Campbell et al., 2011, p. 96). So without a trigger event, markets for CWMs are likely to remain illiquid. Secondly, there is evidence that due to cognitive biases, consumers often focus primarily on the short-term costs of mortgage contracts, even if they might be vastly more expensive in the long run (Gathergood & Weber, 2017, Badarinza et al., 2018). The result in the case of CWMs is that consumers will probably shy away from choosing CWMs because their implicit insurance makes these contracts more costly in the short term. Thirdly, mortgage originators and innovators have little incentive to create contracts such as CWMs if consumers focus on salient, short-term price dimensions of mortgages. Originators find it vastly more profitable to offer superficially attractive products to consumers than offering complex, but potentially better, long-term products (Campbell et al., 2011).

Regulating Information

We have tried to provide some evidence for two claims: Known freedom is instrumental to increasing consumer desire satisfaction and responsibility, and to deal with some of life's adversities, innovative, complex financial products will be necessary. At the same time, known freedom is not always achieved in practice, and the post-crisis attitude towards financial innovation is not very positive to say the least. We here consider two of the policies that regulators consider: providing information to consumers and enhancing their information gathering and processing skills (Clifton et al., 2017).

The degree to which these policies increase known freedom of course depends on the characteristics of the consumers. The first type of policy is appropriate to address information asymmetries inhibiting *rational* consumers' capabilities to make an optimal choice given their needs. But whether a given financial product suits these needs may be difficult to ascertain if information asymmetries cloud the consumer's judgement. For instance, if you contemplate buying a CWM, you must form a judgement concerning the correlation between the price development of the house you own and the development of a given house price index that captures the average house price development in a certain region. If your house is atypical, a CWM may not be the most attractive choice. But whether your house is atypical may be rather difficult for you to find out. The lender, on the contrary, may have private information about price movements of similar houses that they financed before, or it may be much less costly for the lender to obtain the information from other sources.

We believe that this suggests that we may have to face a trade-off between increased innovation, on the one hand, and, on the other hand, increased informational regulation; if we allow for a greater degree of innovation to stimulate the design of products and services that people really need, then it may be reasonable to make sure that sellers face more stringent rules concerning information disclosure as disclosing information to prospective, rational buyers increases their known freedom. Such a trade-off in favour of disclosing information to buyers is, we believe, justified as long as it makes a genuine contribution to the liberal ideal of known freedom.

Information provision only goes so far, though. Consumers won't all benefit from accessible information to the same degree. We are here particularly interested in the negative influence of cognitive biases on financial decision-making; that is, we are concerned with those consumers who economists tend to call 'irrational'. Such consumers are likely users of simple heuristics that make them focus on easily discernible features of a mortgage contract instead of its specific risk characteristics (Thaler, 1985). In such cases, merely providing information is unlikely to enhance known freedom; it may even decrease it.

We focus on two cognitive biases that have attracted some attention in the literature on mortgage contracting: myopia and optimism (Bar-Gill, 2009). The term *myopia* is meant to capture the propensity of consumers to place excessive weight on present costs while ignoring future costs. Optimism refers to the propensity to underestimate the likelihood of certain adverse events. Consumers who are biased in their decision-making due to myopia are much more likely to accept contracts with deferred cost features, which often turn out to be more expensive than contracts that do not exhibit these features. The combination of myopia and optimism is particularly dangerous to borrowers, as it leads them to prefer mortgage contracts with deferred cost features, that is, contracts including low initial interest rates ('teaser' rates) that are compensated by escalating interest rate payments a few years after the origination of the loan. Consumers with these biases don't see the future sufficiently clearly, and to the extent they see the future, it is painted in overly rosy colours. They may, for instance, falsely expect their incomes to increase proportionally with the interest rate on their mortgage or fail to perceive the likelihood of losing their jobs.

These and other biases undermine known freedom: in general terms, consumers suffering from cognitive biases fail to assign accurate probabilities to the consequences of the actions in their choice set, and they may even fail to see that certain actions are available and/or erroneously believe that certain actions are available to them. These biases are well-known. Yet before the crisis broke out, regulators by and large assumed consumers to be rational and to be capable of making informed choices; consumer protection regulation in mortgage markets (and elsewhere) was therefore primarily focused on regulatory interventions of the first type. Even today, regulators globally seem to be aiming first and foremost at information provision. Mortgage Credit Directive 2014/17/EU, which we mentioned earlier, contains rules on the provision of information concerning the amount and duration of a loan, the type of interest rate, the conditions for pre-payment, and exchange rate risks associated with the loan as well as the total costs of the loan, including fees, in terms of annual percentage rates. This has led to the use of disclosure forms known as European Standardised Information Sheets (ESIS), which have a very similar purpose to Truth in Lending Disclosure Statements and the Good Faith Estimate of Closing Costs Form (GFE) in the United States.

Such forms may help consumers turn away from unreliable, simplistic heuristics because they eliminate the information overload that consumers face without these documents. Furthermore, providing relevant information about a particular mortgage contract in a condensed manner decreases the time necessary to evaluate its most salient features. The implicit goal is to enable consumers to engage in side-by-side comparisons of different mortgage loans in a time-efficient manner, thereby increasing the likelihood that they will consider a wider range of mortgages before making a final decision that will suit their needs.

Used with care, such forms may increase consumers' known freedom but not fully. Standardised forms compile information about a specific mortgage contract that the consumer has preselected but do not provide any information about alternative options. Myopia, optimism, and other biases may still interfere with consumers gathering information about alternatives. Moreover, it is questionable whether these forms give consumers a fully adequate view of the consequences the mortgage has under different scenarios.

Let's consider the CWM again. It will probably be a better deal than a fully amortising FRM if there is a real risk that you will accumulate negative equity, particularly during the first years of the repayment period. Taking out the insurance implicit in the CWM can have a positive effect on your mobility. But as long as such information is not reflected in the standard documentation forms, borrowers relying exclusively on such forms may not consider a CWM. In general, it is safe to say that standard disclosure forms only help people rapidly compare mortgages with similar salient risk characteristics; they are not very helpful if consumers want to compare complex mortgage products that differ, for instance, in their interest rate caps or initial fixed-rate periods. This general concern has been pointed out by scholars such as Stark and Choplin (2011), who argue that standardised ESIS forms exhibit shortcomings with regard to disclosing non-salient features of mortgage contracts and key financial concepts, such as the nominal interest rate, to consumers.

In more general terms, the problem here is that information disclosure regulation is mostly designed to provide information concerning the likely consequences of buying one particular product. But to gain known freedom, consumers would need to have information concerning a wide range of different products with different risk characteristics. Information disclosure regulation as presented here is likely to be effective only in mitigating cognitive biases if disclosure forms allow consumers to *compare* (relevant) mortgages, which for all of them, indicate the consequences under a wide variety of (relevant) scenarios. Standard disclosure forms employed so far fall short of that goal and thus inhibit the potential positive impact of financial innovation on known freedom.

Before we proceed, we briefly consider a second type of regulation. Here the idea is not to provide information but rather to prevent consumers from becoming the victims of problematic heuristics, that is, to limit the impact of cognitive biases that stand in the way of weighing options appropriately. Financial literacy education (FLE) initiatives are the key example here. FLE focuses on teaching consumers a range of core concepts including personal finance, information about national legal frameworks, budgeting, and so on. Although such programmes are to be applauded, critics point out that their success depends significantly on participants' motivation (Mandell & Schmid Klein, 2009) and that they do not significantly decrease the impact of cognitive biases on decision-making (Willis, 2008). Thus, it is doubtful whether FLE in principle enhances consumers' known freedom efficiently.

Epistemic Virtues

Let us take stock. We started arguing that consumers stand to benefit from being informed about the characteristics of the products offered by the financial industry and moreover, that complex financial products may be needed to insure them against life adversities. This naturally leads to a tension: Will consumers ever be informed *enough* about complex products? Will they attain the ideal of known freedom? We moved on to look critically at two ways in which regulators attempt to boost informedness amongst consumers, namely, through detailed information disclosure requirements and financial literacy education, and we concluded that there are reasons to be sceptical about effectiveness.

We are not going to propose a cure-all here; gaining, processing, evaluating, sorting, storing and discarding information can be extremely hard work for which people may lack motivation or competence. What we do want to do is to suggest a move away from *regulatory* solutions (at the level of collective, public policy) by considering an *ethical* approach (at the level of individual, private action) to information based on epistemic virtues. A potential worry about such a move is of course that it will lead to the minimalist position that it is entirely and solely the responsibility of individual consumers to make sure that they possess the requisite knowledge. However, as we will show in the final section, an industry committed to the desire satisfaction and/or personal responsibility argument for freedom must contribute to consumer knowledge.

A more philosophical worry might be: Does it make sense to consider belief formation from an ethical point of view? A key paper defending exactly that claim is Clifford's (1877) 'The Ethics of Belief'. His celebrated case of the epistemic vices of a ship owner is worth recounting here. The ship owner considers sending one of his ships to sea. Seeing that it is in poor condition, perhaps not even seaworthy, he considers having it refurbished. However, to do so will cost him a lot of money, which he does not want to spend. As a result of his desire not to spend the required funds, he gradually rejects his negative beliefs about the ship's condition, eventually deceiving himself into believing that the ship will come home this time too, based on an unjustifiable induction from the fact that it has made many successful trips in the past. It does not return, though, and many passengers die at sea. Clifford then blames the ship owner, noting that 'he had no right to believe [in the soundness of the ship] on such evidence as was before him' (Clifford, 1877, pp. 289–290).

Of course the belief was false, and the ship owner had no good reason to hold it. Yet what can it mean to deny him a right to believe a certain proposition and to charge him with moral censure about holding it? Epistemologists and ethicists have recently started developing a full-blooded ethics of belief along Kantian, consequentialist and virtue-theoretical lines. Of these, the concrete insights from virtue epistemology are especially useful in the present context. One of the main tasks of a virtue ethics of belief is to examine what the specifically epistemic virtues are and how such virtues relate to practical, non-epistemic virtues. Epistemic virtues are genuinely Aristotelian virtues in that they are acquired dispositions to strive for the mean between two extremes, and they are constitutive of the good life. (They do not, though, coincide with what Aristotle calls the 'intellectual' virtues such as wisdom and prudence.)

A helpful way to categorise epistemic virtues is the following (Montmarquet, 1993). Firstly, there are the virtues of intellectual *impartiality*. These include dispositions such as open-mindedness, readiness to confront one's ideas with those of others, and an active awareness of one's epistemic shortcomings and fallibility. Next are the virtues of intellectual *sobriety*. Intellectually sober-minded individuals are disposed to steer the middle course between the reckless, overly enthusiastic adoption of beliefs, on the one hand, and the inert disinterestedness that can lead to a reticence to espouse beliefs, on the other. Intellectually sober consumers, for instance, take advertisements with a grain of salt; they are sceptical but not so sceptical as to never adopt a belief. The terminology may suggest that intellectual sobriety is simply the non-epistemic virtue of temperance exercised in an epistemic domain, but that impression would be wrong. Epistemic virtues are acquired in different ways from non-epistemic virtues, and non-epistemically temperate persons are not of necessity intellectually sober minded. This is also true of the next kind of epistemic virtue, intellectual *courage*. Intellectually courageous individuals are eager to subject their beliefs to thorough scrutiny and persist in their inquiry—even if they meet resistance from others—until it has reached completion. Intellectually courageous individuals keep trying to answer the questions they ask, even when this boldly reveals their ignorance. But again, a person who acts courageously on the battlefield is not necessarily intellectually courageous.

Clearly, epistemic virtues do not come cheap: In addition to the aforesurveyed biases (myopia and optimism), there are a host of other biases that negatively affect them; and stress, sleep deprivation, and alcohol have similarly discapacitating effects. But an emerging body of empirical research suggests that acquiring and maintaining epistemic virtues is feasible and that using them is beneficial. Most of this research still concerns medical decision-making (Pritchard, 2005). However, we believe that encouraging findings are coming forward from behavioural finance supporting concrete recommendations to make individual investors aware of their epistemic limitations (Forbes, 2009; Montier, 2007).

Interlucent Communication

That is all very fine of course: intellectually sober-minded consumers will not immediately conclude that the mortgage the adviser claims has the lowest rate is the best choice for them; intellectually courageous consumers will keep asking questions about the specific differences amongst the options on the table; intellectually impartial consumers will actively seek to find counterarguments against particular options. Yet, if finance practitioners give evasive, incomplete, deceptive or plainly false answers, even the most epistemically virtuous consumers will hardly be able to acquire sufficient knowledge about their choice options.

And even if sellers speak without intention to deceive and buyers exercise their epistemic virtues, problems may arise as it is not always clear that communication will succeed. Here is a stylised example. In most countries, one type of mortgage you can buy is a mortgage that does *not* amortise. (So the full principal has to be paid at or after the loan reaches maturity instead of a bit every month.) Such mortgages are called 'interest-only mortgages' in English. We draw our example from a Dutch context, though, where they are called '*aflossingsvrije hypotheek*'. Although the English term emphasises the fact that one only pays interest on the loan, the Dutch term suggests that the most important feature is that the mortgage doesn't need to be repaid (the literal translation is 'repayment-free mortgage', as in Dutch parlance '*aflossing*' [repayment of principal] and '*rente*' [interest] are distinguished). Personal communication with compliance officers from Dutch mortgage providers (and many customer complaints on online fora, TV programmes, etc.) attest to the fact that a sizeable number of people didn't realise that a repayment-free mortgage *does* in fact require you to repay.

Did providers mislead consumers? We don't necessarily think so. We are sold 'skin rejuvenation treatment' but don't think this actually decreases the age of our skin, and we buy stain removers despite the fact that we are aware that the ads overstate their effectiveness. We use euphemisms and hyperbole all the time. Game theorists might describe situations in which, despite understatement and overstatement, speaker and hearer possess *common knowledge* about the meaning of the words and thereby succeed in communicating effectively (Chwe, 2001). Common knowledge captures a particular kind of epistemic situation in which a particular proposition P is open to all members of a given group G. All members of G individually know that P is the case. But in addition, each member also knows of all other members that they know that P, each member knows that all other members know that each other member knows that P, and so on.

So the issue with the interest-only mortgages in The Netherlands is that it is *not* common knowledge amongst sellers and buyers that 'repayment-free' doesn't mean one doesn't have to repay. This is more than just saying that some consumers didn't know this. It is also, amongst other things, to say that the providers didn't know that some consumers didn't know.

If our diagnosis is accurate, an additional recommendation should be to foster common knowledge of the relevant type. We have elsewhere described this as the virtue of *interlucency* (de Bruin, 2015). Interlucency has to be exercised in communication by both speaker and hearer, seller and buyer. What does it require? Suppose that S keeps his or her knowledge about some proposition P to him- or herself. S fails to tell T that P. Clearly, as long as T is unaware of P, then T will remain ignorant about P. But if T knows that P, but S doesn't tell T about P, T will remain ignorant about the fact that S knows that P, and S will remain ignorant about whether T knows that P. In other words, not providing sufficient, relevant and accurate information frustrates the establishment of common knowledge. What we need, then, is a kind of *generosity* in the provision of information.

Yet interlucency isn't correlated only with generosity. Perhaps even more important is that speakers make sure they *track* whether the hearer has received and processed the information they have provided. S not only informs T about P but also makes sure that S knows whether T has received the information, whether T pays attention to what S says about P, and whether T understands what S says. Generosity is insufficient here because if S shared insights generously, but used unfamiliar terminology, S wouldn't contribute to establishing common knowledge about P.

Unlike the earlier epistemic virtues of impartiality, sobriety, and courage, interlucency has two dimensions: It means different things to senders and recipients of information. So far, we have dealt with the sender only. How do recipients contribute to common knowledge? An interlucent recipient T will not only pay attention to what S says, but also ask questions in an attempt to gain clarification, and otherwise attempt to maximise her understanding of what S tells her about P. T will also try to make sure that S is aware of the fact that T listens to what S tells T, and that T understands it. That is, T will *acknowledge receipt* of the information concerning P. This requires T to assume an active posture: If it looks as though T is not paying attention, common knowledge will not be achieved between S and T. Interlucent communication then requires of both individuals that they keep a keen eye on possible *failures* of common knowledge.

This might raise the issue of who is responsible for such failures. Establishing common knowledge is not the responsibility of the finance industry only. Consumers exercising the virtue of interlucency will easily spot possible failures if they concern technical terms. Take a mortgage provider that, questioned about fees, says that if the par rate on sub-prime loans is 9 per cent, they earn one point in YSP (yield spread premium) if the mortgage sells at 9.5 per cent. Firstly, rather than using standard, everyday words in non-standard ways, the mortgage provider is using technical terminology in the standard way used in the profession. It is certainly possible that they realise that the explanation is not going to help this particular customer very much. Yet given that par rates and YSPs are things mortgage providers deal with rather frequently, they may well believe that consumers understand these terms sufficiently well and hence may not suspect a lack of common knowledge about the meaning of terminology. (Doctors may just as well come to believe that all of their patients understand certain technical medical terms.) Customers, by contrast, will immediately spot the lack of common knowledge because they realise they don't understand what 'par rate' and 'YSP' mean. Moreover, customers also know that the provider knows that they, the customers, are best placed to spot *such* failures. So here it is the interlucent consumer rather than the service provider who has to take action to generate common knowledge.

Conclusion

Freedom has value due to its contributions to the satisfaction of desire and the enabling of increased responsibility. Yet freedom concerning choices of which consumers are unaware doesn't increase the satisfaction of their desires or the extent of their responsibility: What they need is knowledge about what choices are available. Finance is one of the main sources of information about the availability of a range of choices such as insurance policies, retirement plans, mortgages, and so on. Its practitioners ought to be truthful and abstain from lying and deception; and consumers ought to exercise the epistemic virtues of impartiality, sobriety and courage. But consumers' knowledge of financial products will not increase if salespeople and consumers do not establish the common knowledge necessary for successful communication.

One might wonder about the extent to which our argument succeeds in making the case for certain moral obligations on the part of financial service providers. In particular, what normative grounding does the virtue of interlucency have? In typical interactions amongst salespeople and their customers, the virtue of interlucency as developed in this chapter is instrumentally necessary if a customer is to understand what a salesperson tells him or her about his or her options. Without interlucency there can hardly be common knowledge about the relevant terms, and without such common knowledge, the customer will find it difficult to acquire any knowledge about financial products. Although this demonstrates the importance of the virtue of interlucency for consumers, service providers may remain unmoved as long as they do not see it as their task to contribute to their customers' known freedom.

The starting point of this chapter is a liberal conception that seeks to find a justification for freedom of enterprise in terms of the two ideals of consumer desire satisfaction and personal responsibility. One way to address an industry unmoved by our earlier argument is to note that this liberal view is actually fairly popular within finance itself: Many finance workers justify their activities at least partly in terms of increasing the general satisfaction of consumers' desires. As a result, if increasing consumer satisfaction is indeed what they think justifies their work, it follows from what we have said here that just designing more products won't do. The industry has to ensure that known freedom grows too. Further, given that known freedom cannot be attained in the absence of common knowledge, interlucency is an immediate second ideal.

This line of reasoning is entirely general in that it applies to a wide variety of industries. Yet it will not be very convincing if you don't share its normative starting point. In that case a second (admittedly less general) answer can be given. As we noted at the beginning of this chapter, desire satisfaction and personal responsibility are ideals that many people in Western countries subscribe to and are frequently used to motivate legislation. Reagan-Thatcher style liberalisation is a case in point. Without 1980s deregulation, sub-prime mortgage lending would have been (largely) illegal, and the market for private retirement plans would have been much smaller than it is nowadays. Legislators justified these changes precisely on the grounds that liberalisation would lead to increased consumer satisfaction and responsibility. Often it did not, though (and the argument about known freedom may show why not, at least in cases where deregulation wasn't accompanied by increased knowledge). If the motivation for changing the law is that we wish to increase consumer satisfaction and responsibility, then we should change it in such a way as to lead to an increase in consumers' known freedom. The state can only marginally contribute the relevant knowledge itself: Financial education may become part of a mandatory school curriculum, but its effects are not very promising; moreover, information about the precise characteristics of financial products will come mainly from those that design and sell these products. So if the finance industry isn't motivated to contribute to the ideal of known freedom through information provision and interlucent communication, there is reason for the state to require them to do so.

Acknowledgements

We would like to thank Matthew Braham, Chris Cowton, Clément Fontan, Martin van Hees, Frank Hindriks, Jan-Willem van der Rijt, Joakim Sandberg and Tom Sorell for stimulating discussions about the topic of this chapter. This chapter builds on and extends ideas from de Bruin (2013, 2015) and de Bruin and Floridi (2017).

References

Badarinza, C., Campbell, J. Y., & Ramadorai, T. (2018). What calls to ARMs? International evidence on interest rates and the choice of adjustable-rate mortgages. *Management Science*, 64(5), 2275–2288.

Bar-Gill, O. (2009). The law, economics and psychology of subprime mortgage contracts. *Cornell Law Review*, 94(3), 1073–1152.

Brown, A. (2009). *Personal responsibility: Why it matters*. London: Continuum.

Campbell, J. Y., Jackson, H. E., Madrian, B. C., & Tufano, P. (2011). Consumer financial protection. *Journal of Economic Perspectives*, 25(1), 91–114.

Carter, I. (1999). *A measure of freedom*. Oxford: Oxford University Press.

Case, K. E., & Shiller, R. J. (1989). The efficiency of the market for single-family homes. *American Economic Review*, 79(1), 125–137.

Chwe, M. S. (2001). *Rational ritual: Culture, coordination, and common knowledge*. Princeton, NJ: Princeton University Press.

Clifford, W. (1877). The ethics of belief. *The Contemporary Review*, 53, 289–309.

Clifton, J., Fernández-Gutiérrez, M., & García-Olalla, M. (2017). Including vulnerable groups in financial services: Insights from consumer satisfaction. *Journal of Economic Policy Reform*, 20(3), 214–237.

de Bruin, B. (2013). Epistemic virtues in business. *Journal of Business Ethics*, 113(4), 583–595.

de Bruin, B. (2015). *Ethics and the global financial crisis: Why incompetence is worse than greed*. Cambridge: Cambridge University Press.

de Bruin, B., & Floridi, L. (2017). The ethics of cloud computing. *Science and Engineering Ethics*, 23(1), 21–39.

Dworkin, R. (1981). What is equality? Part 2: Equality of resources. *Philosophy & Public Affairs*, 10(4), 283–345.

Forbes, W. (2009). *Behavioural finance*. Chichester: John Wiley & Sons.

Gathergood, J., & Weber, J. (2017). Financial literacy, present bias and alternative mortgage products. *Journal of Banking and Finance*, 78, 58–83.

Haughwout, A., & Okah, E. (2009). Below the line: Estimates of negative equity among nonprime mortgage borrowers. *FRBNY Economic Policy Review*, July, 31–43.

Hurka, T. (1987). Why value autonomy? *Social Theory and Practice*, 13(3), 361–382.

Kramer, M. H. (2003). *The quality of freedom*. Oxford: Oxford University Press.

Mandell, L., & Schmid Klein, L. (2009). The impact of financial literacy education on subsequent financial behavior. *Journal of Financial Counseling and Planning*, 20(1), 15–24.

Montier, J. (2007). *Behavioural investing: A practitioner's guide to applying behavioural finance*. Chichester: John Wiley & Sons.

Montmarquet, J. (1993). *Epistemic virtue and doxastic responsibility*. Lanham, MD: Rowman & Littlefield.

Pritchard, D. (2005). Virtue epistemology and the acquisition of knowledge. *Philosophical Explorations*, 8(3), 229–243.

Shiller, R. J. (2012). *Finance and the good society*. Princeton, NJ: Princeton University Press.

Shiller, R. J., Wojakowski, R. M., Ebrahim, M. S., & Shackleton, M. B. (2017). *Continuous workout mortgages: Efficient pricing and systemic implications* (Cowles Foundation Discussion Paper No. 3016). https://cowles.yale.edu/sites/default/files/files/pub/d30/d3016.pdf

Stark, D. P., & Choplin, J. M. (2011). Consumer protection initiatives in the EU mortgage market: A behavioral economics based critique and proposal. *Temple International and Comparative Law Journal*, *25*, 1–42.

Thaler, R. (1985). Mental accounting and consumer choice. *Marketing Science*, *4*(3), 199–214.

White House. (2009). *Remarks of the president on regulatory reform*. www.whitehouse.gov/the_press_office/Remarks-of-the-President-on-Regulatory-Reform

Willis, L. E. (2008). Against financial literacy education. *Iowa Law Review*, *94*(1), 197–285.

7 Aristotelian Lessons After the Global Financial Crisis

Banking, Responsibility, Culture and Professional Bodies

Christopher Megone

Introduction

This piece is not going to offer an analysis of the factors contributing to the global financial crisis (GFC). Its primary focus is the relationship between individual responsibility for good and bad behaviour and organisational culture. However, the reason for this focus is that it is widely supposed that one thing that did occur in the lead-up to the GFC, and contributed to it, was the development within major banking organisations of 'toxic' cultures. Such 'toxic' organisational cultures had the effect of encouraging or permitting ethically bad behaviour and discouraging individuals from speaking up, or raising concerns, about that bad behaviour.[1] In other words the organisation's culture militated against the organisation's staff developing as ethically mature, virtuous individuals.[2] This in turn led to unethical decision-making, which was one factor contributing to the crisis.

Such a rather general story has implications for the analysis of the responsibility of staff within an organisation for such bad behaviour. It suggests complex links between the culture of an organisation and the behaviour of individual staff and consequent repercussions for our judgement of those individuals.[3] It will be argued in what follows that these links involve both ways in which the culture of an organisation can affect an individual's ethical development and also ways in which individuals in an organisation, and the nature of their ethical development, can affect organisational culture. Thus the responsibility of individual staff for bad behaviour within an organisation turns out to be a complex matter.

However, if individual responsibility and organisational culture are intertwined, and if toxic culture was a contributory factor to the GFC, then in drawing lessons it may be beneficial to reflect on the factors, both internal[4] and external, that can affect the development of organisational culture. What can be beneficial and what harmful? What factors contribute to the existence of 'toxic' cultures?

The aim of this chapter is to set out an Aristotelian framework regarding the development of ethically mature, virtuous individuals, which facilitates an analysis of the responsibility of individual staff within an organisation such as a bank for ethically bad behaviour. This will in turn serve to bring out some of the complexity of the interactions amongst individual development, judgement and responsibility for behaviour, on the one hand, and organisational culture, on the other.

Having set out the Aristotelian framework, and the consequent analysis of the relation between individual responsibility and organisational culture, I will apply this analysis to reflect on contemporary banking culture. In particular, I will identify the role of some key internal factors within banks themselves and that of relevant external factors (such as the UK's Banking Standards Board [BSB], regulators, and professional bodies) in creating positive cultures that can support and encourage staff in developing as ethically mature, virtuous agents and acting accordingly. Although the argument here focuses at this practical level on the banking and building society sector, it could be applied in a similar way to other financial sectors and organisations. For example, it might be applied to accountancy and accounting firms, also in the limelight regarding issues of organisational culture and individual staff responsibility.[5]

Broadly speaking, what I shall claim is that individual employees within an organisation *shouldn't* (morally shouldn't) conform in a simple-minded way to 'how things are (or seem to be) around here' or shouldn't think that ethical behaviour is achieved by unreflectively following the rules (set within or by a regulator). In a similar vein, individuals shouldn't think of ethical behaviour in the workplace as a simple matter that can easily be read off from a knowledge of the organisation's values. This leaves people at the level of a child in terms of moral development.

Thus I will also argue against an organisational culture that encourages or even coerces its staff to adopt such an ethically immature outlook. By contrast, an organisation needs to see itself as developing a culture for adult humans that is, as Socrates emphasised, beings with rational potential, the potential to live an examined life, so agents capable of developing character within which judgement is crucial. In effect, lists of values, rules, regulation, even ethical 'training', *if taken (or provided) in the wrong way*, can all encourage staff to try to deflect responsibility for ethical judgement rather than develop as responsible rational agents. This does not mean that such values, rules, and regulation (and appropriate ethical training) have no place and that staff should be left without guidance and support.[6] Indeed, the Aristotelian framework will suggest that these are important aspects of an organisation's ethical culture. But support must also include the opportunity for rational reflection and discussion, working through what the values and rules actually mean in practice and whether current approaches are in fact correct.

This last point illustrates, I will claim, why organisational culture can depend not just on internal factors but on external ones such as a professional body. For discussion within an organisation may be very difficult, and the opportunity for reflection with fellow professionals may be very valuable. Furthermore, sometimes eyes accustomed to viewing matters a certain way find it hard to see them any other way, so an external review by an organisation such as the BSB can be helpful.

In sum, the Aristotelian framework will suggest that organisational culture needs to give staff the opportunity to develop ethical maturity, to *be* or *become* a wise, just, generous person in the workplace, not merely someone who does wise, just, or generous acts, following rules like a child.

As Aristotle notes in the *Nicomachean Ethics Book II* (Aristotle, 2009; henceforth NE II,4 1105b 7–9; II,6 1106b 21–23, etc.), there is a significant difference between doing a virtuous act and doing a virtuous act as the virtuous person does, namely, in the right way, for the right reasons. This distinction is not merely important because of its significance for the development of the individual. It is also important because, if an organisation leaves individuals in a childlike, unreflective state with respect to 'how we do things around here', that will itself be a major contributory factor in the development of a 'toxic' organisational culture.

So careful thought is needed as to what kind of *internal* practices are required to create an organisational culture that enhances the development of virtuous character and reflective judgement in staff and also as to how other *external* organisations, such as the BSB, the Financial Conduct Authority, and professional bodies, can support the development of such a culture.

Despite this attention to organisational culture, it will also be argued that on the Aristotelian analysis of responsibility, the individual employee pretty much always retains some degree of responsibility for his or her acts and for the contribution of those acts to organisational outcomes. Indeed, even an agent working in a coercive culture remains blameworthy for negligent ignorance of general moral rules. Thus staff do not lose the responsibility to act in ways that can change the culture of their workplace and in particular the responsibility to stand up against obviously morally wrong practices in a 'toxic' culture.[7]

The Aristotelian Framework

Necessarily, the Aristotelian framework here will be a sketch of an Aristotelian position rather than a fully detailed scholarly account, but I take it to be a plausible reading of some of his central ideas.[8]

My aim in setting out this framework is to make it possible to distinguish different senses in which an individual may be responsible for action in an organisation such as a large bank. Following Aristotle, I will argue that there is a sense in which an individual is responsible for those acts they do voluntarily, or intentionally; there is a different sense in which an individual is responsible for his or her character and for actions that flow from that character; and there is a further sense in which an individual is responsible for acts that reflect negligence on the individual's part.

I will also claim that individual responsibility is a matter of degree—individuals can be responsible for actions to a greater or lesser degree.[9] In light of this, individuals can be more, or less, blameworthy for actions. And a significant factor affecting the degree of responsibility is organisational culture. (But there are in fact two connections between individual and culture: the individual's responsibility for his or her acts is affected by organisational culture: But the individual, by her or her behaviour, is a shaper of culture.)

Putting matters somewhat colloquially, one rather common occurrence in the workplace can be that individuals in an organisation become people who do things simply because 'this is how we do things around here'. This can be partly a reflection of a coercive culture, one that encourages such unthinking behaviour, but it may also reflect a lack of mature ethical development that leads to a different kind of responsibility for action. It can also result from a form of negligence on the part of the individual. The claims set out above will help analyse these points.

Hekousion, akousion, ouk akousion

In the first chapter of *Nicomachean Ethics Book III*, Aristotle begins his discussion of actions for which an agent is responsible, hence acts that can be judged virtuous (worthy of praise) or vicious (worthy of blame).

> Since virtue is to do with feelings and actions, and since voluntary feelings and actions are praised and blamed, while the involuntary ones are pardoned and occasionally pitied, presumably anyone considering virtue must determine the limits of the voluntary and the involuntary. It will be useful as well for legislators, in connection with honours and punishments.
>
> (NE III,1 1109b 26ff)[10]

Having indicated in this passage the relation of virtuous action, in the first instance, to the notions of voluntary, or intentional, action, Aristotle then develops his account by providing an analysis of what it is for an act to be voluntary or intentional. He also provides a survey of types of action to distinguish more carefully those for which people are held praiseworthy and blameworthy. The upshot is that he distinguishes three types of action, all of which are relevant for analysing the notion of an agent's responsibility for action. He picks out voluntary, involuntary and 'mixed' acts.

He begins with involuntary acts. These are acts that are performed *by force* or *through ignorance*. What is forced is what has an external first principle (*arche*) such that the agent or person acted upon contributes nothing to it—for example, cases in which the wind blows him or her or people with power over him or her compel him or her (NE III,1 1109b

28ff). In other words, an agent's action is involuntary when he or she is compelled to act by virtue of physical force, but there could also be cases of psychological compulsion involving techniques such as hypnosis or brainwashing. In these cases, the agent is not responsible for his or her action.

The second type of ground for an act being involuntary is its being performed through ignorance. But Aristotle is careful to distinguish the kind of ignorance that is involved. For as he observes, 'Now every wicked man is ignorant of what he ought to do and what he ought to abstain from' (NE III,1 1110b 24ff). So it is not ignorance of universal claims, like the claim that stealing is wrong, that makes an act involuntary.

The ignorance that is relevant for involuntary (or unintentional) action is 'ignorance of particular facts, that is, of the circumstances of the action and the objects with which it is concerned' (NE III,1 1110b 24ff). So, for example, Oedipus knew he was killing a man, but he did not know that the man was his father. So his act was voluntary (or intentional), and one for which he was responsible under the description 'killing a man', but involuntary (or unintentional), and one for which he was not responsible, under the description 'killing his father'.[11]

By contrast, then, 'voluntary [action] would seem to be that of which the moving principle is in the agent himself, he being aware of the particular circumstances of the action' (NE III,1 1111a 22–24). In other words, two conditions must be met for an act to be voluntary, one for which the agent is responsible. Firstly, it must be motivated by a moving principle (an *arche*) within the agent (NE III,1 1110a 15–18), that is, a desire. Second, the agent must have appropriate beliefs concerning the relevant particulars of the action. Thus children (and animals) are capable of voluntary acts, of being responsible for acts of this sort, and praised or blamed for them (NE III,2 1111b 8–10).[12] This point will be important in what follows.

However, Aristotle is also interested in a third category, namely, 'mixed actions'. What leads Aristotle to introduce this category is his reflection on the question of when an act is genuinely motivated by a starting point (*arche*) within the agent or of what kind of external force counts as compelling. He mentions the examples of an agent who is being threatened by a tyrant who is holding the agent's family hostage and of a ship's captain who is caught in a storm and so throws luggage overboard save the lives of the passengers (NE III,1 1110a 5ff).

Such actions, he says, are mixed, although they seem more like voluntary (intentional) ones, because at the time they are done, they are worthy of choice, and the end of an action depends on the circumstances (NE III,1 1110a 7ff). And he goes on to add that they are voluntary because the power of moving limbs, the first principle, is in the agent, and where this is in him or her, it is in his or her power to act or not to act. But, considered without qualification, they are involuntary because no one would choose any of them in itself (NE III,1 1110a 9ff).

These remarks about mixed acts, in which Aristotle reflects on the notion of force or compulsion, and the sense in which the act really comes from a starting point within the agent, are interesting here with respect to the way in which organisational culture, or peer pressure, might be seen as coercive.

Thus, where there is physical force such as the wind blowing, or psychological intervention such as brainwashing, and possibly a threat of sufficient strength, such as a gun against the head, it seems clear there is sufficient coercion to imply the act is not voluntary at all. The agent is not responsible for such acts.

However, what this account of mixed acts suggests is that in a mixed act, the agent is still responsible for the act but to a lesser degree. This implies that responsibility is gradable and consequently that there can be degrees of praise and blame for such acts. So for our present purposes, the question will arise as to how coercive organisational culture is. This may vary, of course. Perhaps on occasion it can be very coercive. But acts performed in such circumstances still look more like those of the ship's captain in a storm, so voluntary at root. I will return to this point in due course.

This then is the first stage in the Aristotelian account of ethically assessable acts, providing one sense in which the agent is responsible for acts. Voluntary or intentional action is ethically assessable (praiseworthy or blameworthy), although the point of assessment may vary in the cases of animals, children, and adults. (In animals the aim might be to steer action, in children to steer action and rational development, in adults for the purposes of rational development and to mark desert for punishment or reward.)

In this discussion of voluntary and involuntary acts, Aristotle has also touched on a second way in which an agent can be held responsible and thus praised or blamed. This concerns cases in which the agent's culpability lies in negligence. For in the argument set out here Aristotle noted that ignorance of universal claims is not the kind of ignorance that makes an act involuntary and thus excusable. His reason was that to claim otherwise would imply that wicked people act involuntarily—because they are ignorant of what they should do. Thus he implies that a certain kind of ignorance is itself blameworthy (NE III,5 offers a long discussion of this issue). Not knowing certain universal truths, or not acting in respect of those truths, may be blameworthy negligence. This is because the agent is responsible for such negligence. The agent has failed to recognise (or act on) truths he or she had the rational power to recognise. This then is a second aspect of the Aristotelian account of responsibility.

Prohairesis

Having discussed *hekousion* and *akousion* acts, Aristotle next turns, in NE III,2, to the concept of *prohairesis*, which has been translated as rational choice, preferential choice or election. (So note that it is a technical term in Aristotle's account.) He gives the following reason for addressing this topic: 'For it is thought to be very closely tied to virtue, and a better guide to men's characters than their actions' (NE III,2 1111b 3–4). Although agents can be responsible for voluntary actions and those actions can be assessed as worthy of praise or blame, it is only when acts are chosen (involve *prohairesis*) that they are in a fuller sense morally assessable because only then do they reflect the agent's character.

Thus an agent is responsible for a voluntary act in the sense that the act came from him or her and he or she knew what he or she was doing, but when an agent's act involves *prohairesis*, he or she is more fully ethically responsible for it in so far as the act not merely came from him or her but reflects his or her character.

This can be explained further by attending to some of Aristotle's additional remarks about *prohairesis*, or preferential choice. He begins by noting that chosen acts are a subset of voluntary (or intentional) acts. Acts involving choice are voluntary, but not the same as voluntary acts, because children and animals can perform voluntary acts, but they cannot make choices or perform chosen acts (NE III,2 1111b 7ff). The reason for this is the nature of the desires (and evaluative beliefs) involved in making choices, of which children are not capable. (That is why children's acts are not fully morally assessable.)

This is explained further when Aristotle notes that choice is a deliberate desire of things in our own power (NE III,2 1113a 9ff). So arriving at a preferential choice is part of a process of reasoning that leads to action. Thus arriving at *prohaireseis* or choices is something that humans can do in virtue of being rational animals and of actualising some of their rational powers. Deliberation, for Aristotle here, involves working out the means to the agent's ends or goals. Thus to make choices, the agent must have such goals or ends.

Choice is a significant component in the development of character. Thus it is part of Aristotle's definition of virtue (NE II,6 1106b 36–1107a 2), but it is also a feature of other states of character (vice, *acrasia*, *encrasia*). A state of character is a settled disposition of the mind—this does not mean it is unchanging, but it does mean that an agent's character will involve a tendency to form certain beliefs and desires in response to circumstances. The virtuous agent's choices are distinguished by being made in light of true beliefs and correct desires. This is how their choices differ from those of other types of character (NE VI,2 1139a 20–25).

The reason choice is a significant component of virtue, part of its definition, as well as significant for other states of character, is that it is what makes a settled state of character settled. For the desires that are involved in forming choices are themselves formed in response to the agent's conception of what is good. This therefore distinguishes the motive of the virtuous agent who does a virtuous act from that of an agent who merely performs a virtuous act voluntarily.

On Aristotle's account, habituation is the process through which agents become capable of choice. Through habituation rational agents come to desire the object of their desire as good; and in that same process they come to see for themselves what is (or appears to them to be) worthwhile or good. Thus, such desires are formed in response to the goodness of their objects. By contrast, non-rational agents simply have appetitive desires that just come upon them.[13] The responsiveness of the desires of rational agents to their conception of what is worth pursuing, or good, is what makes such desires (and thus the agent's character) more settled. This state is settled in contrast with that of non-rational agents who are the subjects of mere appetitive desires (and perceptual beliefs) that simply come upon them.

This is why the development of the capacity for making preferential choices bears on the nature of the agent's responsibility for actions. When the agent acts in the light of a preferential choice, that act is performed in the light of the agent's conception of what is, or appears to them to be, good. It is not merely a voluntary act performed, as in the case of a child, in response to a desire that he or she simply finds him- or herself having.

Habituation

As noted, on Aristotle's view, it is a process of habituation that is crucial for development of the kind of desires that make possible the deliberation in the light of ends or goals that result in preferential choices for action. And as is already implicit, such a process, resulting in such desires, is also central for the development of (good) character.

A full account of the nature of habituation on Aristotle's view is beyond the scope of this chapter (see Burnyeat, 1980; Jimenez, 2016; Kraut, 2012; Vassiliou, 1996). The aim is, therefore, to identify those fundamental features that explain its role in the formation of character and illuminate the role that organisational culture can play in that process. This will help explain the importance of the culture of organisations for individual responsibility and, thus, in the present case, the importance of banking culture in particular.

Aristotle sets out the importance of habituation in *Nicomachean Ethics* when he states, following Ross's translation, that 'moral virtue comes about as a result of habit' (NE II,1 1103a 16–17). The use of the term 'habit' can be misleading here as there is more to what Aristotle has in mind than merely making something a matter of habit, more than a process of conditioning.

Aristotle goes on to explain further that

> the virtues we get by first exercising them, as also happens in the case of the arts as well. For the things we have to learn before we can do them, we learn by doing them, e.g. men become builders by building

and lyre-players by playing the lyre; so too we become just by doing just acts, temperate by doing temperate acts, brave by doing brave acts.

And he immediately adds that 'this is confirmed by what happens in states; for legislators make the citizens good by forming habits in them, and this is the wish of every legislator' (NE II,1 1103a 31-b 5).

These remarks already bring out the fact that habituation has three stages. It requires: (i) guidance (as indicated in this last quote concerning legislators); (ii) practice or action; and (iii) (at least often) repetition.

A brief account of each of these factors will elucidate the Aristotelian view. If we consider a child's ethical formation, then on Aristotle's account in the early years it will simply be motivated by whatever desire happens to arise (*epithumia*). The development of virtue will require guidance (e.g., from family and school). Take an example of courage. A parent might advise a child that he or she needs to stand up to a bully at school. The child will then only want to do this insofar as he or she trusts the parent. The second stage involves action—the child following the parent's guidance and actually standing up to the bully. This is crucial in transforming the child's desire. Aristotle's thought is that through acting, and only through acting, the child comes to see for him- or herself the point of the courageous act. As Burnyeat (1980, p. 73) puts it, 'practice has cognitive powers'. Repetition is then important for two reasons. In some cases, the point of action may not be grasped the first time—the point may be difficult to grasp because being courageous is sometimes difficult, or the child's (rational) ability to grasp it may have been distorted by other pressures. But also, courage can be manifested in different ways on different occasions, with the common feature not necessarily obvious, so grasping the point of courage across different circumstances will require repeated courageous actions (and reflection).

Putting these features together, through guidance, repetition, and action a person undergoing ethical formation (which is not, of course, confined to childhood) comes to form desires for actions, or the goals of action, in virtue of the point of those goals. Thus, rather than having the desires of an infant or small child, which come upon the agent and simply aim at the object as what satisfies the desire, the agent comes to have desires that are responsive to the (perceived) value or worth of the goals. This in turn enables the agent to form *prohaireseis*, deliberated preferential choices for the acts that will achieve those desired goals in the present circumstances.

For present purposes it is the role of guidance in this account of habituation that is most important. As Aristotle's remark about legislators indicates, guidance need not be given simply by explicit orally expressed advice from a parent or authority figure but can be provided by the laws of the land (or by other regulation—e.g., school rules). Thus communities, not just individuals, can provide guidance. But guidance within a community is more complex than that because it need not be explicit at all. It can be implicit in the way exemplars conduct themselves. So those who lead others, whether in virtue of position or in virtue of fame, can convey guidance through the way they behave. Similarly, the behaviour of groups, especially of groups of peers, can express implicit guidance. Furthermore, what is rewarded or penalised within a community, whether explicitly or implicitly, can provide guidance on practice and thereby influence habituation (and thus ethical formation). And all of these forms of guidance can obviously be found as components of an organisation's culture.

The key features of this Aristotelian framework can now be summarised. From the point of view of an agent's responsibility for action, Aristotle begins by distinguishing voluntary (or intentional) actions, involuntary (or unintentional) actions, and mixed actions. When the starting principle (*arche*) is within the agent and the agent has the relevant knowledge, the act is voluntary, and the agent (whether animal, child, or adult human) is responsible for it in that first sense. Where an act is involuntary the agent is not (usually) responsible for it. In mixed actions the agent acts under some kind of external pressure that raises a question as to whether the act is really motivated by a starting principle (desire) from within the agent. However, Aristotle claims that in a genuinely mixed act, the act remains voluntary, so one for which the agent is responsible. The degree of pressure in such acts can vary, which suggests responsibility in this sense can be gradable—the agent can be more or less responsible depending on the degree of pressure.

There is a form of ignorance that does not prevent this kind of responsibility, namely, ignorance of general moral rules or principles. If an agent acts from such ignorance, then this will reflect negligence for which the agent is responsible. (One might think that this could even affect an 'involuntary' act in which the agent acts involuntarily because of failing to take sufficient care, when he or she should have known that such care was required.) In these cases, then, even though there is a sense in which the agent does not know what he or she is doing, he or she remains responsible for what occurs.

However, there is a further (third) type of action in which the agent is more fully responsible, from an ethical point of view, for what he or she does. Such acts are those that stem from the agent's preferential choices (*prohaireseis*). But the agent is only capable of such acts when he or she has undergone habituation and thus come to have the type of desires that are necessary for forming such choices.

Applying the Aristotelian Framework to Learn Lessons From the Financial Crisis

This Aristotelian account of responsibility and character formation can now be applied to an analysis of the relations between ('toxic') organisational culture and individual behaviour and to the lessons that might be learnt from the influence of such 'toxic' cultures during the banking crisis.

To begin with, when an employee (in a bank, say) acts voluntarily, that is motivated by a desire from within him or her and having knowledge of relevant particulars, then the employee is responsible (in the first sense) for the outcomes of that action.

However, Aristotle's discussion of mixed actions suggests that when an employee is working in an organisation with a 'strong' culture, the employee will be subject to significant external pressures. These might sometimes be analogous to those on the ship's captain who throws luggage overboard in a storm. The organisation may provide very strong incentives to behave in certain ways, and failure of the employee to act in ways so incentivised might significantly affect career progression, family opportunities, and so on. Nonetheless Aristotle seems right to say that the employee's acts remain voluntary, so ones for which he or she is responsible. However, it might be held that the degree of responsibility here is less, and so he or she is less worthy of blame (or praise) for his or her acts. (This would, of course, depend on whether he or she would have done the acts irrespective of the pressures.)

However, the framework here suggested more complex ways in which organisational culture can bear on individual responsibility for action and in particular two ways in which a 'toxic' culture can affect individual behaviour adversely.

The most obvious way in which organisational culture can affect individual behaviour is through providing the kind of guidance that plays a crucial role in habituation. Thus a 'toxic' culture will provide guidance that contributes to the development of bad character. And to the extent that the employee's character involves a tendency to choose and behave in certain ways, the organisational culture will have had a part in the agent's bad actions. As noted, there are a range of factors—both explicit and implicit—that can constitute components of an organisational culture that provide guidance and so a variety of ways in which a culture can be 'toxic' and form bad character. But before turning to these in more detail, it will be helpful to note the second way in which a 'toxic' organisational culture can encourage adverse ethical formation and thus bear some significant responsibility for the bad behaviour of employees.

Whilst a misguided organisational code of conduct, or poorly thought-out incentives, can directly guide character formation and thus bad behaviour, the other damaging effect of a 'toxic' culture is more subtle. Some forms of organisational culture can encourage employees to become agents that simply unreflectively act in the way they take to be 'how we do things around here'. Various factors can contribute to this result. Organisations can imply that all an employee needs to do is follow the code of conduct or adhere to values. Leaders can imply that employees should simply do what they are told. Those who raise questions about values or practice can be stamped upon. Peer behaviour can imply that conformity to the group is all that matters and that failure to so conform will result in isolation. Spheres of responsibility for action can be left very unclear to discourage employees from taking any responsibility for action. Ethical training can be poor, implying that ethical decision-making is obvious or simple so not something worthy of reflection.

An organisational culture that comprises all or some of these factors (and there may be others that produce the same effect) will encourage employees to the view that what is required in the workplace is unreflective conformity to how things are currently done in the organisation (as they perceive it). This kind of culture leaves an employee in an ethically childlike state, simply voluntarily following perceived rules but making no effort to go beyond that to discern for him- or herself the value or otherwise the goals implied by the rules. Such a culture is 'toxic' for two reasons.

First it fails to enable employees to develop as ethically mature humans. Human beings are rational animals, as Aristotle claimed (NE, I,7 1098a 3–14). But what he meant by that is that all humans have rational potential, potential that is developed if things go well (no disease/illness, or injuries, or other harms) and if nurtured properly. And the nurturing of such potential is part of flourishing. So organisational cultures that encourage their employees to remain in an ethically childlike state are harming them and preventing them from becoming fully ethically responsible beings.

But the second effect of an organisational culture that encourages such unreflective conformity is that it adversely affects the ability of such employees to raise concerns if the behaviour to which they conform becomes ethically flawed—dishonest, greedy, exploitative, untrustworthy, and so on. A 'toxic' organisational culture that fails to encourage employees to see for themselves the point of what they are doing, undermines their ability to develop an independent perspective, a necessary pre-requisite for having the courage to challenge existing practices. But organisations can often incentivise unethical behaviour inadvertently as a side effect to other objectives, and an important safeguard is having ethically mature employees, capable of forming their own preferential choices, who can speak up in such circumstances.

These last remarks actually lead into noting the third way in which individuals within an organisation can be held responsible for outcomes of behaviour, given the Aristotelian framework. There is a form of ignorance that does not make an agent's action involuntary, namely, ignorance of ethical rules or principles. When an individual can reasonably be expected to have known such rules or principles (where the individual is of a certain age and the rules or principles are basic or fundamental), such ignorance constitutes negligence, and the corresponding behaviour is negligent.

Thus even in a strongly 'toxic' organisational culture, individual employees remain responsible not only for doing bad acts but also for failing to speak out against bad guidance, implicit or explicit in the culture, where they could have been expected to know of its badness.

This last point is connected to the fact that although guidance, and thus organisational culture, is an important part of the formation of employee character through habituation, our character is still to some extent up to us. As Aristotle observes,

> If, then, as we suggested, virtues are voluntary, (because we are in some way partly responsible for our states of character, and it is by being the kind of people that we are that we assume such and such as our end), vices will also be voluntary, for the same is true of them.
> (NE III,5 1114b 21–26)

One explanation for this is that as rational agents, we have the power to recognise, even when adversely guided, fundamental goals that are worth pursuing or avoiding. Thus to that extent we always retain an irreducible ability to contribute to the development of our own characters even in adverse circumstances. Thus ignorance can, in relevant circumstances, constitute negligence.

The remarks in these latter paragraphs point to a final intersection between individual employees and organisational culture. Individuals, through their behaviour in the workplace (hence exemplars), and through what they speak up for, what they question, and how they advise others, contribute to the development of organisational culture for the future. Although not leaders, each individual is still an exemplar via their actions (or lack of them) to their fellow employees, thus also guiding (but with less influence than a leader) the behaviour of their fellows in a small way. Those who merely conform unreflectively contribute therefore to an ossifying and stale culture. To the extent that a 'toxic' culture encourages this, in the way explained previously, it fosters a vicious circle.

Practical and Policy Implications

So values, rules or codes, ethical training, and leadership can all, if poorly implemented, contribute to a 'toxic' organisational culture, and such a culture may have been a contributory factor in the financial crisis. This does not mean that banks and building societies should seek to avoid guiding employees in ways that affect character. Organisations will have a culture—there is no neutral place to stand here—and it will affect employees' character and behaviour. So the important thing is to focus on the factors that are most significant in creating an organisational culture that has a positive effect on ethical character and behaviour.

Previous work on promoting integrity in organisations is relevant here (Baxter et al., 2012). Although the current focus is on developing an organisational culture that promotes formation of virtuous character, the factors identified are equally important in that context. (Indeed, an

Aristotelian might argue that there is a close link between virtue and integrity [Megone, 2009].)

The work on integrity identified a number of factors, some of them familiar, that bear on organisational culture. These included, in ranked priority, leadership or tone from the top, organisational values, an open culture, space to raise concerns,[14] the availability of advice, codes of conduct, and ethical training. These can now be understood in the Aristotelian framework in terms of the way they bear on character formation as forms of guidance. Leadership provides guidance in the form of an exemplar; the leader embodies a character to be adopted, and the fact that the leader has such a character implies that it has the imprimatur of the organisation, which emphasises to the employee the value in becoming of like character. Obviously it is important that there is consistency between the leader as an exemplar and the organisation's stated values and code of conduct. If the leader's behaviour is in conflict with these, the employee is not given clear guidance, which undermines the process of habituation. (Worse than that, of course, if the leader does not merely behave in ways inconsistent with stated values, but behaves ethically badly, such an example directly poisons the culture by implying that behaving badly is the way to progress in the organisation, so implicitly guiding employees towards behaving in that way.)

Leadership, values and a code of conduct give direct behavioural guidance. The employee can act on this guidance and, assuming it is well-founded, come to see for him- or herself the point or worth of the goals of the behaviour it encourages, the second stage in the formation of (virtuous) character. An open culture, space to raise concerns, the availability of advice, and well-designed ethical training are all relevant to avoiding the indirect way in which a 'toxic' culture can harm the development of character in an employee. It has been argued that a 'toxic' culture can harm the development of virtuous character indirectly by encouraging mere unthinking conformity to organisational practice. In so doing it discourages the employee from seeking to see for him- or herself the point of the behaviour guided.

Employees in such a culture, left in a childlike ethical state, at best do the right thing, but fail to do the right thing for the right reasons, so merely do virtuous acts but do not become virtuous. However, the four features identified are aspects of organisational culture that will encourage employees to exercise their rational powers to identify the point of the practices encouraged in their organisation. An open culture and well-designed ethical training, for example, encourage employees to reflect on why the organisation guides behaviour in the way it does, constructively engaging with such guidance. Indeed, in the context of the financial crisis, an organisation fostering the development of good character in this way might have found its employees querying the goals or practices of those organisations and whether their approaches sat well with the true purpose of banking.

A recently introduced policy, the implementation of the Senior Managers Regime (SMR) in the UK may also make a positive contribution to organisational culture. For another cultural factor that can cause employees to deflect ethical responsibility away from themselves is the absence of clear spheres of responsibility for action and outcomes. The SMR addresses that issue. Furthermore, to carry out that role effectively, managers will need to have fully developed ethical characters (not be mere conformists). They will need to have a critical grasp of the values and goals of the organisation, and of its practices. But this means that if banks and building societies are to nurture staff well-equipped for those roles, they will need to have organisational cultures that foster the development of virtuous character.

Such internal features in banks and building societies will create an organisational culture that guides behaviour in a way likely to encourage good character and employees equipped to be critical friends with respect to the overall purposes of the organisation as well as with regard to details of particular practices. However, external factors can also have an important bearing on organisational culture, so I will end by identifying three such external factors.

Firstly, there is the role of regulation. One response to the GFC has been to focus on regulation in the bank and building society sector. However, one danger with an over-emphasis on regulation, in the present context, is that organisations develop a culture in which employees believe that they need only to conform unthinkingly to the law or to the regulator's rules. So again, there is the risk of a culture encouraging a childlike ethical formation. To the extent that such a culture prevails, this prevents employees developing a perception of the point of the rules. They simply follow them without knowing why. It will also mean that a sector fostering such attenuated ethical development will be ill-equipped to engage constructively with the need for new practices as the banking environment changes, for example, as technology develops. This does not mean there is not a role for regulation—it means that organisations need to be conscious of the pitfalls of developing an uncritical regulatory culture internally and the adverse effects that can have on the development of ethically mature employees.

Another response to the banking crisis in the UK has been the development of the BSB, tasked with raising the quality of ethical and technical practice across banks and building societies. In the present context one significant activity that is carried out by the BSB is the annual survey of culture. (It also surveys behaviour and competence.) The Aristotelian framework presented here has made it possible to identify the way in which a 'toxic' organisational culture can adversely affect employee character and behaviour both directly and indirectly. It has also provided a critical basis for assessing factors that can contribute positively to organisational culture.

It should be clear from the argument thus far that cultures that encourage mere behavioural conformity are 'toxic' in an important way, even when the behavioural guidance is good. But the risk of an organisational culture becoming merely conformist is probably as strong for cultures that have well-judged values as for those whose values encourage vice in their employees. So the need for a further set of eyes to examine an organisational culture on a regular basis is a critical factor in avoiding such degeneration. Thus this work by the BSB is something that from the current perspective would seem to be in principle of significant value for all banks and building societies, at least those that take seriously the ethical formation of their employees. The GFC should be sufficient motive for doing that. Clearly the BSB's own work in assessing culture will itself benefit from being informed by Aristotelian insights that clarify the complex relation between organisational culture and character formation.

The third external factor is professional bodies. The argument already presented has claimed that whilst employee ethical formation is affected by organisational culture, employees can also contribute to the development of organisational culture. In part this is because employees are formed by other guidance and experience outside their workplace. These might include, for example, their family, the clubs they participate in or their religious practice. But one obviously relevant community might also be their professional body.

Developing this point depends on a view of the nature and role of a professional body. Sir Philip Mawer offers some helpful thoughts here. In a 2010 speech, Mawer identified 'an additional pillar of professionalism—the culture of a profession' and noted that

> initial training and CPD need to be seen, not just as being about the acquisition of skills but as being about the shaping of members in the culture of a profession. We [the Institute and Faculty of Actuaries] are not in the business simply of training, but of formation of members in the values and expectations of the Profession of which they seek to be, then are, a proud part.[15]

As Jim Baxter and I have argued elsewhere (Baxter & Megone, 2016, p. 94):

> [This] is a picture which helps to explain how members of a profession can develop a shared language and foster good practice and a sense of common purpose in ways which help [them] to develop a sense of pride in what they do. Taken together these can in turn create a notion of professional identity, a sense in both the individual and the professional community that what the professional does is not just work, but a meaningful way of life.

On this account a professional professes a way of life, and part of the role of a professional body is formation in that way of life.

In terms of the development of a positive organisational culture within a bank or building society, then, a professional body can support employees that belong to it in various ways. Insofar as the professional body also contributes to the formation of character, it provides another guide that can help the employee become a virtuous agent rather than at best merely a conformist to good practice and at worst an unthinking conformist to bad practice. An example can illustrate this. It was argued that a positive organisational culture will be open and allow employees to raise concerns. However, raising concerns can be a difficult matter even within a supportive culture, for it will usually involve in some way criticism of other employees, and that can be hard for them to receive, with the potential to undermine other important factors in an organisation, such as trust. A professional body can provide another community within which to raise one's concerns with fellow professionals, talking through whether they are justified, reflecting on how they relate to organisational values, and so on. Thus a professional body can be a useful aid in strengthening a positive organisational culture.

Conclusion

In this chapter I have sketched an Aristotelian framework concerning individual responsibility for action and its relation to the culture of a community. This identified three types of individual responsibility for action, that which arises from voluntary action, that which arises from action flowing from preferential choice (so reflecting character), and that which arises in cases of negligence. It also identified the role of the culture of a community in guiding members of that community in ways that are relevant to habituation and thus the formation of character.

I have argued that this framework is helpful in analysing the nature of a 'toxic' organisational culture, and the way in which such cultures in banks and building societies may have contributed to the GFC, but also the responsibility that lies with individuals despite the influence of organisational culture. In that light I have suggested factors, internal and external to organisations, that can contribute to cultures that will positively support the development of ethically responsible employees, making those employees better placed with respect to the actions for which they are responsible.

Notes

1. In this chapter I mean the term 'ethical' to be interchangeable with the term 'moral'. So ethically bad behaviour is morally bad behaviour. Although some philosophers have suggested drawing a distinction between the ethical and the moral, 'moral' (and 'morality') is simply derived from the Latin word for

the Greek word '*ethike*', which is the root of 'ethics'. So a standard view is that ethics and morality cover the same ground.

2. I use the term 'virtuous', in Aristotelian mode, to pick out individuals of good character, with the opposite being vicious, meaning people with vices or of bad character. So justice and courage are paradigm virtues, whereas injustice and cowardice are paradigm vices.

3. 'Culture' is another term that is widely used in different disciplines but may mislead because of different disciplinary nuances. Here I mean by it, with respect to an organisational context, roughly 'the way we do things around here', expressed explicitly in guides to staff behaviour from statements of values to codes of practice to staff handbooks but also, and often at least as importantly, expressed implicitly via implied assumptions about behaviour. For example, if a member of staff has finished work for the day and begins to leave at 5:30, the official time for leaving work, but is met by comments from more senior staff such as 'taking an early bath, then', the implication might be both that 'we don't leave work at 5:30 around here' and also that this is not a culture in which one questions such practices (so 'speaking up' is frowned upon).

4. By 'internal factors' I have in mind here structural features of an organisation, but it will be argued that one relevant internal factor is also the behaviour of individual staff.

5. Obviously the argument could in fact be generalised beyond the financial world.

6. So far as ethical training is concerned I must declare an interest insofar as my organisation offers such training! But inappropriate ethical training can encourage staff to think that ethics is simple, so obvious, so not in need of reflection.

7. This has the repercussion that to the extent that individuals can change culture in the workplace, they are responsible for the development of virtue in others as well as in themselves.

8. The most detailed recent discussion is Meyer (2011). See also Irwin (1980) and Roberts (1989).

9. In other words, responsibility is a gradable concept.

10. The words '*hekousion*' and '*akousion*', here translated as 'voluntary' and 'involuntary', are sometimes translated 'intentional' and 'unintentional', so in what follows that alternative translation is sometimes mentioned (see Charles, 1980, Chapter 2).

11. Aristotle gives various examples (NE III,1 1110b 26ff).

12. Animals are capable of one of the kinds of desire that Aristotle identifies, *epithumia*, desires for the object that fulfils the desire, desires that one finds oneself having, and they are also capable of perceptual beliefs or quasi beliefs, states provided by their perceptual organs that have content that represents the world.

13. For Aristotle (like Plato), desire is a genus (*orexis*) with three species— appetitive desire (*epithumia*), *thumetic* desire, and *boulesis*, where only rational animals, such as humans, are capable of the latter types. See, for example, NE I, 13.

14. In the work for the ICAEW this was identified as whistleblowing, but arguably a staged approach to raising concerns is what really counts here.

15. From a speech by Sir Philip Mawer made at a one-day conference, 'Public Trust in the Professions: Ethics, Trust and Integrity', London, 25th February 2010; quoted by Doodson (2016).

References

Aristotle. (2009). *Nicomachean ethics* (W. D. Ross, Trans.). Oxford: Oxford University Press.

Baxter, J., Dempsey, J., Megone, C., & Lee, J. (2012). *Real integrity: Practical solutions for organisations seeking to promote and encourage integrity.* London: Chartered Accountants' Trustees Limited.

Baxter, J., & Megone, C. (2016). *Exploring the role of professional bodies and professional qualifications in the UK banking sector.* London: Banking Standards Board.

Burnyeat, M. F. (1980). Aristotle on learning to be good. In A. O. Rorty (Ed.), *Essays on Aristotle's Nicomachean ethics* (pp. 69–92). Berkeley, CA: University of California Press.

Charles, D. (1980). *Aristotle's philosophy of action.* London: Duckworth.

Doodson, R. (2016). *Professional integrity.* Dissertation submitted for the MA in Applied and Professional Ethics, University of Leeds, Leeds.

Irwin, T. H. (1980). Reason and responsibility in Aristotle. In A. O. Rorty (Ed.), *Essays on Aristotle's Nicomachean ethics* (pp. 117–155). Berkeley, CA: University of California Press.

Jimenez, M. (2016). Aristotle on becoming virtuous by doing virtuous actions. *Phronesis, 61*(1), 3–32.

Kraut, R. (2012). Aristotle on becoming good: Habituation, reflection, and perception. In C. Shields (Ed.), *The Oxford handbook on Aristotle* (pp. 529–557). Oxford: Oxford University Press.

Megone, C. (2009). Integrity, virtue and the financial crisis. In S. Gregg & J. Stoner (Eds.), *Profit, prudence and virtue: Essays in ethics, business and management* (St Andrews Studies in Philosophy and Public Affairs) (pp. 195–210). Exeter: Imprint Academic.

Meyer, S. (2011). *Aristotle on moral responsibility* (2nd ed.). Oxford: Oxford University Press.

Roberts, J. (1989). Aristotle on responsibility for character and action. *Ancient Philosophy, 9*(1), 23–36.

Vassiliou, I. (1996). The role of good upbringing in Aristotle's ethics. *Philosophy and Phenomenological Research, 56*(4), 771–797.

8   Professional Responsibility and the Banks

Christopher Cowton

Introduction

The global financial crisis (GFC) led to much blaming of banks and bankers. Suggestions for restitution or punishment flow quite easily from the attribution of blame, as do proposals for making banking better in the future, the latter being the focus of this chapter. However, although fixing past problems can be helpful, it is possible that paying attention to other factors, not obviously implicated in the crisis, has something—perhaps a great deal—to offer. With that in mind, the aim of this chapter is to examine how the development and exercise of *professional* responsibility might make a valuable contribution to a good future for the banking sector and all those affected by it.

Professionals are taken to have an extensive set of responsibilities that go beyond ordinary morality and the law (Davis, 1997); and professions are a notable means of organising and conducting certain activities (e.g., medicine, law) in some societies, particularly in countries such as the United States and the UK, which might be seen as the heartlands of the GFC and subsequent financial sector scandals. The motivating idea of this chapter is that the degree to which professions and their members act responsibility can have an impact on the ethical quality or behaviour of business in general and banking in particular. There are some signs that an attempt is being made to develop the professional culture of bankers, in the UK at least, so there is some encouragement for this idea. However, I suggest that a fuller understanding of professions and professional responsibility than has currently been in evidence is critical to making this project a success in the UK and elsewhere. Moreover, having built that understanding of professions, I go beyond bankers to consider how other professional groups might also contribute.

The chapter is structured as follows. The next section sets out some remarks on the banking sector. It is not directly concerned with the causes of the GFC, which have been analysed at length elsewhere (e.g., Cable, 2009; Davies, 2010; Mason, 2009; Tett, 2010) but rather with some features of the banking sector that are relevant to the subsequent analysis.

This can be seen as initial ground clearing in which space is found for the exercise of professionalism. The following section examines the nature of professions in general. One of its tasks is to address the criticism that in spite of their rhetoric, professions are self-interested endeavours that fail to work in the public interest—which includes not adhering to high ethical standards. The conclusion is that the critics point to real risks but that professions *can* make a desirable contribution. I then turn to the idea of banking as a profession—what scope there might be for the professional organisation of bankers to improve ethics in the sector. A subsequent section extends the discussion by recognising that other groups of professionals are involved in the banking sector and that they might provide further resources for enhancing the quality of the banking sector's behaviour. The final section summarises the key points of the chapter.

Some Remarks on the Banking Sector

In discussions of the GFC, blame has been ascribed to various parties, including regulators, boards of directors, and consumers. Yet it is primarily the banking sector itself that has been the focus for the attribution of blame. 'The banks', usually collectively rather than individually, are a common target, with calls often made for changes in things like culture and incentives. 'Bankers'—sometimes the highly remunerated, occasionally ennobled (in the UK), senior bankers—are likewise frequently targeted, often with notions of restitution or punishment in mind. Modern 'banking' is sometimes critically examined, perhaps with a nostalgic looking back to 'traditional' practices—even if banking crises are nothing new. These three 'b-words' (banks, bankers, and banking) are clearly interconnected. For the purposes of this chapter, it is worth saying a little more about each of them in turn.

First, there are various sorts of bank. Most countries have a central bank that has, inter alia, certain macroeconomic responsibilities (especially related to monetary policy) and acts as lender of last resort to the banking system. They do not fall within the scope of this chapter. There are ways of categorising the other banks. For example, the U.S. distinction between investment banks and commercial banks—introduced by the Glass-Steagall Act of 1933—is now commonly employed internationally. An investment bank supports and advises organisations on their capital market activities, including mergers and acquisitions and the underwriting of security issues, and it often engages in proprietary trading. Commercial banks accept deposits, make loans and offer related products and services. If they focus on households and small businesses rather than corporations, they are sometimes termed 'retail' banks. In this chapter I shall primarily have in mind commercial banks, although much of what I have to say could also apply to investment banks, which played a full role in the GFC.

Secondly, many types of personnel work in banks. Not all would be thought of as 'bankers'. It will be of some significance to the argument of this chapter that some of those employees have their own, different professional backgrounds. It is debatable which of the remaining staff might be considered bankers. Ancillary staff, such as cleaners, would presumably not be and counter staff, for example, might be considered (mere) retail assistants. But what does it mean to be a 'banker' anyway? In times of blame, who might appropriately be accused of being one? Or, assuming that they are willing to do so, who might legitimately lay claim to the title? When it comes to the senior people who have been publicly vilified, were they truly bankers, or were they just highly paid managers who worked for a bank?

Finally, regarding 'banking', commercial banks have changed a great deal in recent decades. Two changes have been particularly problematic. Firstly, there has been the transformation of commercial banks from relatively simple takers of deposits and lenders of money (traditional financial intermediation) to providers of a wide range of financial services. Some of these newer activities have got them into trouble as a result of mis-selling. Secondly, the financial intermediation process itself—which has been at the centre of many previous banking crises with runs on banks and bad debts—has itself been subject to alteration.[1] Long-term reliance on short-term borrowings on the money markets instead of retail deposits and the securitisation of loans, especially mortgages (many of them sub-prime and inappropriately priced) caused major problems that were at the heart of the GFC. For the purposes of this chapter, the crucial points are, first, that banks do more than would traditionally have been understood by the term 'banking', and second, that the more sophisticated financial activities undertaken and the wider range of services provided to customers (both individual and corporate) bring with them a new set of challenges regarding not only ethics but also competence.

It should also be noted that banking and other financial services have been increasingly provided by other sorts of organisations, particularly since the deregulation of the 1980s (the 'Big Bang' of 1986 in the case of the UK). Thus mutual building societies (UK) or savings and loans institutions (United States), although declining in number, have been able to offer a wider range of services, as have credit unions; and there has been huge growth in so-called shadow banking. Islamic financial institutions have also grown in importance. Such alternative providers not only offer different models, some of which might be considered ethically superior in certain respects, but they also add to the intensity of competition in the sector—as has the increased globalisation of financial services.

Competition in product markets places demands and constraints on participants. This sometimes leads senior managers to think, or at least to claim, that in an era of intense competition, their actions are simply responding to the diktats of the market. Yet even in the period of 'irrational exuberance' leading up to the GFC, different banks did different things, even as they also perceived themselves to be under pressure from investors desiring increasing returns: some were relatively responsible; some were negligently caught up in what was happening; whereas others were decidedly reckless in their approach. Such differences suggest that banks did have a degree of strategic choice. Putting to one side the debate over corporate moral agency, some banks may be considered more blameworthy than others when it comes to the GFC; and some might even be without any blame at all. Operating a bank was not simply a matter of reading from a script supplied by the market. As Lucas (1998, p. 59) remarked,

> Economic determinism is false. The iron laws of supply and demand are not made of iron, and indicate tendencies only, without fixing everything, leaving no room for choice. In economic affairs we are often faced with decisions, and often can choose between a number of alternative courses of action. It is up to us what we do; we are responsible agents, and may fairly be asked to explain why we did as we did.

This is not to say that there were not real pressures on banks; but even if they were great, there was choice, which is consistent with being able to attribute blame. There are still pressures post-GFC, but they are likely to have reduced in certain respects (e.g., the previous push to display 'strategic ambition' to investors by engaging in certain very risky behaviours), and boards of directors are probably warier of sanctioning herd behaviour. Some choices will be ethically superior to others. But what if they entail some sacrifice of financial performance? Those who are against such choices often quote Milton Friedman:

> There is one and only one social responsibility of business—to use its resources and engage in activities designed to increase its profits so long as it stays within the rules of the game, which is to say, engages in open and free competition without deception or fraud.
>
> (Friedman, 1970)

Friedman is much misconstrued, but for current purposes we need only note that the inference often drawn is that shareholder primacy (again, often misunderstood—see Cowton, 2011) should force out consideration of 'nice-to-have' things like ethics and corporate social responsibility. However, Friedman himself recognised that ethically desirable actions were not always a drain on profitability but, indeed, might be positively aligned with it. Such possibilities were not a problem for him. This 'business case for ethics' has been hotly debated over many years, and much research has been undertaken to discover whether being ethical (broadly defined and in various ways) does actually pay.

Such research is not easy to conduct, and the results have been described by some as inconclusive (Jones & Wicks, 1999). However, it is possible to draw some clear conclusions from a broad range of studies. Overall, the research certainly doesn't prove that being ethical always pays, but it suggests that it might do so, at least some of the time (see Margolis and Walsh, 2003, and Orlitsky et al., 2003, for widely cited reviews). The findings imply that it would be wrong to think that being ethical *never* pays or, to put it colloquially, that the good guys always finish last.

In conclusion, there is strategic space, albeit constrained, for banks that permits a more or less ethical approach to be taken. Moreover, within that space it is likely to be possible to make money while being ethical and to lose it by being unethical; and banks, like other businesses, vary in their 'ethical positioning', intentionally or not.

Similarly, individuals in banks have a degree of choice, with which comes responsibility. In the case of senior managers, some of that room for manoeuvre relates to the strategic space that banks enjoy because those managers have a degree of influence on the positioning of the organisation. Furthermore, discretion will exist at all levels of an organisation; the existence of many forms of organisational resistance, diversion, adaptation and deliberate policy slack, and the regular modification of control systems in the light of senior management concern, are evidence that management control is not total (Dermer & Lucas, 1986).[2] Thus, whether explicitly and deliberately granted or not, individual employees have a degree of agency.

To focus briefly on one area, one of the criticisms of banks during the GFC was that their incentive systems were such that staff engaged in inappropriate behaviour, such as taking on reckless amounts of risk or mis-selling products to customers. These were almost certainly poor systems. However, to the extent that employees were simply pursuing more remuneration or promotion, rather than, say, protecting their job, they were not forced or even significantly pressured to act in the inappropriate ways signalled by the incentive scheme. This is without considering the options of 'voice' or 'exit'. Moreover, some banks have significantly modified their incentive systems post-GFC, so there should now be a better, if still not perfect, alignment between incentives and good behaviour—or at least less reward on offer for bad behaviour.

None of this is to suggest that employees have total discretion. The environment in which they work places on them many demands and constraints, to use Rosemary Stewart's terminology (Stewart, 1982); but as Stewart's 'demands, constraints and choices' model makes clear, there will also be some room for choice, the extent of which will be a contingent matter. Of course, perception of that choice is critical to its exercise, and use of Stewart's model with managers in similar roles will tend to find that some of the variety that was a matter of choice by managers had previously been seen by them, individually, as a matter of demand and constraint. There are many potential influences upon how individuals perceive their environment and how they behave, for better or worse. One set of influences for good, at least potentially, relates to their professional identity, if they have one in the sense discussed in the next section.

The Potential of Professions

The terms 'professional' and 'profession' are used in a variety of ways in everyday speech. As an adjective, 'professional' can mean, for example, highly competent (as opposed to amateurish) or paid (as opposed to having amateur status), and 'profession' is used to apply to many occupational groups. However, the meanings are narrower and more technical in the academic literature on professions. Jary and Jary (1991, p. 501), for example, define a profession as 'any middle class occupational group, characterised by claims to a high level of technical and intellectual expertise, autonomy in recruitment and discipline, and a commitment to public service'. This definition is expanded in literature that seeks to distinguish 'true' professions from other occupational groups by identifying the characteristics that professions are expected to possess.

The classic examples of professions are medicine and the law, but the increased complexity and level of development of societies and economies has thrown up new occupational groups that have aspired to professional status. A good business-related example that will feature later in this chapter is accountants, but other occupational groups that display some professional features and perhaps have the potential to do so to a greater extent include marketers, human resource (HR) managers—and bankers.

A profession's key characteristics and their relative importance are subject to considerable debate, but the literature (e.g., Abbott, 1988) tends to agree on the importance of the following, all or most of which will need to be present for an occupational group to be considered a profession. Firstly, there should exist a widely agreed and extensive specialist skill and knowledge base, the latter often of a relatively theoretical or abstract kind. Secondly, acquisition of the skills and knowledge involves a long period of training, with formal certification of competence (usually involving written examinations) and, many would emphasise, some form of licence to practise (but I will come back to that). Thirdly, operation as a professional entails the use of discretion and judgement, not just the application of rules (however complex) to routine circumstances. Fourthly, independence and self-regulation are jealously guarded by the occupational group, with control over the requisite knowledge base, setting of entry standards and criteria for membership, and responsibility for the disciplining of members. Fifthly, in many cases there are high levels of personal and financial reward. But sixthly, beyond self-interest a profession is expected to operate in the public interest. And finally, one of the ways in which public interest should be served is through the implementation of an ethical code (often formal but not exclusively so) independent of contract or regulation. Self-enforced by professional bodies, such codes should demand more than ordinary morality and the law (Davis, 1997). Therefore, what might be judged as praiseworthy in others might be considered simply a matter of professional responsibility and blameworthy if not met.

Given analyses of the causes of the GFC, it is striking that the standard list of professional characteristics just enumerated revolves around both competence and ethics (de Bruin, 2015). The two strands are not separate, though; they can be regarded as linked in various ways. For example, a key reason for consulting a professional or employing one is that they have expertise. However, this creates a power asymmetry that can be exploited by the unscrupulous, such as a rogue dentist who recommends complex treatment that isn't in the patient's best interests but which generates large fees. The professional has a duty not to exploit inappropriately the specialist expertise that he or she possesses. Likewise, he or she has a duty not only to acquire but also to maintain that professional expertise, refreshing his or her knowledge base and keeping up with recent developments—and to know the limits of his or her expertise and demur accordingly.

Although the discussion so far has been in terms of professions and professional characteristics, the existence of professional associations or bodies, in which the idea of a profession takes flesh, has been implicit. It is they that, for example, admit or discipline members. In practice, professional bodies and organisations that look rather like them differ in the range of things that they do. I have suggested elsewhere (Cowton, 2009) that one way to think about this variety is in terms of three types of professional body that can be distinguished according to their level of development and the degree to which they display the characteristics listed earlier.

The first is the professional body that is little more than an educational and examining institution: the 'qualification' body. It can be seen as principally an awarder of qualifications. Yet even this limited agenda can have a valuable role to play if it is accepted as a gateway to significant career progression in a particular field or sector. It can help ensure that influential positions tend to be held by individuals who have an appropriate background in terms of theoretical knowledge and high-level skills.

The second type of professional body—which I have termed 'customer-focused'—is one that also provides a wide range of other services to its members. For example, it offers continuing professional development (CPD) so that members are able to maintain and enhance their expertise in the light of new developments and opportunities. The cost-effective provision of useful benefits to members, who may view themselves as customers as they pay an annual subscription and seek value for money, is a business challenge familiar to the managers of professional bodies.

Finally, there is what I have termed the 'membered' body. This is a deliberate choice of word to resonate with the way in which a human body is an organic whole made up of its 'members', or limbs. One feature of this type of professional body is that it requires its members to engage in appropriate CPD. It is not just that the opportunity for CPD is provided; members have a responsibility to ensure that they are up-to-date and fully competent to fulfil the tasks they undertake. Moreover, membership of this type of professional body will entail ethical as well as technical responsibilities. There will not only be a code of ethics but also guidance and support as necessary (e.g., an ethics advice line) as well as disciplinary processes for those who do not abide by the code. When it works well, the professional body will develop a strong culture amongst its members and might even be seen as a moral community. With a shared professional culture, members 'just know' how to act and 'wouldn't think twice' about behaving in certain ways. Such professionals will tend to possess a common set of virtues, not just a common set of skills. It is this type of body that is capable of realising the fullest public benefits of professionalism.

For those who hold a positive view of professions—such as functionalist sociologists in the tradition of Talcott Parsons—a profession is a valuable technical and ethical endeavour, and its members deserve the financial rewards and respect they receive. The 'membered' professional body is most likely to realise the ideal.

However, the 'membered' professional body is also the most likely kind to be the target of critics who see professions as a successful conspiracy against society that seek to justify considerable personal reward with a smokescreen of talk about ethics and public benefit. Marxist and, more recently, consumerist commentaries are critical of the way in which professions seek to pursue and protect economic advantage by attempting to secure monopoly in the market through the establishment, protection, and extension of an effective monopoly jurisdictional claim (Reed, 1992). Whereas professional bodies might claim to be exercising control of quality as they restrict membership, the counterargument is that the intention is primarily to restrict supply and so drive up fees and remuneration.

However, to the extent that they rely on an assumption of the existence of a licence to practise in a particular sphere, such critiques overstate the general case against professions. In some cases, particular professions do indeed have a degree of control through legislative or other regulatory backing. If so, only members in good standing with a particular professional body (or bodies) will be permitted to undertake a particular task, although that might not always seem unreasonable (e.g., performing surgical operations in hospitals or auditing large companies perhaps). However, professional bodies differ in the extent to which they control their particular domains. Many don't. For example, although auditing is a restricted area, it is worth noting that only a minority of the 150,000 or so members of the Institute of Chartered Accountants in England and

Wales (ICAEW), to pick one major professional body, hold practising certificates. The remainder are employed in a wide range of financial (e.g., management accounting) or managerial roles for which there are no formal qualification requirements. A professional qualification might often be deemed desirable by service users and employers, but in the absence of regulatory protection, it is far from clear that this preference is inappropriately exploited. Other examples of business-related professional bodies in a UK business context that vary in their degree of market power include the Chartered Institute of Purchasing and Supply (CIPS), the Chartered Institute of Logistics and Transport (CILT), the Chartered Institute of Marketing (CIM) and the Chartered Institute of Personnel and Development (CIPD).

It is therefore better to see the criticisms of professions as indicators of potential problems or risks rather than as general descriptions of the behaviour of all professional bodies. Just as it was argued in the previous section that banks make different strategic choices, which can be more or less praiseworthy or blameworthy, so too different professional bodies vary in the contributions they make. My contention is that the actual contribution of a particular profession is a contingent matter, not an inevitability. It is to be empirically assessed, not theoretically determined. Negative discourses that treat professions in a homogeneous manner leave little or no room for considering whether some professions, in some places or circumstances, at some times, are of significant value—even if the members are well rewarded. If professions do live up to their rhetoric on ethics and the public interest, at least to a significant degree, then so much the better. And if there can indeed be variation in the social contribution that professions make, then it is worth considering how that can occur and how it can be encouraged—an avenue that sceptical, not to say cynical, general positions on professions tend to close off.

Moreover, critics of professions are likely to be comfortable in joining in with the criticism of the excessive remuneration of (senior) bankers that has been a feature of the debate about the GFC. However, it is worth noting that such financial rewards were accomplished without any exploitative 'professional project'. De George (2006, p. 93) comments that '[p]rofessions carry with them special obligations that members of that profession take on, both individually and collectively'. Perhaps the addition of a stronger sense of professional responsibility on the part of bankers would go some way towards justifying their rewards. The next section considers the idea of bankers as professionals.

Banking as a Profession

Is banking a profession? In some countries there are long-established professional bodies in operation, so the institutional potential, at least, appears to be there, but even in such countries only a minority of employees who might reasonably be identified as bankers are members. For this reason, banking would probably not be considered a profession, even before a detailed analysis is conducted of whether the standard characteristics are present. However, the idea of bankers having a deep knowledge of their subject, exercising sound judgement (e.g., not being reckless), acting ethically and in the interests of customers (rather than mis-selling to them), and being disciplined if they fall short of expected standards all fit well with being professional, so it seems a development that would be welcomed. The causes and consequences of the GFC, the strategic and organisational space for the choice of more ethical behaviour, and the potential improvement to competence and ethics of this significant occupational group suggest that there is a strong case for the proposal that bankers should become, or at least make significant strides towards becoming, professionally organised.

There come risks with professionalisation, but the scope for exploitation tends to derive from the granting of an exclusive jurisdictional claim and the restriction of the number of licences to practise. This is currently far from the case in banking; and given that banking is closely monitored and any increase in professionalisation is likely to require policy support, discussed below, policy-makers can intervene if the disadvantages of greater professionalisation come to threaten the benefits to be derived from it. Furthermore, current critics of banking make the point that many bank employees have reaped, and continue to reap, very substantial financial rewards (especially at senior levels, where the ascription of 'banker' might seem to apply most appositely) yet without even the pretence of subscribing to the public benefit-serving characteristics of a profession. Hence, any progress on this front might be viewed positively, as a kind of payment for the rewards already enjoyed. Although some of the biggest critics of the banking sector might be amongst the most sceptical of professions, a more nuanced view of professions opens up the possibility of recognising that a well-functioning professional body with real influence in the sector would offer some measure of what the critics of banking seek.

Although my analysis has emphasised the way in which professional bodies can influence the competence and ethics of their members, a 'membered' professional body is fundamentally a collective endeavour; the professional body is not separate from its members in the way in which a bank is separate from its customers. One possible corollary of this is that the professional body not only prescribes and examines required knowledge—which will tend to be broader than the on-the-job training provided by individual banks—but also seeks to develop the body of knowledge related to banking. Likewise, a well-functioning professional body helps develop a common professional culture that, in some respects, is different from and transcends the corporate cultures of individual banks.[3]

This, then, is my main, if interim, conclusion: that professionalisation has, notwithstanding some possible risks, something positive to offer in the post-GFC era, alongside other attempts to improve the operation of the banking sector. The chapter thus opens up a possibility that has been little considered, at least in the way I have done, even when the opportunity has appeared to be at hand.

For example, Graafland and van de Ven (2011) provide a very good summary of the antecedents of the GFC and identify, from a MacIntyrean perspective, the virtues implicit in the codes of conduct of eight banks. Noting that the banks did not live up to their professed standards, they conclude that the core virtues to be expected of professionals in finance will be successfully realised only if attention is paid to the institutional context. However, the term 'professionals' in the title of the paper remains unexamined, and perhaps surprisingly, no mention is made of professional banking bodies as a feature of the institutional context that might be able to contribute to the renewal of virtue.

Similarly, Llewellyn et al. (2014, p. 2) provide the following lucid summary of the GFC as

> a calamity that has its origins in the profligate and irresponsible action of a significant number of bankers and banking institutions, urged on by a banking culture that was at its core fundamentally self-serving [. . .] The banking sector had, in short, lost its ethos. Instead of a culture that prioritised its own self-interest, it should look towards the fulfilment of a broader common good and its wider social purpose.

This passage seems to promise support for the kinds of suggestions in this chapter, especially given their interest in culture and character—and their desire for a bankers' oath in the UK, as in The Netherlands. However, although they make some interesting recommendations, they do not explore the contributions that professional banking bodies might make, whether as they currently exist in the UK (Llewellyn et al.'s focus) or as they might become. What is particularly concerning is that they don't even explicitly dismiss professional bodies as a possible source of positive leverage for the sector, despite their having been operating in the UK for about 150 years. Hence, the principal aim of this chapter, namely, to encourage consideration of professionalisation as a force for good in banking, seems all the more important.

How that agenda might be promoted would require a greater amount of space to do it justice than I have remaining in this chapter, especially given some other issues that I wish to cover. Nevertheless, some indications of the issues involved would seem to be in order. I shall do this primarily with the UK in mind because it is the context with which I am most familiar; but it is in any case a good context for examining the issues because the UK was a key centre in the GFC and it has a long tradition of the operation of professional bodies in general and of professional banking bodies in particular.

One of the issues raised at the beginning of the chapter was: Who might be considered a 'banker'? This question might be answered as anyone who is a member in good standing of a banking professional body. Other persons might perhaps have a claim, but such members have the automatic right to be recognised as bankers. It should be acknowledged, though, that banking has changed a great deal since the professional bodies were founded—1875 in the case of the Chartered Institute of Bankers in Scotland (the oldest professional banking institute in the world, now trading as the Chartered Banker Institute) and 1879 in the case of the Institute of Bankers (now known as the London Institute of Banking & Finance). One trend is that although individual members of staff within a bank retain a degree of discretion in how they behave (i.e., choice within demands and constraints), many banking judgements have been removed from the customer interface—including the local branch environment. This change reflects other trends, such as centralisation, standardisation and automation. It means that the locus for the exercise of higher professional skills and judgement has shifted to higher organisational levels, while at the same time greater demands are made through increased complexity, as well as dynamism, within the sector. This might reduce the proportion of staff needing to be professionals, although there is still a need for staff who might move into such positions in the future to acquire a professional grounding, and inculcation of a good professional culture more widely is unlikely to be without value.

A second significant trend that has affected professional bodies is the increase in the proportion of young people taking higher education qualifications. Historically, when a small proportion of the UK population went to university, it was not unusual for 'bright grammar school boys' to enter a retail bank when they left school at the age of 16 and still to be able to reach a senior position in due course. Over a number of years, they would be trained in the skills of branch banking, which was far less standardised and automated then. They would be introduced into a very specific culture, but they would at the same time be undertaking study, perhaps by correspondence course, for the examinations of a professional banking body. Over time, this pattern became less common as more and more young people went to university and therefore acquired high-level qualifications before entering the bank, in which case they were much less likely to take a professional banking qualification. This had two significant effects. Firstly, the graduates came from many different academic backgrounds, and few held a banking degree, which have never been common in the UK, especially at the undergraduate level. This means that although recruits to the sector might possess generic skills, many do not have a broad and deep knowledge of banking. Secondly, and as a consequence of this, the significance and viability of professional bodies became more problematic. The response of the Institute of Bankers is an interesting case.

Founded in 1879, it gained a Royal Charter in 1987, becoming the Chartered Institute of Bankers. The change was a mark of prestige, yet in 1997 it changed its name to the Institute of Financial Services. This was the year after it began offering a BSc (Hons) in financial services as a dual award with the University of Manchester Institute of Science and Technology (UMIST), which was the first professional award to be linked to a university degree. The innovation can be interpreted as, at least in part, a response to the growing presence of graduates in the sector and the increased demand for degrees from young people themselves. More changes were to follow. In 2006 the organisation was renamed the 'ifs School of Finance', which was granted Taught Degree-Awarding Powers in 2010. In 2013 the ifs School of Finance was granted University College title and became 'ifs University College', then in 2016 it changed its name yet again to 'The London Institute of Banking & Finance'. The number of name changes might be interpreted in different ways. On the one hand, it might indicate, particularly after gaining the prestigious chartered status, an organisation that has lost its way. On the other hand, more positively, with the development of its power to award prestigious qualifications, it might be viewed as an example of successful organisation innovation in response to changed circumstances. However, as a professional association it now looks more like a 'qualification' body than a 'membered' body. It is interesting to compare it with the Chartered Banker Institute, which is the current trading name of the Chartered Institute of Bankers in Scotland. It looks more like a traditional professional body and has recently introduced an 'experience' route to membership. Although this development might seem to undermine the educational aspect of a professional body, it is worth noting that this is how professional bodies usually start out, and as long as it is well administered, with appropriate accreditation of prior learning, it increases the number of people coming within the professional body's ambit, rendering themselves subject to its requirements and processes.

To make a significant contribution to the development of a better banking sector, any professional body not only needs to become 'membered' but also to have an important place within the sector. For this, support will be needed. As Graafland and van de Ven (2011) comment, the return to what they term the 'core virtues' of the sector will be successful only if a renewed sense of responsibility is supported by institutional changes. This will tend to vary from country to country. The banks themselves will have an important role to play, but this will necessitate the reversal of a long-term trend of becoming less closely linked to the professional bodies. Perhaps the following anecdote illustrates the position as it had developed. Following the onset of the GFC, I was invited to a two-day roundtable meeting of parties, including bankers, board directors, and regulators, to discuss what had happened and how to respond. One of the many interesting pieces of information to emerge was that one major London-based bank represented at the meeting had contacted one of the professional bodies to find out which of its staff were members because it did not know.

The attitude of regulators could also be important. Early in the GFC, one UK government minister suggested that bankers who had been implicated in causing the crisis should be banned from practising as bankers in the future. This is the language of professional membership; but of course, no licence to practise was in operation that could be taken away. However, in due course, after various iterations, the SMR commenced operation in March 2016. Covering banks and similar financial institutions (e.g., credit unions), the aim of the SMR is to focus accountability on a narrow range of individuals, encourage individuals to take responsibility for their actions, and make it easier for both banks and regulators to take greater responsibility for their actions. Thus the SMR seems to be capable of delivering what the government minister wanted and, more generally, to open the way to blame being more clearly attributed, with appropriate actions, in the event of a future crisis or, indeed, particular mishaps. With its requirement for senior managers to take reasonable steps to prevent regulatory breaches from occurring or continuing to occur in their area of responsibility, the SMR seems to be a step forward in incentivising responsible behaviour in the future.

However, anyone who thinks the SMR will lead to a significant culture change is likely to be disappointed, and its effects will fall far short of what the analysis of this chapter is reaching towards. One reason for this is that the system is, in effect, largely a matter of compliance, even if banks can choose exactly how they comply, in terms of the 'Management Responsibilities Map' that they produce. As long as things are properly documented in senior managers' 'Statements of Responsibilities' and 'reasonable steps' are taken, senior managers are likely to feel that they are covered. Moreover, the reverse burden of proof if the regulator alleges that something has gone wrong has now been removed, so the regulator will now have to prove not only that something has indeed gone wrong but also that the senior manager—who will presumably engage a good lawyer—failed to take reasonable steps. It will be interesting to see how many successful cases emerge over the years to come. Thus the SMR does increase individual accountability, but how substantial an effect it will have is open to question.

Furthermore, there are two other concerns with the SMR that are highlighted by the earlier discussion. Firstly, the SMR is concerned only with regulatory breaches. In other words, it is trying to make sure that individuals meet the minimum requirements—a useful addition to the regulatory regime armoury, perhaps, but hardly likely to be culturally transformative. Secondly, with its emphasis on individual accountability, it does nothing to stimulate the deep cultural change that many critics have called for (except to the extent that it might change attitudes to some aspects of accountability in the sector). It does little or nothing to drive cultural change in banks as corporate entities, and it does nothing to bolster the position of professional bodies—which it could do, for example, by finding a way of placing significant weight on being an active member.

However, the SMR does not preclude regulators also supporting the mission and activities of professional bodies, and there are other institutions that might help. For example, the BSB was established in 2015 to promote high standards of behaviour and competence across banks and building societies in the UK. Funded by subscriptions from financial institutions, it is not a trade association but exists to 'provide challenge, support and scrutiny for firms committed to rebuilding the sector's reputation' (Banking Standards Board, 2018). Nor is it a professional body, but it has seen the relevance of such institutions, sponsoring research that explored whether and how the role of professional bodies could be strengthened. The report by Baxter and Megone (2016) provides much useful detail. It provides support for the conclusion of this chapter: that the potential does exist for professional bodies to play a significant role in raising levels of competence and ethical behaviour in the sector. However, it identifies several challenges that will need to be addressed to fulfil this potential, including remedying the lack of clear links between qualifications and career progression within firms. Thus the strong engagement and support of banks and building societies whose staff are (or might be) members is crucial, as is the commitment of the professional bodies themselves; at least they have already shown their ability to adapt in recent years. As stated earlier, the stance of the regulatory bodies is also important.

In conclusion, there are reasons to suppose that strengthening the professional culture of bankers, whatever bank they happen to work for, would improve the likelihood of developing and maintaining 'good banking'. Given the current situation, it seems likely that there is much to gain and little to lose when the espoused benefits and possible risks of professionalism are considered. The GFC suggests that the public interest would be served by an improvement in bankers' competence (de Bruin, 2015) and ethics, not just their individual accountability (per SMR), as offered by well-functioning professional bodies with real reach in the sector. Professionalisation has its risks, including restriction of supply and the creation of high salaries. But many (senior) bankers are well, not to say excessively well, paid already; and if they were to act more professionally as an occupational group, they might not only be closer to justifying their pay, but they might also regain some of the respect they have lost.

The degree to which the benefits of professionalisation might be realised, and the ways in which it could be done, will depend on many local, national contextual factors—although serious international moves would be welcome, especially given that finance has become increasingly globalised. Some remarks have been made about the UK context that might provide food for thought about other countries' banking sectors too. Whatever the way forward, the support and active participation of regulators and the banks themselves will be important. At best, it will be a long-term project. However, this does not exhaust the benefits that the banking sector might derive from the exercise of professionalism. Those other possibilities are the subject of the next section.

The Contribution of Other Professions

In thinking further about the contribution of professionals, three possible positions in relation to a sector might be recognised. Firstly, there are what I term 'sector professionals', whose activities lie at the heart of the sector's operations. Physicians in hospitals are a clear example, and bankers in the financial sector might be too.

Secondly, there are professionals that are external to the sector but provide services to it. They might be viewed as helping to support and safeguard the sector's activities. This is the classic position of a professional; an independent expert, singly or in a professional firm, provides services to clients, whether individual or corporate. Following the demise of Enron, John Coffee wrote an influential analysis of auditors (specifically, Arthur Andersen), credit-rating agencies and other external parties that he referred to as 'gatekeepers' (Coffee, 2006). Although that term might not naturally encompass all the external services that professionals provide to banks, it will be used here, not least because, like Coffee, I am interested in responses to a major crisis and how future crises might be averted or diminished in their impact.

The classic gatekeepers, auditors, tend to be the target of criticism whenever there is a major corporate failure (at least they are still around to be sued!). The GFC was no exception. This is understandable because corporate failure not long after the publication of a seemingly satisfactory set of audited financial statements seems less than satisfactory and might, to some, suggest incompetence, a lack of professional ethics, or even both. To some extent, such a reaction might betray a misunderstanding of what auditing is intended to achieve—the so-called expectations gap (Porter, 1993). However, auditors certainly need to live up to their professional status, which includes keeping pace with the evolving challenges of accounting for novel activities in a dynamic banking sector; an issue in the lead-up to the GFC was how to value some of the sophisticated financial instruments that had been developed. The same might be said of other gatekeepers, some of which (e.g., credit raters) might be encouraged to take on the mantle of professionalism (see Cowton, 2008), as I argued for bankers in the previous section.

However, I am more interested in the third type of professional in this current typology: the 'embedded professional'. These are professionals who are employed in a particular sector but are not 'sector professionals'. Instead, they typically provide support services. Thus, for example, banks employ accountants, human resource (HR) managers and marketers, who may well hold professional qualifications. The choice of the term 'embedded', which echoes the embedding of journalists with the armed forces during military operations, signals more than just being inside or within an organisation; it connotes being firmly and deeply situated. Thus, in contrast to gatekeepers, who are usually engaged for a fixed period of time to undertake a limited range of tasks, embedded professionals have an extended opportunity to contribute professionally to a single organisation.

Thus bankers are not the only potential sources of professional competence for the banking sector and not the only type of employee who could shoulder some of the blame for the GFC, for that matter. Embedded professionals can exercise their knowledge and skills in various ways. They design and operate systems to monitor and support banking activities, they offer advice, they can act as a 'critical friend' and so on. Thus, for example, management accountants are able to assemble information that can show where reckless or questionable activities might be taking place; HR managers should be able to assess aspects of the corporate culture and design or critique incentive schemes and promotion criteria; and marketing professionals should be capable of highlighting where mis-selling might be a risk. All such actions, and more, could make a valuable contribution to a more responsible banking sector.

Furthermore, all members of a properly developed professional body will have an ethical code to follow—which might include, but will certainly go well beyond, the requirement to be competent. This gives those staff an additional set of considerations—demands and constraints—to take into account as they go about their work. Those codes will vary in the nature of the demands they make, but in the case of accountants who are members of a body such as the ICAEW, which has adopted the International Ethics Standards Board for Accountants (IESBA) Code of Ethics for Professional Accountants, it is worth noting that embedded accountants are subject to the same code as auditors (albeit the latter face additional requirements and guidance). Therefore, it might be said that embedded professionals march to a slightly different beat from other employees; given that they are supposed to act beyond the requirements of ordinary morality and the law, this provides a further possible influence for good upon the banking sector.

However, to the extent that an embedded professional feels that he or she should act in a way that is not in accordance with the bank's culture or particular demands, they experience dissonance. This dissonance is known as organisational-professional conflict (OPC). It occurs when a professional's employing organisation seeks to set aside professional autonomy (Davis, 1996) or demands adherence to organisational norms that are incompatible with professional ethics (Sorensen, 1967). Organisational norms may be expressed in a variety of ways, from the formal, such as organisational regulations, through pressure exerted within the managerial hierarchy, to the informal social expectation of organisational loyalty and other local cultural values.

Many variables can be associated with the experience of OPC,[4] but the key point for the argument is that to the extent that the professional seeks to follow his or her professional ethics, there is an input to the bank's workings that is likely to represent high standards.

There are at least three significant differences between an embedded professional and an ordinary 'ethical' individual who works for a bank. Firstly, the member of a (good) professional body has an ethical code to which they can refer for guidance and which can be pointed to in discussions within the organisation, with the authority of the professional body that stands behind the individual concerned. Secondly, they have a degree of support from the professional body if they decide to provide some sort of challenge. This might take the form of advice, perhaps on an 'ethics hotline', which can help them think through the issue and determine their next step. The professional body might also continue to provide support as the episode unfolds.

The third difference that professional membership can make is at an earlier stage though. James Rest's well-known social psychological model of ethical decision-making (Rest, 1986) is an acknowledged simplification, but it usefully distinguishes four stages: awareness, judgement, intention, and action. When considering a particular issue, the professional body's resources can, as explained, help its member to form an appropriate judgement and intention (through the detail of the ethical code and any advice that is sought) and support its member, if needed, when action is taken. But the first stage, awareness, is of critical importance. An otherwise ethical individual who does not have a professional reference point might not even notice an issue when immersed in a particular working culture, or they might have a sense of discomfort without being able to identify what the problem is, whereas a professionally qualified person should possess a developed understanding of the application of an ethical perspective to his or her professional work situations and how ethical risks can arise. They should therefore have greater sensitivity to the possibility of ethical issues in the workplace.

None of this is to suggest that such episodes are easy to deal with, but membership of a professional body can increase the likelihood that an individual is able to make a positive impact. In this sense, OPC is a 'good thing' for the ethics of a particular sector, such as banking, and professionals should not expect to go through their careers without experiencing it at some time—particularly if working in a sector that is widely criticised for its ethical climate.

In conclusion, 'other', 'embedded' professionals offer the potential to help bring professionalism to banking, which might be especially valuable as its sector professionalisation remains under-developed. Both the ethical code that they are meant to follow and their professional duty to develop, maintain and exercise competence mean that embedded professionals have obligations that if fulfilled, should make a significant positive contribution. Although they have professional resources to draw upon in exercising their responsibilities in the banking sector, it would be helpful if banks also committed to respecting their status and encouraged them to exercise their professional judgement to a fuller extent than seems to have been the case, at least in some respects, in the lead-up to the GFC.

Conclusion

In this chapter I wished to open up for examination the possibility that professionals, with their supposed commitment to competence and ethics and hence the public interest, provide one source of influence to make banking, and business more generally, better than it might otherwise be.

There is considerable scepticism, not to say cynicism, towards professions and their contribution to society. Of course, the same is true of business, particularly banking after the GFC. However, the position taken in this chapter is that the contribution of both is a contingent matter; anything near to perfection might be unattainable, but in both cases there is at least the possibility of their being better rather than worse. And if there is scope for banking to be better, it makes sense to think about how this might be brought about. The more that professional bodies can act as moral communities, exerting influence over their members—in particular those employed by banks—the more likely it is that we will have the kind of banking sector that we all wish to see. Professional influences might be a relatively minor factor, at least in the short term, but they offer potential that should not be ignored.

In the case of the classic professional position of gatekeeper, the issues in relation to banking do not seem to be much different from those in other types of business—which is not to say that it is not important. To be sure, auditing or credit rating a bank is different from undertaking the same for, say, a manufacturer, but what is required is high quality in both cases—a competent approach undertaken without any conflict of interest. In the case of embedded professionals, they are supposed to have a significantly different 'script' (especially when the setting is not upholding high ethical standards) from that given to other employees. Given the importance of the banking sector, it might be useful for non-banking professional bodies to put together special interest groups of their members who work in the banking sector who can share ideas and provide mutual encouragement in relation to the working out of their professional commitments in what can be a challenging context. This would be one way in which such professional bodies could demonstrate that they really are committed to the public interest. Finally, perhaps the greatest potential lies in the mission to create, or indeed recreate, a professional ethos amongst bankers through the strengthening of their professional bodies. This will need considerable support, especially from regulators and the banks themselves, but with appropriate encouragement, hopefully future generations of bankers will act more professionally than the previous one to the benefit of all of us.

Notes

1. I examine some of the ethical issues relating to traditional financial intermediation in Cowton (2002) and Cowton (2010).
2. Blaming tends to carry an assumption that things could and should have been otherwise, along the lines of 'ought implies can'. When accused of wrongdoing, a person might make the defence that he or she had no choice but to follow a particular course of action, although in the case of employees, exit would seem to be an option (although it might be a difficult option to exercise). And it can be argued that blame may still be attributed even when an agent undertakes an unavoidable action, if he or she would have chosen it if some (hypothetical) alternative had been available. However, I am less interested in blame for the past than in the opportunity to exercise responsibility in the future.
3. I explore some implications of this in the next section when I examine 'organisational-professional conflict'.
4. For a meta-analytic review of studies of accountants, see Brierley and Cowton (2000). The concept also applies to bankers who are members of a professional banking body.

References

Abbott, A. (1988). *The system of professions*. Chicago, IL: Chicago University Press.

Banking Standards Board. (2018). *What is the BSB?* www.bankingstandardsboard.org.uk/what-is-the-bsb/, accessed 21 September 2018.

Baxter, J., & Megone, C. (2016). *Exploring the role of professional bodies and professional qualifications in the UK banking sector*. London: Banking Standards Board.

Brierley, J. A., & Cowton, C. J. (2000). Putting meta-analysis to work: Accountants' organizational-professional conflict. *Journal of Business Ethics*, 24(4), 343–353.

Cable, V. (2009). *The storm: The world economic crisis and what it means*. London: Atlantic Books.

Coffee, J. C., Jr. (2006). *Gatekeepers: The professions and corporate governance*. Oxford: Oxford University Press.

Cowton, C. J. (2002). Integrity, responsibility and affinity: Three aspects of ethics in banking. *Business Ethics: A European Review*, 11(4), 393–400.

Cowton, C. J. (2008). Governing the corporate citizen: Reflections on the role of professionals. In J. Conill, C. Luetge, & T. Schönwälder-Küntze (Eds.),

Corporate citizenship, contractarianism and ethical theory: On philosophical foundations of business ethics (pp. 29–47). Aldershot: Ashgate.

Cowton, C. J. (2009). Accounting and the ethics challenge: Re-membering the professional body. *Accounting and Business Research, 39*(3), 177–189.

Cowton, C. J. (2010). Banking. In J. Boatright (Ed.), *Finance ethics: Critical issues in financial theory and practice* (pp. 325–337). Hoboken, NJ: Wiley.

Cowton, C. J. (2011). Putting creditors in their rightful place: Corporate governance and business ethics in the light of limited liability. *Journal of Business Ethics, 102*(1/S1), 21–32.

Davies, H. (2010). *The financial crisis: Who is to blame?* London: Polity.

Davis, M. (1996). Professional autonomy: A framework for empirical research. *Business Ethics Quarterly, 6*(4), 441–460.

Davis, M. (1997). Professional codes. In P. H. Werhane & R. E. Freeman (Eds.), *Encyclopedic dictionary of business ethics* (pp. 514–515). Malden, MA: Blackwell.

de Bruin, B. (2015). *Ethics and the global financial crisis: Why incompetence is worse than greed.* Cambridge: Cambridge University Press.

De George, R. T. (2006). *Business ethics* (6th ed). Upper Saddle River, NJ: Prentice Hall.

Dermer, J. D., & Lucas, R. G. (1986). The illusion of managerial control. *Accounting, Organizations and Society, 11*(6), 471–482.

Friedman, M. (1970). The social responsibility of business is to increase its profits. *New York Times Magazine*, September 13, 122–126.

Graafland, J. J., & van de Ven, B. W. (2011). The credit crisis and the moral responsibility of professionals in finance. *Journal of Business Ethics, 103*(4), 605–619.

Jary, D., & Jary, J. (1991). *Collins dictionary of sociology.* Glasgow: Collins.

Jones, T. M., & Wicks, A. C. (1999). Convergent stakeholder theory. *Academy of Management Review, 24*(2), 206–221.

Llewellyn, D. T., Steare, R., & Trevellick, J. (2014). *Virtuous banking: Placing ethos and purpose at the heart of finance.* London: ResPublica.

Lucas, J. R. (1998). The responsibilities of a businessman. In C. Cowton & R. Crisp (Eds.), *Business ethics: Perspectives on the practice of theory* (pp. 59–77). Oxford: Oxford University Press.

Margolis, J. D., & Walsh, J. P. (2003). Misery loves companies: Rethinking social initiatives by business. *Administrative Science Quarterly, 48*(2), 268–305.

Mason, P. (2009). *Meltdown: The end of the age of greed.* London: Verso.

Orlitzky, M., Schmidt, F. L., & Rynes, S. L. (2003). Corporate social and financial performance: A meta-analysis. *Organization Studies, 24*(3), 403–441.

Porter, B. (1993). An empirical study of the audit expectation-performance gap. *Accounting and Business Research, 24*(93), 49–68.

Reed, M. (1992). *The sociology of organizations.* London: Harvester Wheatsheaf.

Rest, J. (1986). *Moral development: Advances in research and theory.* New York: Praeger.

Sorensen, J. E. (1967). Professional and bureaucratic organization in the public accounting firm. *Accounting Review, 42*(3), 553–565.

Stewart, R. (1982). *Choices for the manager: A guide to managerial work and behaviour.* New York: McGraw-Hill.

Tett, G. (2010). *Fool's gold: How unrestrained greed corrupted a dream, shattered global markets and unleashed catastrophe.* London: Abacus.

9 Liability for Corporate Wrongdoing

James Dempsey

Introduction

The global financial crisis (GFC), broadly construed, became a focal point for exerting pressure on legal and regulatory approaches to assessing and enforcing liability for corporate wrongdoing. In particular, repeated cases of systematic wrongdoing were exposed at big financial institutions but in the aftermath led to responses that jarred with public judgement of what is appropriate. A few individuals were found criminally liable, but the vast majority of the punishment was levied on institutions themselves in the form of fines. Often, there was not even any admission of wrongdoing by the institution as this was avoided by negotiating a payment with the regulator. The sense is that the majority of those working within such institutions avoided any liability whatsoever, although there is a strong suspicion that many were at least as culpable as the pensioners and investors who, ultimately, hold shares in the banks and footed the fines. Indeed, a leader in the *Financial Times* lamented that 'shareholders [are] punished for the sins of the trader', saying that 'fines are an expensive way of forcing a bank to change its culture' but that 'regulators may lack any better way of forcing banks to treat the [bad] behaviour as seriously as they should' (Financial Times, 2015).

Part of the reason regulators may lack any better way of forcing banks to take the bad behaviour of individuals seriously is a lack of clarity on how to answer three questions central to the issue of liability for corporate wrongdoing: Who is liable? Why are they liable? And what are they liable for? It is these questions that are the point of departure for this chapter. Although I am interested in determining the best legal and regulatory approaches to assessing and enforcing liability for corporate wrongdoing, the *justification* for such measures is to be found in an assessment of *moral* liability—that is, an assessment of who is liable for what consequences based on moral, as opposed to legal, argument.

I start with the idea that the most compelling reason to hold a person morally liable for corporate wrongdoing is that he or she is morally *accountable* for that wrongdoing. I then offer an account of moral accountability for corporate wrongdoing that implicates the directors and employees of those corporations. This argument grounds claims that those individuals are liable on the basis of the wrongdoing, although such claims are not mutually exclusive with those that may be levelled at other parties. I go on to argue that two other ways in which moral liability may be grounded, aside from considerations of moral accountability, both provide further support for holding directors and employees liable. Building on this account, I move on to the legal and regulatory question and explore how such liability may be assessed and enforced in practice. As noted, these questions gained strong public attention following the GFC, with respect to the financial services sector. In response, significant changes were made in the legal and regulatory regime in the UK financial sector, so I outline some of the most important of these changes and argue that they go a long way to implementing the recommendations of this chapter. However, in some respects, gaps remain. I outline what these are and sketch a way to plug them in the fifth section.

Moral Accountability in Business Organisations

In discussing liability my primary focus is on moral rather than legal liability. That is, I am interested in who should be held liable for what, morally speaking, and in particular the moral justification of these conclusions. With these conclusions in hand we are better equipped to determine how laws and regulations should be shaped and enforced. Generally speaking, the most compelling reason to hold an individual morally liable for corporate wrongdoing is that he or she bears moral accountability for that wrongdoing. Moreover—as I will argue—it is often possible for moral accountability for corporate wrongdoing (and hence liability) to be extended quite widely amongst the directors and employees of a business organisation.[1] Standard approaches to moral accountability in group settings—such as business organisations—are based on the idea of action. Accountability is grounded either when an individual acted alone to perpetrate wrongdoing or acted jointly with others to do so. Attempts to expand the group of people who may be held accountable typically rely on explaining how this broader group all participated in the relevant joint action.

My account does not start with the idea of acting but rather with valuing. Groups generally, and business organisations in particular, are settings in which people come together to share values. Although people may share values in a variety of different ways, I focus on value sharing as characterised by the forming of *joint commitments* amongst organisation members to hold certain things as valuable. This mode of value sharing is based on Margaret Gilbert's conception of joint commitment and in particular her account of how values may be the subjects of such commitments (Gilbert, 2005). To say that organisation members share values is equivalent, I argue, to saying that that organisation has a culture. More importantly, when organisation members enter into joint commitments to share values, they enter into normatively significant agreements with each other to pursue those values, and so each contributes to the reasons that all others have to act in ways that fulfil these agreements. It is this relation of mutual reason giving that is the basis for my argument that when cultural values of this kind predictably promote wrongdoing and one or more organisation members act wrongly in their promotion, accountability is shared amongst all those organisation members who participated in the culture, that is, those who are party to the commitment to share those values.

Of course, this approach to moral accountability in business organisations relies on being able to justify a number of claims: that a culture exists within one or more such organisations that predictably promotes wrongdoing; that, in fact, wrong has been done in pursuit of those cultural values; and that organisation members have culpably participated in that culture, so grounding their responsibility for the wrong. In the context of the GFC I have argued that these conditions were met in financial sector organisations (Dempsey, 2018). The culture that predictably promotes wrongdoing in this case is one in which the value of short-term gains— both corporate and personal—is pursued above other values that those organisations and their members are under an obligation to promote, specifically the values of good risk management and customer interests. It was neglect of good risk management practices in pursuit of short-term profits and bonuses, particularly through the development and supply of debt-based securities, that precipitated the central events of the GFC.

Some organisation members bear moral accountability for these actions and the harm they caused because they were personally involved in these central events. Many others, however, bear accountability, even though they were not personally involved, because they participated in the enabling culture nonetheless. The ways in which this wider group participated in the culture are varied, but I argue, they all involved engaging in habitual behaviours and practices that exemplified the promotion of short-term financial gains over good risk management or customer interests; it is through such habitual, value-laden activity that a willingness to enter into a joint commitment to endorse these values is exhibited (Dempsey, 2015). An example of such activity is that related to another banking scandal, the mis-selling of payment protection insurance (PPI) at a variety of UK financial institutions, with Barclays being one of the first institutions where dubious practices came to light. Various parties throughout the Barclays organisation were implicated in the mis-selling: front line sales staff who sold policies to people who could never claim against them; the middle management that directed those staff; the senior leadership who foresaw criticism but did not act; human resources professionals who designed inventive incentivisation contracts; and financial professionals who saw how profitable the PPI product was. Although none of these people was, through these actions, directly connected to the central events of the financial crisis, nonetheless their share of accountability for those events and their outcomes is grounded by the actions they took with respect to PPI mis-selling because of the values that those actions instantiate.

Although this is just an example of how moral accountability for a certain incidence of corporate wrongdoing can be grounded for many members of a business community, the operation of this mechanism and hence widespread moral accountability for corporate wrongdoing throughout business organisations is, I claim, quite common. The sheer volume of scandals that have rocked the financial sector in recent years is itself evidence of this widespread culture, especially given that they have not been limited to just one organisation or one narrow part of the sector. Moreover, the applicability of this model to corporate wrongdoing in general is leant weight by the frequency with which such activities are explained at least partly by recourse to the idea of a bad or unethical corporate culture. Here we might think, for example, of the collapse of Enron or the BP Deepwater Horizon disaster in the Gulf of Mexico (Dempsey, 2015).

Moral Liability Without Moral Accountability

Moral accountability is a major reason why liability for corporate wrongdoing should be extended to organisation members. It also, however, provides the starting point for an argument for why such liability should be extended even in the absence of moral accountability. The approach to moral accountability in business organisations that I have offered might be thought susceptible to various objections. In particular, even if organisation members do engage in joint commitments to promote certain values, and in doing so predictably promote the wrongdoing of others, there may be reasons for thinking that they may still be exonerated. This may be because they are justified in their actions because on balance the good that comes from promoting a certain culture outweighs the bad; or it could be because the individuals' circumstances excuse them participating even when the culture overall cannot be justified.[2]

It is this second type of case that particularly interests me in arguing for extending liability for corporate wrongdoing to organisation members. Consider the situation of a member of a business organisation who is excused moral accountability for participating in an unethical culture. Imagine, for example, that the person is an employee who joined the organisation without knowing that its culture is morally defective, after having taken all reasonable steps to try to find out if this was the case. Also imagine that once the true nature of the organisation becomes clear, that person is bound to it in a way that would make it excessively personally costly for him or her simply to leave. Nonetheless, although he or she recognises that he or she is not expected to make the personal sacrifices that would be required were he or she to leave, he or she takes other less extreme measures in an attempt to mitigate the harm caused by the deficient culture and to improve it as far as he or she is able.

Although these circumstances give us reason for excusing this employee from moral accountability for harms caused as a result of the culture in which he or she participates, nonetheless he or she has still engaged in wrongdoing. The circumstances do not make his or her participation in the culture an act which is, on balance, morally acceptable; rather they allow him or her to escape moral accountability for that wrongdoing. Setting out the situation in this way allows a more nuanced appreciation of the issues at stake in answering the further question of whether he or she should be found morally *liable* for participation in this corporate culture. To be clear, this question asks whether there is a moral case for him or her incurring certain repercussions for his or her participation. We may think that the obvious answer to this question is that there is no case. After all, we have just seen that he or she may not be held morally accountable on this basis. However, I want to argue that moral accountability need not be the only basis on which liability is determined. In particular, I want to suggest that there may be cases in which a person *deserves* to be held liable, even though desert does not provide sufficient ground to establish moral accountability. Participation in corporate wrongdoing provides an archetypal example of such a case.

Corporate wrongdoing is particularly interesting for an investigation of liability because it often results in the generation of significant costs for one or more parties. In many cases these parties are entirely innocent of any wrongdoing connected to those costs: take, for example, the foreign exchange customers of banks who were charged a mark-up without their knowledge, and—apparently—sometimes despite an explicit denial from the salespeople that this was the case (Arnold & Fortado, 2015) or the taxpayers in the UK whose money was used to bail out RBS and Lloyds Bank. In both these cases costs have been incurred by—let us suppose—completely innocent parties. Let us also suppose, for the sake of argument, that although these costs were generated by wrongdoing in financial institutions by a wide range of members of those organisations, all those involved have an excuse that allows them to avoid moral accountability for their actions. The question now becomes: In such cases, is anyone morally liable?

To put it succinctly, here is the situation with which we are faced: One group of people has undertaken wrongful actions and in doing so has harmed another group of people. Neither group may be blamed (morally) for what has happened, but nonetheless, three aspects of this situation play strongly to the intuition that the financial sector workers are (morally) liable to bear costs and this on the basis that such liability is deserved. Firstly, it is they who caused costs to be incurred; secondly, they did this through engaging in wrongful actions; and thirdly, by imposing costs on them as a practical instantiation of holding them liable—and transferring the resources to the other party, assuming the costs levied are financial—the impact on that other party may be alleviated. Moreover, in at least some of the examples I have given, financial sector employees have benefitted personally from the wrongdoing in which they have engaged.

All these considerations support the conclusion that financial sector employees are morally liable to bear costs that result from corporate wrongdoing to which they have blamelessly contributed. Indeed, they support the conclusion that it is these individuals who deserve to bear the costs. The reason liability is appropriate while accountability is not is this: There is no necessity to ascribe moral accountability, and so whether any particular individual deserves such accountability may be considered simply on its own merits. When certain actions, such as those that constitute corporate wrongdoing, impose costs, however, it is not the case that liability can be entirely avoided—costs have been incurred, and someone must bear them.[3] In such cases, the question of *relative* desert becomes relevant. Rather than asking whether this person deserves to be held liable, we ask: Does this person deserve to be held liable more than other potentially liable parties? It is because we ask questions of absolute desert when assessing moral accountability and relative desert when assessing liability (at least in cases in which costs are inevitable) that liability may be established even when accountability is not.

An account of moral liability based on desert is 'backward looking' in that it determines who should bear costs by reference to past actions. A different basis for assigning liability, however, is forward looking and is to be found in the identification of instrumental benefits that a particular principle of liability will achieve, independent of what anyone deserves. This is the second consideration that may ground moral liability even when moral accountability cannot be justified. Whether such a basis can justify holding people liable on its own is, perhaps, controversial. However, in this case instrumental reasons can be seen to be in tune with those grounded in desert, offering at least the possibility of further support for the position I have developed: By holding liable members of business organisations who have engaged (blamelessly) in wrongdoing, positive incentives are created for such members, and others like them in other organisations, to avoid participation in the future. These conclusions generalise to all those cases in which members of business organisations have participated in corporate wrongdoing, which I have suggested will frequently be the case where corporate wrongdoing has occurred.

Enforcing Liability in UK Financial Services

I started by motivating the need to address liability for corporate wrongdoing by reference to cases in which financial sector institutions have been subjected to huge fines on the basis of wrongdoing by their employees.

Although these fines have largely been borne by shareholders, the individuals who have participated in the wrongdoing appear, in general, to have escaped any form of personal liability. Dissatisfaction with this state of affairs, however, has not been ignored, and indeed since the onset of the financial crisis, steps have been taken in the UK to improve the way that accountability—and liability—for wrongdoing is determined within the financial services sector. These measures go a long way to satisfying the requirements that I have outlined in this chapter. However, in some crucial respects they do not go far enough. To argue for this conclusion, a brief outline of the measures and their implications is needed.

In 2012 the UK parliament established the Parliamentary Commission on Banking Standards to consider and report on the 'professional standards and culture of the UK banking sector, taking account of regulatory and competition investigations into the LIBOR rate-setting process' and 'lessons to be learned about corporate governance, transparency and conflicts of interest, and their implications for regulation and for Government policy'. The Commission published its final report in June 2013 and recommended that significant reforms be made in a number of areas of banking supervision and regulation (Parliamentary Commission on Banking Standards, 2013). Some of these reforms were to be primarily structural: It recommended that certain banking functions—those that are central to the functioning of the economy and to meeting the basic banking needs of customers—should be 'ring-fenced'; this involved separating them from other non-vital (and more risky) activities. In the same vein, the Commission also recommended that clear plans be put in place for the continuation of vital banking services should, despite the ring-fence, an institution providing those services fail.

The measures that are most relevant to the determination and enforcement of liability within the sector, however, focused not on the structure of banks but on the individuals within them. These measures were primarily contained in proposals for a new regulatory regime for individuals and backed up with proposals regarding the appropriate structure of remuneration within the sector. The proposed regulatory regime consisted in two main components: a 'Senior Persons Regime' and a 'Licensing Regime'. The starting point for both of these new regimes was the need to identify explicitly those individuals within the financial system who hold roles that would enable them to engage in particularly harmful kinds of wrongdoing. The intention of the new measures was, firstly, to enable the effective vetting of individuals who are appointed to such roles, and secondly, to ensure effective enforcement of liability against role holders who do wrong. As the name suggests, the Senior Persons Regime (which was renamed the 'Senior Managers Regime' when the measures were implemented in The Financial Services [Banking Reform] Act 2013) was aimed at the most senior people within banks: those with responsibility for running the organisation. It was based in the requirement to establish an explicit record for each institution within which individuals hold which key responsibilities in the form of a 'responsibilities map'.

Similarly the Licensing Regime (renamed 'Certification' in the Act) was aimed at all those who, although not responsible for running the bank, could nonetheless cause serious harm to that bank, its reputation, or its customers. The aim of this development was to extend accountability to a wider group than under the previous regulatory regime in recognition of 'the need for a wider sense of responsibility and aspiration to high standards throughout the banking sector'. The intention was that the primary responsibility for monitoring the behaviour of those who qualify for certification would fall with the banks themselves and similarly that banks would be responsible for enforcement when necessary through individuals' contracts of employment. The role of regulators would then be to monitor banks' implementation of these measures and only take enforcement action where this was found to be insufficient. These two regimes can be understood as putting the framework in place for establishing accountability for certain kinds of wrongdoing in the financial sector. Beyond this, however, the Commission also recommended further measures be implemented to enable such individuals to be held liable should accountability be established.

With respect to those falling under the SMR, two measures were recommended: a new criminal offence of 'reckless misconduct in the management of a bank' and, in cases of civil misconduct against senior managers, a reversal of the burden of proof. The former was intended to be pursued only in the most serious cases in which substantial failings resulted in the failure of an institution with significant costs to the taxpayer; the latter was intended to build upon the establishment of a responsibilities map for each institution, the idea being that if the institution itself was found to have committed a regulatory breach, it would be assumed that those senior managers with responsibility for the relevant areas had also breached regulatory standards unless they could prove otherwise. Indeed, once the proposals were passed into legislation and the relevant regulatory bodies—the Financial Conduct Authority (FCA) and the Prudential Regulation Authority (PRA)—published consultations on how they would implement the new rules, it became clear that the scope of the changes would be even wider than the Commission itself envisaged.

Similarly, a new tool was proposed to support the enforcement of liability with respect to the certification regime. Notwithstanding the fact that primary enforcement responsibility would rest with the banks themselves, the Commission proposed the creation of a set of 'Banking Standard Rules' on which the responsibilities of those under the certification regime would be based and which would be set out by the regulators. Although the Act made provision for these rules, changing the name to 'Rules of Conduct', it again went further than the commissioners were imagining, giving the regulators leeway to make them applicable to all bank employees. And although the PRA proposed a narrower application, the FCA proposed to apply the rules to all but 'ancillary staff' (e.g., security guards and cleaners), opening up the possibility of enforcement action being taken against nearly any bank employee in the case of non-compliance. Given my earlier argument regarding corporate liability, it should come as no surprise that I support this broader interpretation, a view that I will develop in more depth in the next section.

Before this, however, it is worth outlining some of the further recommendations made by the Commission regarding remuneration. The important aspects of these recommendations relate, broadly speaking, to two aspects of the remuneration system: the length of time that bankers' variable remuneration payments are deferred and the mechanisms by which awards may be recouped in the case that evidence at a later date shows that they were not, in fact, appropriate. I take these aspects to be the most important for current purposes because they establish in practice a further mechanism by which liability may be enforced within the financial sector. The Commission recommended longer deferral periods for variable pay. Further, two mechanisms were proposed by which awarded pay may be recouped. The first, building on the deferral proposals, was to enable the cancellation of deferred pay before its maturity date were it to transpire that the original award was unjustified. This would be achieved through the development of legal and contractual arrangements. The second and more extreme measure, termed 'clawback', was to enable the recovery of pay that had already vested, and should be reserved for only the most serious cases.

Again, however, differences arose regarding the scope of application of the remuneration code. This time it was the regulator, the PRA, that pursued a narrower scope, arguing that the code should apply just to 'material risk takers'; a broader scope than this, they argued, would go beyond international standards. However, the commissioners originally proposed that it should apply to all who fall under the Senior Managers and Certification Regime. And they were concerned that the PRA's proposal would exclude many who, although not 'material risk takers', fall under the FCA's certification regime due to their ability to cause significant harm to the reputation or customers of an institution.

Enforcing the Liability of Members of Business Organisations: A Proposal

The new measures enacted in the UK financial services sector are clearly significant for the establishment of accountability and—most importantly for the purposes of this chapter—the enforcement of liability. But do they go far enough? And what lessons can be learnt for the enforcement of corporate liability more generally? To answer the first question, they do not go far enough, but they do provide the tools necessary to extend liability along the lines I proposed in my earlier argument. To recap, I argued that given certain conditions, accountability for corporate wrongdoing can be extended widely throughout the members of a business organisation. This accountability is established on the basis of widespread participation in a corporate culture, understood as a system of shared values that promotes the kind of wrongdoing in question. By sharing values in the way that creates corporate culture—through entering into joint commitments to promote those values—each member of that culture gives each other member positive reasons to act in their pursuit, and so they all share accountability for the wrong that is done when those reasons are acted upon. Moreover, moral accountability of this kind entails liability.

It is clear that the reforms in the UK financial sector since the GFC have extended the ability of regulators to hold members of financial sector businesses accountable for wrongdoing and to enforce liability on that basis. This extension is, in theory, in line with the framework for liability that I have set out. However, in practice it looks likely that the implementation of the new regime fails to fill the gap that I have identified. The Senior Managers and Certification Regime is the primary mechanism for the extension of accountability and liability, and in both cases the focus is on ways in which particular identified individuals might directly, through their actions, cause serious harm to a bank, its reputation, or its customers. Although the FCA's list of certified positions commendably goes beyond senior managers and material risk takers, the extensions it offers are still based on this relation of direct harm—for example, by including benchmark submitters and individuals in customer-facing roles such as investment advisors.

In contrast, the mechanism for grounding accountability—and hence liability—in business organisations that I have set out is indirect. Indeed, in developing the full account of this mechanism I have argued that people participating in inappropriate cultures do wrong because they are *complicit* in the primary wrongdoing of others (Dempsey, 2015). The current interpretation of the rules does not capture such complicity in its framework for identifying accountability and enforcing liability. It would not, however, require significant adjustment for this gap to be plugged. Indeed, the FCA has already put in place the basis for such an adjustment by extending the scope of the new conduct rules, upon which enforcement may be based, to all employees of banks with the exception of ancillary staff.

This extension in place, appropriate recognition of how broad accountability can be grounded in secondary wrongdoing may be established through appropriate specification of the conduct rules. Specifically, those rules should recognise that individuals or groups engaging in practices and behaviours in one part of a bank, where those activities clearly promote a certain culture—or set of values—can exert significant influence on the behaviour of those in other parts of the bank who participate in the same culture. Therefore, the conduct rules should explicitly prohibit such activities, for example, activities that systematically undervalue the promotion of customer interests, even when those activities do not *directly* lead to customer harm and run little risk of doing so. Of course, to do this more work would be required to specify exactly the kinds of practices and behaviours that should be prohibited in this way, although there will be no shortage of evidence from events over recent years on which to base this work.

Two further challenges would remain, however: to monitor financial institutions in such a way as to determine when these conduct rules are being breached and to determine the appropriate way to enforce the liability of those found guilty of a breach. On the first challenge I suggest a solution already implemented with respect to the SMR—the reversal of the burden of proof. Just as it is fair to presume, without specific evidence to the contrary, that a regulatory breach by a firm could have occurred only if the relevant senior manager also committed such a breach, it is also fair to presume that it could not have occurred without a conducive corporate culture. The upshot of this would be that in the event of a regulatory breach by a firm, it would be assumed that all non-ancillary staff should acquire a degree of accountability for the breach. This assumption would be made in the absence of proof that behaviours and practices satisfied requirements for not promoting—or appearing to promote—inappropriate corporate values. It would be the responsibility of each business area to provide such proof, if it was available.

This recommendation may appear draconian, but it need not be. In pretty much any significant organisation, business processes and the way in which they should be undertaken are documented. Moreover, those processes are—or at least can be—monitored on an ongoing basis to ensure that they are being undertaken in compliance with documented guidelines. To demonstrate that they should not be held accountable for a regulatory breach by their firm, organisation members could start by demonstrating that the standard practices in which they are engaged have been documented and followed in such a way as to avoid promoting a culture that would encourage such activity. Of course, not all practices and behaviours within an organisation are formal in this way; this said, methodologies exist that firms might employ to record less formal activities and assess their impact on corporate culture, either demonstrating compliance with the conduct rules (clearing organisation members of accountability) or identifying steps that must be taken to ensure compliance. Such record keeping and assessment would have to be verified by the regulator, but similar to the role that the FCA and PRA play with respect to the certification regime, those bodies could perform a secondary function, undertaking spot checks of institutions on an ongoing basis and assessing appeals against presumptive accountability in cases of regulatory breaches by a firm.

If such an appeal were unsuccessful under the proposed regime, then non-ancillary staff at a bank found to have breached regulations would be liable to enforcement action. The kind of actions that would be particularly appropriate in such cases are the cancellation of deferred pay and, if necessary, clawback of pay that has already vested. Such remuneration-based action would have at least two significant features to recommend it. It would, firstly, be highly scalable. Reluctance to extending accountability and liability within business organisations often seems to stem from a perception that such an extension would be disproportionate. However, just as it is possible to ascribe relatively mild levels of accountability on the basis of relatively low levels of wrongdoing, it is also possible to impose low levels of liability—provided the right tools are put in place. Financial penalties are ideal for this purpose. Secondly, financial penalties have the added benefit that they generate revenue. As noted earlier, corporate wrongdoing often leads to relatively high levels of harm being caused to entirely innocent parties. Given that one of the justifications for imposing liability is the transfer of costs from those least deserving of bearing them to those most deserving of bearing them, remuneration-based penalties provide a ready mechanism for promoting this outcome.

Noting this justification for imposing liability brings me back to the argument I made earlier regarding grounds for such justification that go beyond the establishment of moral accountability. Despite arguing that moral accountability for corporate wrongdoing may commonly be established on the basis of participation in inappropriate culture, I also noted a potential objection to my account. This objection holds that members of business organisations will commonly have excuses for such participation and as such may not be held morally accountable. However, my response to this objection was that even if it goes through, those organisation members will still have engaged in wrongdoing and so will be more deserving of bearing costs than other parties, justifying enforcing liability when costs are inevitable. Moreover, I argued that this approach to liability will also have positive incentive effects. These considerations further support the specific measures that I have recommended here because they significantly reduce the situations in which it would be inappropriate to assume the general liability of organisation members in the case of a regulatory breach by a firm.

Of course, in practice no regime will be perfect, and it is inevitable that there must be a balance between attempting to capture as many liable individuals as possible under an enforcement approach and risking penalising those who should not be held liable. The suggestions I have made here will, inevitably, capture some who should not be held liable. However, they should establish a better balance than approaches that either impose blanket penalties on shareholders or those that rely only on identifying direct connections between particular acts by given individuals and particular harms.

Here I have focused on the question of whether the reforms to the liability regime that applies to UK financial services go far enough and how they should be augmented to reflect the conclusions regarding corporate liability that I have outlined in this chapter. I have not discussed the second question with which I started this section: What lessons can be learnt from this for the enforcement of corporate liability more generally? In general, the answer should be that a lot can be learnt, given that there is no obvious reason why the best approach to liability within the financial sector should be completely different from that which is appropriate in other sectors of the economy. Of course, there are differences that will affect the exact implementation of any regime. Financial services are regulated and, since the crisis, increasingly heavily regulated for good reasons. Such reasons have to do, for example, with the degree of harm that the sector can do to the rest of society and the degree of specialisation that makes it hard for outsiders—including customers—to assess performance.

The cost of regulation will mean that a full application of the Senior Managers and Certification Regime is not appropriate in all sectors of the economy. Nonetheless some aspects of these approaches may be suitable for widespread use. More directly in line with the arguments of this chapter, the development of rules of conduct that might be enforced through financial penalties against corporate employees is a measure that could be translated directly to other sectors. At the very least, the default approach in cases of corporate wrongdoing of fining the shareholders should be augmented with the imposition of financial penalties on all organisation members in the absence of proof that they were not complicit through their participation in an inappropriate corporate culture.

Conclusion

The action, or rather lack of action, taken against individuals in the aftermath of the GFC and the banking scandals that followed it—PPI mis-selling, LIBOR fixing, and manipulation of the markets for foreign exchange—focused minds on how liability for corporate wrongdoing should be identified and enforced, particularly in the financial sector of the economy. I have set out one model for grounding such liability, a model based primarily in the possibility of establishing widespread moral accountability amongst organisation members for incidents of corporate wrongdoing. It suggests that in such cases of corporate wrongdoing, there are grounds for enforcing liability equally widely amongst those members. Moreover, this model of liability is supported by further considerations: that organisation members will often be the most deserving bearers of liability even when moral accountability cannot be established and that by enforcing liability in this way, beneficial incentive effects will be generated.

In practice, reforms of how the UK financial sector is regulated have put in place much of the infrastructure necessary to implement these recommendations. However, extensions in the way the reforms are interpreted are necessary. It is important that the scope of the conduct rules covers all non-ancillary staff. Further, the rules themselves must be specified to capture misconduct through secondary wrongdoing in the form of contributions to inappropriate corporate cultures that encourage or facilitate primary wrongdoing. When a firm is found to have breached regulations, it should be assumed that organisation members generally have breached these conduct rules unless they can provide evidence to the contrary. The remuneration code, extended to cover all non-ancillary staff, provides a tool for enforcing liability for corporate wrongdoing on this basis.

Although I have focused particularly on the financial services sector, I see no reason why a version of this liability regime could not be adapted for use across the whole spectrum of corporate wrongdoing. It fills the gap that currently exists between the indiscriminate punishment of shareholders and the overly focused identification of only those few individuals most intimately involved in any particular corporate wrong.

Notes

1. I have made a detailed argument for such an approach to moral accountability in business organisations elsewhere; see Dempsey (2015).
2. I will continue to discuss the case for liability drawing on the approach to understanding moral accountability in business organisations that I have set out. However, the following discussion of liability in the absence of moral accountability (due to the person in question having a valid excuse) is equally applicable to other approaches to understanding moral accountability and its proper application conditions.
3. Given that it is within society's power to determine where these costs fall, at least an implicit ascription of liability is inevitable.

References

Arnold, M., & Fortado, L. (2015). Lawsuits loom after $5.6bn forex settlements. *Financial Times*, 22nd May.

Dempsey, J. (2015). Moral responsibility, shared values and corporate culture. *Business Ethics Quarterly*, 25(3), 319–340.

Dempsey, J. (2018). Banking culture and moral responsibility for the financial crisis. *Midwest Studies in Philosophy*, 42(1), 73–94.

Financial Times. (2015). Shareholders punished for the sins of the trader. *Financial Times*, 22nd May.

Gilbert, M. (2005). Shared values, social unity, and liberty. *Public Affairs Quarterly*, 19(1), 25–49.

Parliamentary Commission on Banking Standards. (2013). *Changing banking for good: Report of the Parliamentary Commission on Banking Standards*. London: The Stationery Office.

10 The Bankers and the 'Nameless Virtue'

Tom Sorell

Introduction

Morally conscientious people sometimes blame themselves for things that are not within their control. The driver who unavoidably kills someone nevertheless kills someone, and because it is normally awful to have killed someone, it makes sense for the driver to blame him- or herself. It makes sense, although the death was not the driver's fault. Blame also makes some sense where a driver who does not kill anyone but who does not maintain his or her car properly, identifies with someone else who runs a child over through failure to maintain the car. Although there has been no bad outcome of the second agent's negligence, the second agent feels guilty for having carelessly increased the risk of the same kind of road death that the first agent is actually responsible for. This sort of expansive self-blame is probably not entirely rational; but it can be admirable all the same.[1]

Susan Wolf (2004) has connected scruples about matters outside one's control with a 'nameless virtue' that acknowledges our involvement in a world where things are inevitably affected by luck and chance. This context of contingencies, according to her, should not be taken to be irrelevant to ascriptions of responsibility, as if the only thing we can take blame or take responsibility for is how we direct the will. Human agency is not just a matter of what is willed but of what happens for better or worse when one's will is translated into action. Expansive self-blame is, according to her, an expression of this mixed context of human action (see also Walker, 1993). It gets over the gaps in responsibility otherwise created by moral luck. It is not just open to individuals acting on their own behalf, she says, but to powerful role holders acting *ex officio* in institutions. It is the virtue that is displayed when leaders of businesses or governments are quick to take responsibility for bad outcomes even when they or their institutions are not strictly or wholly at fault. When we are dissatisfied with the reluctance of leaders to respond appropriately to bad things that happen on their watch, we may be sensing a failure to exercise a virtue that Wolf's account identifies and helps to define.

There is a connection between the nameless virtue and the global financial crisis (GFC). Many ask why the bankers have been so slow to apologise or why their apologies have been so meagre when taken together with the cost in public money of bank bailouts. Wolf's account suggests an answer: namely, the lack of the nameless virtue. The bankers' lack of this virtue also explains the half-heartedness with which they have introduced a new culture into banks after the GFC. In short, the absence of this virtue helps make sense of the disapproval we feel for the principal players in the crisis. On the other hand, the arguable *presence* of the virtue in one exceptional UK banker—Sir James Crosby—may explain why, virtually uniquely, he seems to deserve admiration for the way he responded to his role in the GFC. In other words, the presence or lack of the nameless virtue seems to rationalise reactive attitudes it has been natural to direct towards some bankers since 2008. The nameless virtue does not function merely, as Wolf suggests, to allow attributions of responsibility to stick in conditions of moral luck.

I shall try to say something about the *limits* of expansive self-blame as a virtue. Sometimes that sort of blame is insufficient for taking responsibility appropriately, even when it is accompanied by public expressions of remorse or regret. One reason is that taking responsibility appropriately sometimes requires an agent to submit to judgement by *others*, paradigmatically through legal proceedings and, in particular, by exposing themselves to proportionate punishment determined by independently devised and independently applied standards.[2] Self-blame often does not meet these independence requirements. Again, except where it is psychologically so far-reaching that it dominates one's consciousness and is, for a time at least, inescapable, self-blame need not reach the threshold for being punishing at all. Minimal self-blame—a matter-of-fact acknowledgement of fault—is sometimes not enough for taking responsibility appropriately, even when self-blame is heartfelt and is expressed publicly.

This point seems particularly compelling where an agent—either an individual or an organisation—takes blame for a very bad outcome but is so rich or powerful that bearing even major money costs is easy and hardly alters the quality of life. In cases like these, self-blame by itself seems not to register on the scale for appropriately taking responsibility. Even if rich and powerful wrongdoers feel so bad about something that they are put off their champagne and caviar for a week, that cost may be so slight and forgettable for them, all things considered, as to be hardly any payment at all.

This is where the nameless virtue appears to come in, for it is expressed not in minimal but expansive self-blame. In fact, however, the nameless virtue does not even help with understanding the one case in which a leading banker has gone beyond feeling bad about the crisis and has given up money and symbols of status to demonstrate his or her contrition even when not directly responsible for a bank failure. To the extent that postulating the nameless virtue helps us admire the atonement of James Crosby, it produces the illusion that his response sets the pattern for the morally appropriate banker's response to the crisis. It does not, for two reasons: Firstly, it does not impose a sufficiently high financial cost, and secondly, personal roles in systemically important banks are subject to more than norms of personal character, norms that are properly legal and impersonal.

The Nameless Virtue

A good place to begin is with the following passage from Wolf's 'The Moral of Moral Luck':

> There is a virtue that I suspect we all dimly recognize and commend that may be expressed as the virtue of taking responsibility for one's actions and their consequences. It is, regrettably, a virtue with no name, and I am at a loss to suggest a name that would be helpful. It involves living with an expectation and a willingness to be held accountable for what one does, understanding the scope of 'what one does,' particularly when costs are involved, in an expansive rather than a narrow way. It is the virtue that would lead one to offer to pay for the vase one broke, even if one's fault in the incident was uncertain; the virtue that would lead one to apologize, rather than get defensive, if one unwittingly offended someone or hurt her. Perhaps this virtue is a piece or an aspect of a larger one, which involves taking responsibility not just for one's actions and their consequences but also for a larger range of consequences that fall broadly within one's reach. One may offer to pay for the vase one's child broke or offer to take the blame for the harm someone suffered as a result of the practices of an agency of which one is the head. Like other virtues, this one is a matter of offering the right amount (whether it be of compensation, apology, or guilt) at the right time to the right person in the right way. It's not the case that the more responsibility one takes for the harms that lie at increasing distance from one's control, the better. Yet one ought to take responsibility for more than what, from a bystander's view would be justly impersonally assigned.
>
> (2004, pp. 121–122)

Wolf distinguishes here between the nameless virtue and a larger one of which the nameless virtue is a part. The larger virtue—which involves taking responsibility for things beyond what one does but still within 'one's reach'—will turn out to be more relevant to the case of the bankers and the financial crisis than the narrower one. But before we come to that, the nameless virtue deserves discussion.

Firstly, the nameless virtue may not be nameless. 'Conscientiousness', which is Wolf's own gloss at times, comes close to it, and that is the term I shall use throughout. Conscientiousness in the relevant sense is not quite the same as 'conscientiousness' in ordinary English. In the ordinary sense, 'conscientiousness' might mean the disposition always to try to do the right thing, including by not doing harm or by making up for harm that one has done, including despite oneself. A conscientious agent in this sense might *not* go in for expansive self-blame, knowing that he or she had characteristically done his or her best to do the right thing. Again, the conscientious agent in the ordinary sense of 'conscientious' might behave as he or she does if he or she alone expected him- or herself to do right or abstain from harm. Wolf's nameless virtue, on the other hand, operates specifically in response to a convention of being held accountable (the central case of which is being held accountable by others), and it appears to be a matter of internalising a communal or social standard and applying it to one's own actions and to actions of those suitably related to oneself.

Although Wolf does not spell this out, conscientiousness in the relevant sense seems to lie somewhere between, and to counteract, two character defects—one of underestimating one's socially assigned sphere of responsibility for harm and one of over-estimating it. Underestimating one's socially assigned sphere of responsibility might be characteristic of a self-indulgent person. To the extent that such a person is disposed to take responsibility for things at all, it might take the form of offering to do the least inconvenient thing in response to harm. At the other extreme is the uncommon trait of over-estimating one's responsibility. This might occur in a person who is treated or treats him- or herself as some kind of jinx, or as irremediably clumsy and disruptive, and who apologises even for things that are not his or her fault. Alternatively, it might be the trait of someone who self-importantly exaggerates the effects of his or her actions or his or her power to benefit others. The expression of this latter defect might be or resemble officiousness. To be officious is to take it upon oneself to act in circumstances in which it is neither useful nor requested by others whose interests are at stake. By contrast with officiousness, conscientiousness responds in a timely way to genuine need, sometimes unspoken need, and produces assistance to meet it while being considerate of the beneficiary's feelings about receiving assistance. Unlike someone who is careless or self-indulgent, the conscientious agent also considers whether he or she has fallen short in detecting or acting appropriately to meet need 'within his or her reach'.

When taking responsibility for wrongdoing that he or she is not directly responsible for, the conscientious agent adopts a broad view of the circumstances in which it is appropriate for him or her to benefit those who have been adversely affected. Wolf does not say what happens when the conscientious agent is in a position to take the credit for doing something *right* or beneficial, but because he or she thinks conscientiousness is a kind of acknowledgement of the way the will is enmeshed in a world also containing contingency, one expects that either conscientiousness or some allied virtue will work to make one *minimise* one's estimate of one's own contribution to a good outcome. Here conscientiousness might have the effect of an agent's ascribing to good luck some or all of his or her success in carrying out a rescue or in being at the right place at the right time to offer some particular effective assistance. In this way conscientiousness in relation to bad outcomes in one's ambit might be the other side of the coin of humility or self-effacingness with respect to good outcomes.

Conscientiousness in Wolf's sense must be related somehow to justice. Presumably the just person does not necessarily take an *expansive* view of his or her responsibility, as the conscientious person does; otherwise conscientiousness would not be a nameless virtue but rather justice itself or an aspect of justice. To allow for a distinction in this area, let us call the just but unconscientious person 'merely just'. The merely just person may not wonder whether, when he or she obeys the letter of a legitimate law, his or her actions also reflect its spirit. Suppose he or she claims tax deductions that he or she is entitled to, while thinking that it would be better for the public treasury to have more money to discharge the policies that tax collection finances. This may be where, to forgo the deductions, the agent has to feel the force of the more exacting virtue. Conscientiousness has to take over from justice.

In relation to penal law, one could imagine the conscientious person being prepared to plead guilty to a charge with a more serious penalty than the charge that has actually been brought against him or her, or being prepared to plead guilty to more counts of the same crime, if he or she is in fact guilty of the more serious crime or more counts of the same crime. Suppose he or she is on trial for a breach of a secrecy law in, as he or she thinks, the public interest, and suppose he or she has not confessed to some further illegal disclosures he or she has in fact made that could attract fresh charges. Justice without conscientiousness might involve pleading guilty only to existing charges; justice with conscientiousness might involve confessing and pleading guilty to more. Conscientiousness, then, seems not only to exclude the evasion of legal responsibility, as justice does; conscientiousness also seeks out responsibility where law has been leniently applied or where it gives out altogether. Thus, expansive self-blame can be in place even when the bad things one has done or allowed to happen contravene no regulations.

According to Wolf, what I am calling conscientiousness might be part of a 'larger virtue'

> which involves taking responsibility not just for one's actions and their consequences but also for a larger range of consequences that fall broadly within one's reach. One may offer to pay for the vase one's child broke or offer to take the blame for the harm someone suffered as a result of the practices of an agency of which one is the head.
>
> (2004, p. 121)

We could call the smaller virtue 'personal conscientiousness' and the larger virtue 'wide conscientiousness'. Does Wolf have a coherent conception of this larger virtue? I shall suggest that she does not but that there is something of value to be distilled from the elements of her account. This will have a bearing on taking responsibility in the complicated case of the financial crisis.

Although it is hard to be sure on the basis of the little before us, Wolf may associate with the larger virtue at least the responsibility one takes on by acquiring a certain role, such as *parent* or *agency head*. But there are reasons to think that these do not work well as illustrations of the way the larger virtue, if there is one, works. For example, it is a familiar part of parental responsibility to apologise for one's children's transgressions and even, as in the example, to compensate those adversely affected by what the children have done. Or at least this seems to be part of parental responsibility when children have themselves not reached the age of responsibility. The parent of a careless 40-year-old does not seem to be irresponsible if he or she refuses to pay for the denting of someone's car in an accident. Only so long as one's children are 'under one's control'—typically before adulthood—are their actions widely taken by parents to be the parents' responsibility. It is doubtful, however, that acknowledging parental responsibility in the usual way would rise to the threshold for being *virtuous*. It seems too routine for that. Perhaps the threshold is reached by parents who take responsibility particularly promptly and are such good judges of appropriate compensation that there are never hard feelings on the part of those who have been adversely affected. But otherwise it is too routine a disposition to be given special moral credit.

Holding an office in an 'agency' and taking responsibility for its bad practices is different from conscientiousness as a parent of young children. In Wolf's example, it is possible to take the blame for the 'practices of an agency' as its head, presumably because one has directed people whom one manages to engage in those practices or because, although the practices were engaged in without one's permission, they were supposed to accomplish a purpose which it is one's job as agency head to see accomplished in the right way. That is, although one has not authorised the practices, their connection to the agency's purposes and employees cannot honestly be disowned by the agency, and because one is the head of the agency, then *ex officio* one ought to own them, too. Whether, when one does so, one is exercising a *personal* virtue is far from clear. Perhaps someone who is unconscientious in their personal life could apply an agency policy of taking responsibility without endorsing that policy and perhaps while disagreeing with it. If so, then taking responsibility *ex officio* may come apart from personal conscientiousness. The case that seems to fit in best with Wolf's theme is where the agency has *no* policy and the head is being advised by others to take *no* responsibility. In that case, *the head* acts when he or she takes responsibility or blame: it is not just agency policy or the board acting through him or her. It is as if, in displaying wide conscientiousness, the agent personifies the agency and internalises the blame he or she claims on behalf of the agency.

Under the conception of conscientiousness that Wolf operates with, agents who go in for expansive self-blame both show signs of good 'psychic health' and display a virtue. They show good psychic health because they do not adopt the over-detached viewpoint of a bystander on their own actions, or on the actions of those they are connected with, even when those actions are not in their control. Disassociating oneself from the killing of the dead child when one is the driver is a case of over-detachment and threatens to make one psychologically compartmentalised and conflicted rather than unitary and whole. As for why conscientiousness is a virtue, Wolf's suggestion is that it is similar to, or possibly a case of, an undoubted virtue that does have a name: generosity:

> Perhaps the more obvious reason for regarding [conscientiousness] as a virtue is that, when applied to harmful actions, this trait is a species of, or at least akin to, the well-established virtue of generosity. Generosity generally involves a willingness to give more—more time, more money, more lenience, more, in one way or another, of oneself than justice requires. In offering to pay for the broken vase or in trying to provide comfort to the grieving family beyond what a rationalist assignment of liability would demand, an agent benefits or tries to benefit others at cost to herself. That this should be seen as virtuous is not hard to understand.
>
> (2004, p. 122)

Something goes wrong in this explanation of why conscientiousness is a virtue, but, as I will go on to claim, it is an instructive and suggestive mistake and one that will prove helpful in our discussion of blame-taking in the financial crisis.

What goes wrong is that Wolf runs together two different kinds of virtue—on the one hand, being generous, and on the other, being willing to bear significant costs as a way of being seriously contrite. Being generous is giving more than is required by justice. But to display generosity in this sense is not necessarily to do so at a cost to oneself, or at least an appropriately significant cost to oneself, which is where additional exactingness comes in.

To see this, consider a merchant with 100 melons to sell. If he or she gives away 20 melons to some very hungry passers-by, they will feel much better. The merchant is not obliged by justice to donate the melons: the passers-by are not starving, and although they are not rich, they can afford to buy the melons. In these circumstances, making a gift of the melons is generous. But let us stipulate that had the merchant not given away the melons, they would have remained unsold and would have had to be thrown away uneaten. The stipulation makes it true that the merchant does not forego income by giving away the melons. By the same token, it in fact costs nothing to give the melons away. To the extent that he or she bears a cost it is in the epistemic sense: for all he or she knew, he or she would have been forgoing income. In fact, the merchant gives the melons away at no additional cost and so sacrifices nothing. What is more, let us stipulate, the loss of the melons would make no noticeable difference to the merchant's felt wellbeing or to the wellbeing of those depending on him or her. This is an example of generosity—in the sense of a donation above the level required by justice—but at no personal cost.

It is easy to adapt the point to making reparations in a case in which one is not personally to blame. Suppose your friend has broken a stranger's vase, and you happen to have been given two identical vases, only one of which you have ever used. Let us stipulate that the unused duplicate is a delightful vase so that it amply fills the void left by the now broken vase in the stranger's house. It is generous of you to part with a delightful vase as recompense for someone else's damage. But it is generosity at no cost. Had the vase not been offered in recompense, it would have lain unnoticed, gathering dust in a cupboard. Generosity seems to be a matter of more than satisfying the requirements of justice: It is not this *as well as* sacrifice or taking a loss.

Is the conscientiousness under discussion a kind of generosity? Yes, because it is expansive blame taking with the corresponding willingness to offer more help to whomever is directly disadvantaged than is required by mere decency or even justice. One assumes liability in cases where one is not strictly responsible. One helps as if one had in fact been responsible, not as if one were merely a disconnected bystander. The willingness to give more than is strictly required is what is generous. On the other hand, the appropriateness of giving help *at significant personal cost* comes not from the expansiveness of expansive blame but from its being *blame*. To blame oneself is to have beliefs in common with those who think one ought to be punished: one has done wrong and should somehow pay for it. Feeling bad—experiencing agent regret—is not that payment; compensating the victim might be. But the feeling indicates the willingness of the agent to bear a significant cost. If no significant cost is borne, then agent regret seems to issue in business as usual, not action that is particularly praiseworthy and that reflects well enough on the agent to point to virtue. A payment that is too easy for the agent, although it is a payment, is not a payment that registers as appropriate in both the perspective of a blamer *and* a punisher. I am suggesting that this more exacting test of appropriateness—being costly from the perspective of both agent and punisher—is the one that has to be met by people who display the nameless virtue. The application of this suggestion will become clearer when the discussion turns to bankers.

Now expansive blame-taking is harder to read as virtuous the more it is *ex officio* blame-taking, the more it is blame-taking for large-scale harm or damage, the more that damage is at least partly attributable to an agency much bigger than a single person, and the more the resources used to pay for the harm or damage are not personal resources but those of an agency. To enlarge on these points in turn, *ex officio* blame taking by an individual is not necessarily personal blame-taking nor personally endorsed blame-taking, nor therefore personally virtuous. The individual may simply be the *channel* for apology or payout. Secondly, when what an agency is blaming itself for is large-scale harm or damage, the threshold that has to be reached for simple compensatory justice to be done and certainly to be seen to be done may already be very high—so high that claims of generosity as opposed to mere justice are likely to seem disputable. Thirdly, where an agency is the relevant agent and the agency is large and possibly collective, the agency may not be easily intelligible as a bearer of virtue: virtue tends to be defined for individuals capable of excellences contributing to species flourishing. Fourthly, the greater the resources of an agency, the harder it is to bear out the claim that the agency has paid enough to be generous.

Finally, large-scale disaster seems to *demand* expansive blame taking from even partly responsible agencies and their figureheads: It does not seem to be a case of *noblesse oblige*. If the disaster is big enough, not only regret or blame taking but prompt action to compensate victims seems to be obligatory. In the more extreme sort of case, justice seems to drive out what is discretionary and therefore what can be considered generous. Not only is expansive blame-taking and the appropriate compensatory action *demanded*, but the standard of appropriate action can be very exacting.

Indeed, in the case of very large-scale disasters, less than personal *tirelessness* on the part of relevant agency heads is sometimes thought to be unseemly. When a BP oil well leaked in the Gulf of Mexico in 2010, for example, it did not do for the BP chief executive to take a holiday break during the initial clear-up efforts, even though he seems to have behaved conscientiously before reaching the point of considering a vacation. On the contrary, holidaying while the oil leaked was portrayed as outrageous personal behaviour, notwithstanding the fact that many others at BP were still attending to the problems in the Gulf. Wolf's account does not seem to extend to the case of personal responsibility for the actions of such large-scale agencies, especially when things go very wrong. It is as if the size or power of the agency, or the scale of its bad effects, disrupts the virtue framework. Fault fills up the space that would otherwise have been created by the expansiveness of expansive self-blame, and responsibility-taking that would have looked supererogatory in more domestic settings starts to look obligatory for the agency, with the result that there is not enough discretion left to the head of the agency to act in a way that seems personally virtuous.

Not only is *ex officio* blame-taking harder to regard as virtuous than *in propria persona* blame-taking; in *practice* it also tends to be less of an option. After all, it can be required by one's office to *limit* the acknowledged liabilities of the agency. This requirement, what is more, can be morally inspired, because the money lost by admitting liability can be that of relatively weak or vulnerable people connected to the agency (e.g., small shareholders), or can involve losses to others (e.g., vulnerable clients).

The Global Financial Crisis

Although the damage done to many Western economies by the financial crisis has far exceeded the environmental damage caused by the BP oil spill, few bankers in leadership positions in 'systemically important' banks[3] in the United States and Western Europe have done more than make apologies *ex officio*, and usually ceremonially, in set-piece confrontations with inquisitorial legislators before the television cameras. A *Washington Post* report[4] for 9 April 2010 sets the tone:

> Two top Citigroup executives who guided the bank along its disastrous path toward massive losses and multiple government bailouts expressed regret Thursday during testimony before a panel investigating the financial crisis [. . .]
>
> 'Let me start by saying I'm sorry,' Prince told members of the Financial Crisis Inquiry Commission. 'I'm sorry the financial crisis has had such a devastating impact on our country. I'm sorry for the millions of people, average Americans, who have lost their homes. And I'm sorry that our management team, starting with me, like so many others, could not see the unprecedented market collapse that lay before us'. [. . .]
>
> In an opening statement, Rubin cited numerous factors—including low interest rates, sharp increases in housing prices, misguided credit ratings and excessive risk-taking—that contributed to the unprecedented crisis. But he framed the breakdown at Citigroup and other companies as a collective failure, in which 'almost all of us [. . .] missed the powerful combination of forces at work and the serious possibility of a massive crisis. We all bear responsibility for not recognizing this, and I deeply regret that'.

These comments make it seem as if the failures at Citigroup were failures to discern the effects of complex financial forces to which bankers were related as mere observers. In fact, those forces were unleashed by bankers through the establishment of shadow banks and successful lobbying for permissive regulation on acquisitions of financial services companies by banks, and their ill effects would have come to the notice of top management earlier if internal processes had been more robust. In Citigroup in particular there was a culture of not reporting bad news, and there was misinformation within the firm about the size of its holdings in securitised mortgages. It had been assumed in the company that many of those holdings had been sold on.

In the UK, too, bankers have also gone in for highly detached apologies, where they have made apologies at all. The following exchange[5] in February 2009 between the chair of the Treasury Committee of Parliament and the former CEO of the government-rescued RBS, Sir (now just plain Mr) Fred Goodwin, is indicative:

Q760 CHAIRMAN: Sir Fred, one of the members of the public said to me this morning, 'Do the institutions know what they have done to ordinary people's lives, families and jobs?' Everyone in the room pays some form of tax to the UK Government, and the UK Government has forwarded shed-loads, lots of money, to your institutions. What are we getting? In terms of your approach, some people say you have been hesitant to say 'sorry', so I am giving you your opportunity now.

SIR FRED GOODWIN: Thank you very much for that, Chairman. I apologised in full, and am happy to do so again, at the public meeting of our shareholders back in November. I too would echo Dennis Stevenson's and Tom [McKillop]'s comments that there is a profound and unqualified apology for all of the distress that has been caused and I would not wish there to be any doubt about that whatsoever.

The strangely impersonal 'There is a profound apology' instead of a simple 'I'm sorry' is particularly striking—so striking that certain discourse analysts have studied bankers' expressions of contrition (see Hargie et al., 2010).

Few heads of systemically important banks have voluntarily resigned; none has personally started a programme of recompense to damaged shareholders and people irresponsibly sold inappropriate financial products; and many have resisted regulatory proposals intended to enforce greater prudence in banking and a return to the core banking purpose of intermediation for productive commercial investment. There is a widespread public sense of the insufficiency of *ex officio* apologies by bankers and of their willingness to cooperate with banking reforms. At first sight, it is a strength of Wolf's account that it enables us to articulate the nature of the insufficiency: Did certain bankers fail to take responsibility for things that possessors of the nameless virtue *would* have taken responsibility for? If so, then perhaps what keeps the apologies from being satisfying is the absence of the nameless virtue in bankers making the apologies.

I shall dispute this diagnosis of the bankers' failure to take responsibility. In what follows I shall distinguish between taking responsibility for the financial crisis and taking responsibility for mismanagement leading to bank failure or mismanagement of a systemically important bank leading to a rescue to prevent failure. No one person is responsible for or can take responsibility for the financial crisis. But if they are placed correctly in the power structure of a particular bank, especially a systemically important bank that is known by its management to be systemically important, individuals *can* be responsible or mainly responsible for particular bank failures and also the costs of government pre-emption of a failure (Sorell, 2018). In these latter cases, there is scope for the personal exercise of the nameless virtue. But in these cases, too, the nameless virtue can fail to be sufficient from a moral point of view. I come to such a case in the next section, but I begin with responsibilities in and for the financial crisis as a whole.

The GFC is in part the responsibility of institutions and not only systemically important banks. These institutions include, in the private sector, specialised mortgage lenders, insurers, hedge funds, credit-rating agencies, accounting firms, and lobbying firms. In the public sector, institutions with responsibility in the crisis include sovereign wealth funds, a very wide array of regulatory bodies closest to the biggest financial markets in the United States and the UK, the big U.S. government-backed mortgage providers, Fanny Mae and Freddie Mac, and some sub-departments of the U.S. legislature concerned with the reform of banking law. In addition to institutional agents in the financial crisis, there are a host of irresponsible individual borrowers in real estate markets, individual dealers in derivatives, individual mis-sellers of mortgages, individual risk raters within banks and others.

In considering so complex an array of actors, it may be tempting to think that lines of responsibility are irremediably tangled so that blaming individual institutions, let alone particular people, is out of the question. But this is a mistake, attested to by the fact that no one connected to the banking industry denies the distinction between systemically important banks and others and because all of the systemically important banks had clearly identified leaderships, some of which had been in place for decades, as in the case of Lehman Brothers. Although not all systemically important banks in the crisis needed to be rescued, those that did have all publicly admitted to one kind or another of management failure or market misjudgement or risk miscalculation, and the hierarchies of these banks, and job descriptions of top executives, were well-enough defined to indicate where the loci of *ex officio* responsibility lie. In general terms, those at the top of the hierarchy of a systemically important rescued bank from around 2000–2007 are prime candidates for the ascription of personal responsibility in the crisis.

It is true that over the period that led up to the crisis, the growth of 'shadow banking'—I explain what that is shortly—and the development of new markets in financial derivatives may have proceeded at such speed that no one, not even those at the top of the systemically important financial institutions (SIFIs), would have been able to exercise suitable controls.

If this conjecture is true, conditions for *virtuous* responses to the failure of SIFIs start to be in place. If no one could have stopped the runaway train of shadow banking, then, had more heartfelt apologies been made by top bankers in response to the crisis and stronger gestures of recompense and reform, those apologies and gestures might have started to look like exercises of the nameless virtue.

To come to shadow banking, a number of regulatory changes, mainly in the United States, had the effect over decades, but especially after 1999, of weakening the banking regime that had prevailed in the United States since the Great Depression (see Johnson & Kwak, 2010, especially Chapters 4–6). The decisions to bring in these regulatory changes and create the conditions for shadow banking were neither monumental nor irreversible, but their effects were significant, and crucially, they were made under the active influence of bankers. Under the regime established in the United States immediately after the Great Depression, banks operated under relatively strict requirements to hold capital against liabilities, and there were limits on the interest rates they could offer to both retail and commercial customers. This conservative regime was maintained to avert another banking crisis, not to maximise growth in the banking industry. The banking industry-supported growth of retail and commercial money markets made it possible to sidestep these restrictions—money market funds are not legally banks, although they offer services similar to those of banks and were marketed to customers as facsimiles of banks.

Within money markets, particular funds could legally pay higher returns to retail depositors than in the deposit insurance-protected retail banking sector while also offering checking privileges and on-demand withdrawals or 'redemptions' of holdings. They also enabled commercial organisations to make more profitable use of cash reserves and to exploit the commercial possibilities of financing long-term investment with short-term borrowing. Commercial borrowers with good credit ratings could even insure against defaulting on short-term obligations by paying others—sellers of the class of derivatives called credit default swaps—to take on those liabilities. An important form of long-term investment was securitised packages of mortgages sold in different risk-rated tranches. These securitised products included, at the riskier end, collateralised debt obligations, the market that collapsed for many of the rescued systemically important banks.

Although there is a much longer story to be told here than I have space for (Dempsey & Sorell, 2018), the creation of money markets, along with developments in the sale of securities based on risk-rated tranches of mortgages, are important instalments in the narrative of the financial crisis. Partly on the strength of this narrative, many bankers have disputed the role of immorality in the events of 2007–2008. Instead, they have tended to admit to costly but excusable misjudgements of a wide variety of risks, including risks of illiquidity in money market finance and risks of a downturn in the American real estate market. The less repentant bankers' position can be put roughly as follows:

> Although misjudgements of risks were undoubtedly costly, they were made in good faith, broke no criminal laws, and fell afoul of no financial regulator's requirements at the time. What is more, the risks in question were hard to judge, and considerable intelligence was put by banks into modelling them so that they could be better understood. If the models failed, that is not because they were unsophisticated through negligence but because, despite great expenditures of time, money and brain power, they were not sophisticated enough. In any case, the deficiencies of the models are not to be traced to moral malignancy, and the deficiencies couldn't have been that great; otherwise people could not have made as much money as they did *before* 2007.

This is the sort of position that invites or is consistent with the interpretation of the financial crisis as a case of very bad moral luck for the bankers and therefore as a potential site for the operation of the nameless virtue on the part of those moved to apology, or serious banking reform, in response to the crisis. According to this interpretation, the moral character of any decisions made under uncertainty seems to depend on how they turn out, and the complex lending and borrowing decisions that underlay the financial crisis, although they went well and made many people rich in the early 2000s, eventually turned into a disaster. If bankers, particularly those in the rescued 'systemically important' banks, are amongst those to be blamed for this disaster, then they also deserve credit for the good times. Either that, or both the good and bad times are matters of luck, and neither credit nor blame is in order.

Let us grant, for the sake of the argument, that bad moral luck *was* operating when the collapse of the wholesale money markets drove many systemically important banks to the brink of failure and Lehman Brothers to outright bankruptcy. That is, suppose that many investment decisions made in good faith went wrong through no carelessness on the part of bank management. Had the leaders of the rescued systemically important banks possessed the nameless virtue, they would have taken responsibility even so. This would have meant offering abject apologies at least to those adversely affected. The victims of the financial crisis are legion. They include sub-prime borrowers in the United States, taxpayers across the developed world, elderly savers, poor non-taxpayers whose welfare provisions and other services have shrunk in the period of austerity following the recession, and credit-starved businesses. Foreign sovereign holders of the debt of countries at the heart of the crisis—the UK and the United States—have also been adversely affected. Then there are all those caught up in the global recession that has followed the crisis. In fact, few if any of these groups have been compensated, let alone quickly or spontaneously.

If moral luck creates conditions for exercises of the nameless virtue, does the GFC—with its arguable accretions of moral luck—create conditions for it? Suppose the answer is yes. Then couldn't the nameless virtue have guided the leaders of the 'systemically important' banks to do some of the things—make abject apologies, devise compensation schemes partly funded from personal wealth, or take part in vigorous banking reform—that they have been so roundly criticised for omitting to do?

In considering this question it is important to recall a conclusion argued for earlier:

> Expansive blame taking is harder to read as virtuous the more it is *ex officio* blame-taking, the more it is blame-taking for large-scale harm or damage, the more that damage is at least partly attributable to an agency much bigger than a single person, and the more the resources used to pay for the harm or damage are not personal resources but those of an agency.

The damage of the financial crisis is on too large a scale and too extreme to call for a response informed by a purely personal virtue. Again, as was pointed out earlier:

> large-scale disaster seems to *demand* expansive blame taking from even partly responsible agencies and their figureheads: it does not seem to be a case of *noblesse oblige*. If the disaster is big enough, not only regret or blame-taking but prompt action to compensate victims seems to be obligatory. In the more extreme sort of case, justice seems to drive out what is discretionary and therefore what can be considered generous.

The scope for generosity, and so for the nameless virtue, seems to be very limited in the case of large-scale disasters, including the GFC. This seems to be true notwithstanding the operation of moral luck. The moral luck in the crisis, such as it was, depended on unavoidable loss of control and irremediable uncertainty surrounding investment decisions and innovations such as securitised real estate instruments.

Even if the outcomes of myriad investment decisions involving esoteric financial instruments were indeed beyond senior bankers' control, the establishment of shadow banking and departures from traditional norms of banking prudence were not. The rescued systemically important banks operated actively and deliberately in the shadow banking sector and took advantage of its looser capitalisation requirements and near anonymous, highly leveraged dealings in the derivatives market, which in turn contributed to the liquidity problems and share-selling panics that constituted the crisis proper. As I shall now argue, those actions should be seen as cases of injustice, which are far more serious than failures to exercise the nameless virtue. Claiming as much is perfectly compatible with saying that many investment decisions made within the shadow banking sector were subject to uncertainty and moral luck. But, by the same token, it is not the failure to operate the nameless virtue that justifies our sense of the insufficiency of the bankers' reaction to the crisis but their injustice.

Elsewhere (Dempsey & Sorell 2018), I have contributed to a detailed narrative of the events of the financial crisis in New York and London as background for the claim that some heads of major New York banks were personally responsible, not just *ex officio* responsible, for some of the damaging events of the crisis, including the failure of Lehman Brothers and the near failure of other large banks. There is wide agreement, for example, that most of the systemically important banks over-borrowed in the early 2000s. It is widely agreed that there was an overconcentration of investment in real estate, especially through different kinds of securitised instruments. It is widely agreed that models employed by credit-rating agencies for measuring the risk of investments and the financial strength of banks were deeply flawed. Even if none of these factors was individually sufficient to cause the crisis, jointly they make its outbreak less than surprising. Nor are these just judgements in hindsight. All of these matters were seen as worrying by some in the banking industry before 2008. Some systemically important banks even escaped the need for government rescue by behaving more prudently *against* the trend of risk taking. JP Morgan, for example, was far less leveraged at the height of the crisis than other Wall Street institutions,[6] which put it in a position to acquire Bear Stearns when the latter faced bankruptcy. Similarly, Lehman Brothers executives had raised questions about its exposure in the real estate market quite some time before it failed but were overruled by those at the top (Sorkin, 2009, pp. 124ff).

The point of this narrative is that responsibility in and for the crisis was not exclusively collective or organisational: Some of it was individual responsibility, especially where some identifiable person making high-level decisions in a systemically important bank had held a leading position in such a bank for decades and had great latitude to implement a wide variety of strategies but chose what in retrospect were very risky ones. People meeting this description—Richard Fuld and Sanford Weill to name two—had powerful positions in Lehman Brothers and Citigroup, respectively, and there were other, similarly highly placed, people in some of the U.S. mortgage originators, such as Countrywide.

Some of these figures had to unlearn or actively dismantle the traditional norms of banking to over-borrow, to overinvest in real estate, and to move into financial services that, in the United States at least, had been closed to banks by law ever since the Great Depression. At least one leading banker, Sanford Weill, was actually instrumental in the repeal of the relevant legislation, the Glass-Steagall Act. Because many of the accounting and investment practices engaged in by the big banks in the early

2000s were self-consciously anti-traditional and, by traditional standards, highly imprudent, there were reasons for suspecting that things might go wrong quite apart from the inscrutability of trading algorithms or the complexity of higher-order collateralised debt obligations. In short, there was a flight from traditional prudence in lending and investment practice, although traditional prudence had not been discredited. How does this translate into injustice?

The systemically important banks put at risk deposits and share prices with policies that, because they avoidably increased the probability of losses, were unjust to depositors and shareholders. The banks did not make sufficient provisions to pay back their debts, adding injustice to creditors to their list of wrongs. When their collapse was imminent, they turned to the government they previously claimed had over-regulated them to bail them out, adding to the huge over-indebtedness of the United States and diverting funds that might otherwise have gone through social security and other benefits to the worst-off Americans. Here again there was injustice. Under further U.S. government policies that add to the injustices attributable to banks in relation to taxpayers, banks have been able to divest themselves of 'toxic' assets—without being exposed to the full scale of the losses that they would otherwise have had to face—injustice again.

The Case of James Crosby

We can distinguish the financial crisis from the failure of particular banks. We can also distinguish the difficulty of taking personal responsibility for the crisis from taking personal responsibility for the mismanagement of a particular bank. The leaders of rescued systemically important banks have a personal share in the complex responsibility for the financial crisis, but they may have a much larger share of personal responsibility for the expensive rescue of individual banks that would otherwise have failed.

Are there no cases of leaders of rescued systemically important banks expansively *taking* responsibility? Are there no leaders of systemically important banks, in other words, who displayed the nameless virtue? One apparent exception—perhaps the *sole* apparent exception—to the rule of half-hearted contrition is James Crosby, ex-Chief Executive Officer of Halifax Bank of Scotland (HBOS). He was heavily criticised in a report from the UK Parliamentary Commission on Banking Standards in 2013, which in its turn was a response to the imposition by the UK FSA of a large fine on the HBOS Chief Financial Officer. After giving a short summary of the issues that concerned both the FSA and the Parliamentary Commission, I shall describe Crosby's, at first sight impressive, response to the criticisms directed at himself and other HBOS executives.

At first sight, Crosby's actions seem to show the nameless virtue in action, and what is more, the nameless virtue being displayed by someone at the top of a systemically important bank. Perhaps he did display the nameless virtue. I shall argue that impressive as that was, it was an *inadequate* response to his failings as a bank executive because the costs Crosby imposed on himself do not appear to be to proportionate to the failings for which he was ostensibly claiming responsibility, or to his own resources. We can have a sense of the insufficiency of a banker's response to the financial crisis, then, even when the nameless virtue *is* present.

Crosby's gestures are best understood against the background of the near failure of HBOS and its rescue by Lloyds Banking Group in 2006.

HBOS resulted from the merger in 2001 of a large UK retail mortgage provider (Halifax) and the Bank of Scotland (BoS). Before 2001, BoS had a retail and corporate banking business in Scotland and a smaller presence in England based on telephone banking and niche services connected to high-value mortgages and deposits. In corporate banking it concentrated on commercial real estate lending and servicing management buyouts. Its merger with Halifax gave it a retail depositor base in England, which put HBOS in a position to compete with the so-called Big Four in the UK as a new universal bank.

Crosby set an aggressive growth strategy. He aimed at exceeding the 20 per cent share of the market that Halifax had achieved in its core (retail) markets, and he sought to build its commercial loan book and commercial depositor base. Its international division attempted to establish a presence in Australia. Between 2001 and 2008, according to the Parliamentary Commission on Banking Standards,[7] the group loan book more than doubled. But especially in commercial real estate, the loans were often of very doubtful quality, were often riskily financed in the wholesale money markets rather than from deposits, and were not often enough syndicated, so that HBOS took the risk of default alone. Eventually these big risks materialised on the HBOS books as 'impairments' or large write-downs of the value of loans.[8] In its International Division HBOS's impaired loans as a proportion of its total loans were strikingly high by comparison to its competitors, typically more than twice as high as its competitors in the Irish market.[9] In Australia, nearly a third of its loan book was impaired at a time when Australian banking was avoiding entirely the losses of financial institutions closer to the epicentre of the financial crisis. Even after 2008, impairments continued to be staggering in scale: The Parliamentary Commission estimate for retail loans between 2008 and 2011 is £7 billion.[10]

In addition to bad loans, HBOS was overcommitted to short-dated money market funding for financing them. This was because its deposits were relatively low in comparison to the loan obligations it had taken on. As a result, HBOS was very vulnerable to illiquidity in the money markets. This vulnerability was recognised as early as 1 March 2005, when Crosby was still in charge of the bank, and although steps were taken to increase deposits and bring in longer-dated money market financing, HBOS's overall dependence on short-dated credit was not significantly reduced. The day after Lehman Brothers failed, HBOS, too, had in effect failed. Lord Stevenson, who was chair of HBOS from the time of the merger with Halifax, denied in evidence to the Parliamentary Commission that its failure was due to anything other than the seizing up of the wholesale markets. But the Commission is scathing about that claim. For them, HBOS simply had too little capital. According to the report,

> The HBOS failure was fundamentally one of solvency. Subsequent results have shown that HBOS would have become insolvent without injections of capital from the taxpayer and L[loyds]B[anking] G[roup].[11]

The Parliamentary Commission claims that failings within HBOS were compounded by a malfunctioning regulatory regime in the UK. The FSA, although it raised questions about HBOS credit risks in 2003, about its ability to meet the requirements for a Basel II waiver—allowing it to be its own judge of capital adequacy—and about the effect on HBOS of the turbulence in New York, had been too ready to accept reassurances from HBOS officials that turned out to be ill-founded.[12]

Not that the FSA held no HBOS bankers responsible for HBOS's troubles. It served an 'enforcement notice' on Peter Cummings, head of the Corporate Division, in September 2012. This imposed a fine of £500,000 (reduced after lawyers' negotiations from £800,000) for failure to exercise due skill and care in the management of HBOS and for failure to manage risk at BoS. The fine punished the policy of growing the loan book quickly at the cost of a disproportionately high rate of impairment.

In evidence to the Commission, Cummings complained of being singled out personally and complained, too, of the FSA's targeting HBOS when other banks were in a similar position. Up to a point, the Commission agreed with Cummings. They concluded that not one person but four should have been pursued by the FSA. In addition to Cummings, they named (i) the long-serving chair of HBOS, Lord Stevenson, (ii) Crosby, who served as HBOS CEO until 2005, and (iii) Andy Hornby, who succeeded Crosby. The FSA's simply allowing the 'Approved Person' status of each of these three to lapse was insufficient. All three should have been barred from any further role in UK financial services.[13]

There was no noticeable response from Lord Stevenson and Hornby to this recommendation. Crosby, on the other hand, promptly resigned his remaining (and lucrative) financial services positions and offered to return his knighthood, no doubt having in mind the fact that the disgraced CEO of the government-rescued RBS had had his knighthood unilaterally removed. In addition, Crosby voluntarily took a 30 per cent reduction in his HBOS pension.

At least at first sight, these gestures seem honourable. Certainly they stand out from the meagre apologies and protestations of events beyond their control that have come from other prominent bankers on both sides of the Atlantic since 2008; in addition, they come from someone who left HBOS several years before it failed and who oversaw its considerable growth after the merger. This fact in particular seems to justify the claim that Crosby was being criticised by the Parliamentary Commission for things beyond his control and that, even so, he exercised the nameless virtue. Because there was an opportunity to rethink his strategy after he left and to introduce more prudence, Crosby is perhaps not first in line for the criticism that he brought the bank irresponsibly to the brink. Stevenson, who presided over the bank the whole time, is perhaps the guiltiest of the three.

Although Crosby deserves blame as architect of a policy that was insufficiently attentive to building up deposits and reducing dependence on wholesale markets, the fact that he made his gestures in 2013, eight years after leaving the bank, the fact that he did so promptly (relative to the publication of the Fourth Report of the Parliamentary Commission), and the fact that he did so at some cost to himself, may indeed make his gestures *prima facie* expressions of Wolf's 'nameless virtue'. Admittedly, his relation to the downfall of HBOS is not that of pure bystander, but his hand was not on the tiller when HBOS could have saved itself by changing course. So, in a sense, Crosby accepted a cost for something that he was not fully or directly responsible for: the bank's affairs for the whole period from 2001 to 2008 and in particular the bank's failure and the need for rescue years after he left.

For these gestures to deserve classification as expressions of the nameless virtue, they have to impose a cost on the agent that makes sense not only from his perspective but also from the point of view of someone who wants to mete out punishment. That was the conclusion reached in the first section of this chapter, when I reviewed some of the shortcomings of Wolf's own explication of the nameless virtue purely in terms of generosity. If Crosby had shown his remorse by privately slapping his own wrist, or by depriving himself for a year of a favourite recreation, that would presumably have fallen far short of a *prima facie* expression of the nameless virtue, just because it was too slight a cost relative to the enormity of the HBOS failure and its consequences. By being willing to pay a higher financial and reputational cost in a highly public way, Crosby went much further, far enough to exercise the nameless virtue. But was that far enough?

A relevant consideration is the size of the payment relative to Crosby's resources. The main financial sacrifice he made was to forgo 30 per cent of his pension. But it is a very big pension. The effect of the sacrifice was to reduce the annual payment to himself from £560,000 to £406,000. This hardly puts Crosby in the poor house. On the contrary, it leaves him with an annual income after retirement vastly greater than that of the average private-sector worker in the UK.[14] In addition, because he left HBOS in 2005, Crosby did not suffer the kind of losses that other leaders of distressed and failed or rescued banks experienced when the relevant share prices plummeted. On the contrary, he sold two-thirds of his shares in HBOS in 2006, considerably before the crash. As for the knighthood, that would probably have been taken away (with greater ignominy) if he had *not* given it up. The fact that he surrendered it voluntarily probably left his profile raised and his reputation in a better state than that of many other bankers. In short, reputationally at least, Crosby's gesture *cut* his losses.

As already made clear, it would be unfair to give Crosby no credit for his responses to the Parliamentary Commission. When they are compared with the total inaction of the two colleagues who were criticised alongside him, and the protestations of helplessness from other bankers, one feels that Crosby did *quite a lot* right, even if he did not give back enough or take responsibility early enough. We have already conceded that he exercised the nameless virtue. The problem is that exercising the nameless virtue does not go far enough. I am not claiming that Crosby bore no real costs (although they may have been insufficient) but that he acted as judge in his own case of how high the relevant costs should be, and in the end he was perhaps an overly lenient judge. What is missing in his response to the Commission is the impartiality and independence in the determination of costs that (ideally at least) is associated with institutional justice.

In this respect Wolf seems to me to be wrong to extend the operation of the nameless virtue from personal life to personal action within big public or public-aspected roles. Wrongdoing with big consequences carried out in institutional roles is not answerable only or primarily to norms of personal character or norms of appropriate personal emotional response. The big public roles, including the role of leading a 'systemically important' bank, have an ineliminably impersonal, institutional aspect (Sorell, 2018). This impersonal aspect is captured by some of the *legal* constraints on wrongdoing in office—by the fact that some wrongdoing is classified as crime—and, short of this, by the fact that one can be made legally ineligible to play certain kinds of potentially damaging public roles, including the role of bank director.

The Parliamentary Commission has recommended the introduction of a criminal offence of reckless banking to capture the kinds of wrongdoing that have eluded FSA rules in the UK and that arguably led to some of the worst consequences of the financial crisis. This idea may be impractical because it is hard to define in law the relevant kind of recklessness, because taking risks is inseparable from banking, and because the skills of modelling risk in modern banking are so sophisticated that they are hard for would-be regulators, let alone judges and juries, to understand. The criminalisation of recklessness may also be self-defeating because white-collar crime will inevitably attract sentences that are relatively light, disappointing the punitive intentions of the Commission. Furthermore, prosecuting and imprisoning bankers would add significantly to the financial costs the state has already had to bear in rescuing the banks.

Nevertheless, there is something right about the idea of criminalising financial recklessness in the case of systemically important banks. The proposal correctly recognises the need for independent judgement of the behaviour of those at the top of the relevant banks and the appropriateness of addressing serious damage to the state's resources with serious punishment. Although the UK FSA is not a model institution,[15] it is of the right general type for imposing genuine costs on bankers. Firstly, it is a regulatory authority subject to the oversight of a democratic central government. This not only makes it suitably independent of the banks (at least in theory) but also provides a line of accountability to taxpayers, who have been left having to pick up after HBOS and its ilk. Secondly, a financial regulatory agency is (or ought to be) staffed with people who have a detailed understanding of the duties and performance of high office holders in specific banks. Thirdly, such a body is well-positioned to understand the kinds of costs that office holders who are responsible for recklessness can easily evade when they have a level of legal help only they can afford or shrug off because they are so wealthy.

Leaders of systemically important banks who are reckless in their management should not only be exposed to very large fines, as Peter Cummings was; in the worst cases—the most costly in money terms and those involving the grossest mismanagement—they should be liable to significant periods of imprisonment. Chief executives and chief financial officers of systemically important banks might be particularly exposed to relevant charges when, as in the case of HBOS, borrowing and lending are for years demonstrably badly managed. This suggestion adds courts to financial regulators as arbiters of punishment and twice removes the judgement of appropriate costs from those whose conduct is in question.

Crosby's gestures, honourable as they appear to be when compared to the inaction and shamelessness of other bankers, seem to lack something if all they amount to is his forgoing a little of the icing on his cake. Justice might have required him to surrender a portion of the cake itself; but that is not all: It is risky, probably unjust, and a misunderstanding of a leadership role in a systemically important institution, for the authorities to allow good conduct to depend on the personal conscientiousness of individual bankers.

Notes

1. Our reactive attitudes to ourselves in cases like these have great philosophical interest. If we blame ourselves for something, then we take responsibility for it. Being able to take responsibility—in the sense of acknowledging the

action as one's own—may be as important to *being* responsible as being causally operative in the production of the bodily movements that realise the action. This emerges from consideration of abnormal agents. Someone who feels deeply alienated from his or her actions most of the time is deficient in agency, and this deficiency may call into question attributions of blame (Frankfurt, 1988; Watson, 2003). There is a connection not only between the ability to take responsibility and unalienated agency but also between taking responsibility—in the sense of expansive self-blame—and the intelligibility of moral luck. If blaming oneself expansively makes some sense in the case of the non-negligent car accident in which the child is killed, then so (to the same extent) does the judgement that the agent in that case has bad moral (outcome) luck. In a relatively recent reflection on the arguments for the reality of moral luck that he originally put forward in his ground-breaking paper on the subject (Williams, 1981), Bernard Williams has insisted on the intelligibility and soundness of agent regret even in cases in which bad outcomes are not due to negligence (Williams, 1993). According to Williams, it makes sense to blame oneself for a death that was not one's fault because that outcome is directly connected to what one did or was doing.

2. Taking responsibility can even mean forgoing due process protections (Sorell, 2002).

3. The concept of SIFI has been developed by international regulators since 2008 to apply to banks, insurance companies, and other financial firms whose failure would have large-scale, unwanted economic consequences in economically important jurisdictions or globally. SIFIs, as they are now called, are now specifically required by international banking regulators to meet new (but arguably insufficiently demanding) capitalisation requirements, for example. What are now called SIFIs include the 'too-big-to-fail' banks that were bailed out by Western governments after 2008, such as RBS, Lloyds, and Citigroup. A sufficient condition for systemic importance is that a bank's failure would bring about the more or less immediate failure of many other financial institutions, the widespread loss of individuals' deposits, and widespread runs on other banks, sometimes in more than one jurisdiction. Side effects of such a failure could include, as in the case of the 2007–2008 financial crisis, the paralysis of inter-bank lending, huge reductions in commercial lending, sudden and sharp declines in the values of equities, and protracted deflation. Virtually the only systemically important bank to be allowed to fail during the financial crisis was Lehman Brothers, which was regulated in the United States. Other systemically important banks, including Citigroup in New York and RBS and Lloyds in the UK, received tens of billions in direct financial support from the United States and UK governments. All systemically important banks were in regular and routine contact with regulators before the crisis and in the time leading up to it, and it was common knowledge between banks and regulators that the market positions of these banks made them highly important to their respective national financial systems. Their de facto systemic importance was not suddenly revealed by the crisis.

4. Dennis, B. Citigroup executives apologize for not averting financial crisis. *Washington Post Staff Writer*, Friday, April 9, 2010. http://www.washingtonpost.com/wp-dyn/content/article/2010/04/08/AR2010040804865.html

5. www.publications.parliament.uk/pa/cm200809/cmselect/cmtreasy/uc144_vii/uc14402.htm

6. The bank fared less well later in the 'London Whale' scandal.

7. See its Fourth Report: 'An Accident Waiting to Happen': The Failure of HBOS. (2013). London: The Stationery Office, p. 7.

8. Ibid. ch. 3.
9. Ibid. p. 14 (Table 2).
10. Ibid. p. 17.
11. Ibid. p. 38.
12. Ibid. ch. 5.
13. Ibid. p. 43.
14. Neate, R. James Crosby to give up knighthood and 30% of pension. *The Guardian*, April 9, 2013. www.guardian.co.uk/business/2013/apr/09/james-crosby-give-up-knighthood-pension
15. It has indeed recently been replaced by newly designed specialist agencies dealing with system-affecting balance sheet risks, on the one hand, and mal-administration and mis-selling, on the other.

References

Dempsey, J., & Sorell, T. (2018). Introduction. *Midwest Studies in Philosophy*, 42(1), i–xvii.

Frankfurt, H. G. (1988). Freedom of the will and the concept of a person. In H. G. Frankfurt (Ed.), *The importance of what we care about* (pp. 11–25). Cambridge: Cambridge University Press.

Hargie, O., Stapleton, K., & Tourish, D. (2010). Interpretations of CEO public apologies for the banking crisis: Attributions of blame and avoidance of responsibility. *Organization*, 17(6), 721–742.

Johnson, S., & Kwak, J. (2010). *13 bankers: The Wall Street takeover and the next financial meltdown*. New York: Pantheon.

Sorell, T. (2002). Two ideals and the death penalty. *Criminal Justice Ethics*, 21(2), 27–34. Reprinted in N. Rosenstand (Ed.), *The moral of the story: An introduction to ethics* (pp. 717–720). New York: McGraw Hill, 2005.

Sorell, T. (2018). Responsibility in the financial crisis. *Midwest Studies in Philosophy*, 42(1), 1–17.

Sorkin, A. (2009). *Too big to fail*. London: Penguin.

Walker, M. U. (1993). Moral luck and the virtues of impure agency. In D. Statman (Ed.), *Moral luck* (pp. 235–250). Albany, NY: SUNY Press.

Watson, G. (2003). Free agency. In G. Watson (Ed.), *Free will* (2nd ed., pp. 337–351). Oxford: Oxford University Press.

Williams, B. (1981). Moral luck. In B. Williams (Ed.), *Moral luck* (pp. 20–39). Cambridge: Cambridge University Press.

Williams, B. (1993). Postscript. In D. Statman (Ed.), *Moral luck* (pp. 251–258). Albany, NY: SUNY Press.

Wolf, S. (2004). The moral of moral luck. In C. Calhoun (Ed.), *Setting the moral compass* (pp. 113–127). New York: Oxford University Press.

11 Moralising Economic Desert

Alexander Andersson and
Joakim Sandberg

Introduction

A prominent set of intuitions concerning the just distribution of work-related incomes, such as wages and bonuses, invokes the notion of desert (Freiman & Nichols, 2011; Goya-Tocchetto et al., 2016; Miller, 1992). For example, many people hold that employees who work harder than their peers, or who contribute more to their company's profit, thereby come to deserve a higher level of pay. The justification here is not about the consequences of such pay arrangements—for example, that wage differentiation may spur employees to work harder for increased rewards. Instead it concerns a basic form of justice: The general claim of economic desert, we may say, is that economic 'outputs' (wages or bonuses) should be distributed according to economic 'inputs' (effort or contribution).

But how should this claim be understood more exactly? The present chapter seeks to answer this question as well as to address a central ambiguity in the notion of economic desert concerning the relevance of moral assessments and consequences. According to several previous authors, what separates economic desert from other forms of desert, especially from so-called moral desert, is its salient instrumental and institutional—we may say 'non-moralising'—nature. Economic desert is therefore something quite different from traditional and more moralising variants of desert. However, we will argue that such analyses go too far and that economic desert makes little sense without a stronger moralising component.

Our thoughts on this issue were ignited by the popular reactions to and debates on remuneration practices after the global financial crisis (GFC) of 2008. By many accounts, a central cause of the crisis was the so-called bonus culture of Wall Street firms. By tying remuneration levels too closely to performance, traders and executives were incentivised to take excessive risks that eventually made the whole financial system unstable (de Bruin, 2015; Moriarty, 2018; Sinn, 2010; Stiglitz, 2010). So it is clear that the consequences of these remuneration practices were terrible. But can they perhaps be defended with reference to economic desert? Some people answer yes, partly on the basis of the general claim about inputs and outputs (Kershnar, 2005; Mankiw, 2013). However, most people seem to say no. This is on the basis of more moralising concerns, the general argument being that the relevant trading activity contributed very little to society and instead put us all in great economic jeopardy, which is morally reproachable (Admati & Hellwig, 2013; Lanchester, 2010; Stiglitz, 2010).

This chapter continues as follows. We first give some background on the general concept of desert and discuss whether it is after all a coherent or ambiguous concept. Thereafter, we introduce the prevailing distinction between economic and moral desert and discuss the merits and, most importantly, demerits of the resulting non-moralising conception of economic desert. Finally, we sketch a moralising version of economic desert that is consistent with the findings of previous sections. We find that our version of moralised economic desert can accommodate parts of the public outcry that has been directed towards the executive remuneration practices of Wall Street. With that said, much is left to discuss when it comes to economic desert, and we hope to indicate some ways to progress this discussion with this chapter.

What Is Desert?

There is a wide range of cases in which we make judgements that someone is deserving of a specific treatment or good due to her actions or attributes.[1] Perhaps the most central example, which is typically called moral desert, is when we hold that people deserve to be praised or blamed for their morally virtuous or vicious actions. The related notion of retributive desert concerns cases in which people deserve punishment for breaking the law or for acting immorally. There is also what we can call the desert of merit, in which we say that people deserve high grades, accolades, or prizes for being an excellent student, a brave soldier, or the fastest sprinter. Compensatory desert has to do with cases in which we say that someone is deserving of compensation or rectification for being exposed to a third-party harm—for example, innocent crime victims and people who contract fatal diseases. Lastly, we have the notion of distributive desert, which we can divide into two sub-categories. Firstly, there is the desert of social goods such as welfare benefits, scholarships, and tax benefits. Here it is usually citizens of a state who are the recipients and the state or an organisation that is the distributor. Secondly, there is economic desert, which is our main concern here, in which it is the employers' responsibility to reward their employees for their effort and contribution. The goods considered when it comes to economic desert typically include wages, bonuses, and other work-related incomes (e.g., stock options and restricted stock programmes).

It is an interesting question whether there really is something that unites all of these judgements. In other words, is there a universal sense in which people can be said to deserve things, or is the relation amongst the different kinds of desert more akin to family resemblance? Let us see what can be said for a unified concept of desert.

A common attempt at analysing desert is to regard it as a three-place relation between a person, the grounds on which he or she is said to be deserving (the desert basis), and the treatment or good he or she is said to deserve. Put more formally: X deserves Y on the basis of Z (see Feldman & Skow, 2016; McLeod, 1996; Olsaretti, 2004). It is clear that all of these examples fit into this schema, with simply different things counting as Y and Z: It can be praise for virtue, punishment for wrongdoing, or economic output for input. However, the schema is obviously quite vague, and it may be noted that it is also consistent with many alternative, non-desert-based principles of distribution. For example, entitlement- and rights-based accounts fit this description as well even if the 'desert basis' might differ in these cases—for example, you might have a right to your fair share of social goods on the basis of being a citizen of a state.

According to several authors, an additional criterion of desert is what we may call the responsibility requirement, which states that for X to deserve Y on the basis of Z, X also has to be responsible for Z (see Miller, 1999; Moriarty, 2002; Olsaretti, 2004; Rachels, 1978; Sadurski, 1985). The basic motivation here is that desert must stem from actions or attributes that are properly *yours*; you cannot deserve something on the basis of an action or attribute over which you had no control. For example, it seems wrong to praise a person for a good character trait that is simply innate and does not flow from his or her own volition. Similarly, it is inconsistent with retributive desert to punish people for crimes that they are not responsible for committing. An exception here seems to be compensatory desert, which holds that victims can deserve compensation simply because they were harmed by crimes that they were not responsible for bringing about (Feldman, 1995). But one may understand this example along the lines of a reversed appeal to responsibility: If X experiences Q on the basis of some Z for which they were *not* responsible, they may deserve Y as a compensation for Q.

Some classic and sweeping criticisms of the concept of desert are due exactly to this connection to the responsibility requirement. For example, philosophers who are critical of free will argue that there are in fact no actions or attributes that are properly *yours* in the sense described here, so the concept of desert is a non-starter (see Arneson, 2003; Strawson, 1994). A similar point is made by John Rawls in his well-known argument against desert: Because so much of the basis for our actions and attributes depends on the 'natural lottery' of genes and upbringing, it is difficult to see how the concept of desert can get much traction (Rawls, 1971). We obviously cannot address these criticisms in any depth at this juncture. To proceed, we will simply assume that there is a broad enough set of cases in which the concept of desert has the relevant traction. As noted by

Serena Olsaretti, this amounts to assuming that certain fair background conditions are in place:

> [T]he defensible principle of desert is one which does not make the magnitude of people's unequal desert depend on unchosen, and unequally distributed, factors. People may then deserve more or less than others on the basis of the choices they make or the effort they exert, given certain fair background conditions that enable them to make free or voluntary choices, including the choice to exert more or less effort than others. When these background conditions are in place, people have a fair opportunity to acquire deserts, and their becoming more or less deserving than others is just.
>
> (Olsaretti, 2004, p. 28)

In addition to the responsibility requirement, we think that another condition is important to capture the essence of desert. According to the proportionality requirement, the aim of desert claims is to maintain (create or restore) balance or proportionality between people's actions and attributes (Z) and the relevant outcomes or responses (Y). Put formally, we should add to our analysis that X deserves Y on the basis of, *and in direction proportion to*, Z. For example, retributive desert holds that punishment should be proportional to the committed crime or wrongdoing. In a similar manner, the desert of merits builds on an idea of proportionality between a person's excellence or achievement and the reward that he or she deserves. This is perhaps an obvious, but nevertheless important, point that helps further distinguish desert claims from other kinds of claims.

The proportionality requirement is the source of another oft-debated problem for desert theorists, namely, how to compare the value or gravity of an action (Z) with the value of an outcome or response (Y). For retributive desert, this is often called the 'anchoring' or 'baseline' problem: how to turn the gravity of a given wrongdoing into a proportional punishment—say, for example, a proportional number of years in prison (Walen, 2016). We will see how economic desert faces a similar challenge.

Put together, then, our analysis of the concept of desert (the general schema plus the responsibility and proportionality requirements) amounts to the following: A desert claim is a claim to the effect that a certain person (X) ought to get a certain outcome or response (Y) on the basis of, and in direct proportion to, a certain action or attribute for which he or she was responsible (Z). We think that this analysis covers the majority of desert claims that people make (although there may still be exceptions and counterexamples). However, whether this counts as a *unified* concept of desert obviously depends on more factors, such as whether there are further large and important variations *within* this class of desert claims, for example, between economic and moral desert. It is to this matter that we now turn.

Economic Versus Moral Desert

It has become commonplace in the philosophical literature to analyse economic desert by contrasting it with moral desert. Rather than seeking a unified concept of desert, the literature has focused on purported dissimilarities amongst different desert claims. As Ryan Jenkins puts it, rather than 'erring on the side of parsimony by hoping to account for the desert of different goods within a single theory', we do better to 'focus on desert in wages itself rather than trying to provide an account that captures wages, punishment, and other goods that are seemingly unrelated' (Jenkins, 2011, p. 80).

Judging from the literature, there are three main purported differences between moral and economic desert. Firstly, it is argued that moral desert is concerned with final values, whereas economic desert concerns only instrumental values. Secondly, it is argued that moral desert is essentially non-comparative, whereas economic desert is essentially comparative. Thirdly, it is argued that moral desert is pre-institutional, whereas economic desert is institutional. In this section we will introduce and discuss these purported differences as well as the resulting 'non-moralising' conception of economic desert.

Final Versus Instrumental

A first purported difference between economic and moral desert concerns characteristics of the relevant 'currencies' of the desert claims, that is, the Ys and Zs in the formula presented here. As noted at the outset, moral desert holds that people who perform morally good actions deserve to be rewarded, and virtuous persons deserve praise, pleasure, or happiness (see Hurka, 2003, p. 58; Kagan, 2012, p. 6; Olsaretti, 2004, p. 15). We may say that moral desert is about deserving outcomes or goods of *final value*, such as wellbeing and happiness, on the basis of input or actions of *final value*, such as generosity or sincerity. The relevant distinction is between final and instrumental values, which can be defined as follows:

> *Final value*: A good is of final value if it is valuable 'in itself' 'for its own sake' or 'in its own right'.
> *Instrumental value*: A good is of instrumental value if it is valuable for something other than itself—for leading up to, reaching, or otherwise involving a good of final value.

Turning to economic desert, we have already established that the relevant outputs are taken to be wages, bonuses, and other work-related incomes. With regard to the relevant inputs or desert bases, there are two main ideas. One idea is that workers' income is a reward for their positive contribution to a collective enterprise. That is, the income should be proportionate to workers' production of goods and services or to the profit they generate for the firm (cf. Galston, 1980; Kershnar, 2005; Miller, 1999; Sternberg, 2000). The other idea is that wages and bonuses are compensation for workers' negative efforts and sacrifices. That is, the income should be proportionate to what workers have (had) to endure in or for the job, including its level of seriousness and risk (cf. Feinberg, 1970; Sadurski, 1985; Soltan, 1987). It is also possible to hold a mixed view that combines attention to both contribution and effort (cf. Hurka, 2003; McLeod, 1996; Wolff, 2003).

In comparison with the final values of moral desert, the 'currency' of economic desert may seem more mundane or instrumental. This is at least the position of Thomas Hurka, who is perhaps the strongest advocate for a non-moralising understanding of economic desert. More specifically, Hurka's claim is that moral desert concerns final (or intrinsic) values, whereas economic desert concerns only instrumental ones. The argument has two parts: one concerning the desert basis (Z), the other concerning what is deserved (Y). With regard to the first part, the point is that no moral assessment is necessary of the desert basis: 'If a person contributes to others or does unpleasant work, it does not matter if his motive is an altruistic desire to benefit others or greed for a higher income; so long as he does those things, he deserves income for them' (Hurka, 2003, p. 58). However, this reasoning seems to overlook the issue of how to understand properly the relationship between instrumental and final values.

Our proposition is that it makes little sense to talk about instrumental values without some background assumption about their relationship to final ones. This means that for someone's effort or contribution to have positive instrumental value, he or she must be linked (at least indirectly or on most occasions) to work that ultimately contains, expresses, or produces positive final value. To illustrate this point, we can ask ourselves whether there can be a link to a positive final value in any kind of work task. For example, what about meaningless jobs, such as counting blades of grass? And what about obviously evil tasks and harmful activities, such as inflicting pain on others? Proponents of non-moralising economic desert may perhaps say that as long as there are enough people willing to pay for such services, people counting blades of grass or inflicting pain deserve to get paid the market price for their jobs. But in our view, this waters down the concept of desert to a level of pointlessness.

Perhaps it is better to invoke actual cases in this context. According to one narrative, the GFC was in part caused by executive compensation packages that incentivised excessive risk taking (Kolb, 2012; Moriarty, 2018). This risk taking resulted in financial meltdown, costing countless people their jobs, savings, and homes. The executives, on the other hand, got out of the crisis relatively well-off, even in cases in which their own firms behaved poorly. Bear Stearns was sold to JP Morgan Chase for $10 per share, which is quite a steep fall from the firm's pre-crisis 52-week high of \$133 per share. Lehman Brothers went bankrupt in the midst of the GFC. Despite this, it has been estimated that executives of these firms derived cash flows of about \$1.4 billion (Bear Stearns) and \$1 billion (Lehman) from cash bonuses and equity sales during 2000–2008 (Bebchuk et al., 2010). These executives, then, profited from the system of performance-based compensation that can be seen as one of the cornerstones of the GFC.

As noted at the outset, there has been much public outcry about this situation. At least amongst commentators outside of the financial industry, there seems to be a consensus that the executives' bonuses were undeserved. This reaction can be explained by our proposition that economic desert cannot be completely divorced from questions about final value. More specifically, it seems inconsistent with desert to reward someone for work that is both reckless and causes serious harm to innocent third parties. A similar point has been made by Jenkins:

> This criterion is most controversial and most difficult to elaborate, but it also flows naturally from an investigation of desert and wages. Desert is an appraising attitude, whereby we take a moral stance toward some action. We ought not give wages for pointless actions nor harmful ones. The former are undeserving actions, the latter are deserving of resentment, not a wage.
>
> (Jenkins, 2011, p. 84)

There are of course some that do not share this reaction. They may argue that the financial executives were not morally deserving due to their reckless behaviour but nevertheless economically deserving on the basis of having performed a job that they were contracted to perform. But our view is that this argument is flawed and ultimately rests on concerns that are separate from desert. The reader should take special notice of how the argument focuses on a general procedure (of respecting contracts) more than the balancing between inputs and outputs. It seems like a plausible principle that people who have been contracted to do a certain job for a certain pay should not be disrespected or deceived—that is, they have a legitimate claim to the pay that they were promised by their employer. But this is something quite separate from desert (we will return to this argument).

Our proposition does not concern only the desert basis (Z) but also what is deserved (Y). Hurka writes: '[W]hat he deserves on the basis of his contribution or effort is only income and not happiness; if he does not derive joy from his earnings, that is no concern of economic desert'. Although it seems correct that employees need not derive joy from their wages directly, we once again think than the instrumental value of the wage needs at least some connection to the final value of happiness. To see this, consider the more fantastical example of a society that is dominated by a communist disdain for inequality. In this society it leads to social stigma and hardship to earn a higher-than-average wage. Should we say that Diligent Derek—who always comes first to work, puts the most effort into his job, and therefore also contributes the most to his firm—deserves a higher-than-average wage in this society? Because such a wage would cause Diligent Derek more hardship than enjoyment, it seems that this is not what he deserves.

A hardcore critic may here argue that the communist disdain for inequality in our example is morally unjustified, and therefore it is wrong to base our conclusion about Derek's deserts on it. However, we take it that a plausible account of economic desert should be able to give the right answer even in situations that are suboptimal in various ways. Therefore, we think that this counterargument misses its mark and does not dispute our central point.

Judging from these considerations, it seems that the non-moralising conception of economic desert is far from intuitive. We will return to the issue of the proper connection between wages (or instrumental value) and happiness (or final value) in the next main section.

Non-Comparative Versus Comparative

A second purported difference between moral and economic desert concerns how one derives what is deserved (Y) from the desert basis (Z) in terms of these values. The key question is whether we can determine someone's level of desert based on the intrinsic quality of actions alone or if we need to compare said person's actions with others' actions to make a desert judgement. The former seems possible with moral desert: Joe dedicates his life to help out other people, and he therefore deserves to be happy and prosperous, irrespective of how helpful or happy other people are. Josephine saved a life, and she is therefore deserving of significant praise, irrespective of whether other people also save lives or receive various amounts of praise. Simply put, we are able to determine what Joe and Josephine deserve based on the intrinsic quality of their actions, regardless of what others did or did not do. It is because of this feature that moral desert is essentially non-comparative in nature. Shelley Kagan defines non-comparative desert as follows:

> Non-comparative desert: For any given individual, to determine the intrinsic value of her being at a given level of well-being I need only consider her individual desert line. By determining whether she has more or less than she absolutely deserves [. . .] I learn whether I can make the situation better or worse from the point of view of desert by changing her level of well-being. But I do not need to consider what other people deserve, or how well off they may be; information about the given individual alone is sufficient.

(2012, p. 349)

The centrality of non-comparative moral desert should not be taken to rule out the possibility or relevance of comparative considerations in the same realm. For example, suppose that Bob and Billy are equally deserving, but Billy is getting more than he deserves from a non-comparative perspective. Suppose further that we are able only to change the welfare of Bob. Should we, then, improve Bob's situation so that he will also get more than he deserves? Most people will accept some pull towards improving Bob's situation, which indicates that moral desert also has a comparative component. Kagan describes comparative desert as follows:

> Comparative desert: When I am as virtuous as you, then I should be doing as well as you, no matter how well you are doing. If I am not, then there is something to be said in favour of improving my lot to bring me up to where you are—regardless of where you are. That is the claim of comparative desert. It is an essentially *comparative* claim, since it is concerned essentially with comparing our levels of well-being—in light of how (non-comparatively) deserving we are.
>
> (2012, p. 350)

Turning to economic desert, it has been argued that this is an essentially comparative phenomenon and that non-comparative desert claims make little sense (Miller, 2003). We might say that with an increased level of effort, there should also be an increased level of income, but is there any intelligible way to set the absolute values of pay levels that is not arbitrary? For example, what is an hour's or a day's work worth in economic terms from the perspective of non-comparative desert? It seems as if the only viable way of answering this (and thereby to fulfil the proportionality requirement of desert) is to consider an employee's effort and contribution *in comparison to the work of others*. For example, the structure could be that those employees who make the least effort or contribute the least compared to others (in a given company or organisation) deserve the lowest income, whereas those who make the greatest effort or contribute the most deserve the highest income.

An alternative idea could be to base the value of work on market prices. Although this initially seems like a non-comparative alternative, actually it is not. David Miller demonstrates this by taking the example of market fluctuations. More specifically, he asks us to imagine a case in which a large number of manufacturers simultaneously engage in the production of pocket calculators:

> The product is oversupplied at the prevailing price, and the price falls until eventually a new equilibrium is reached—perhaps restoring the original price, perhaps not. What of the position of Smith, who has been making calculators all along? His income falls, but how have his deserts lessened? The answer is that they *do* lessen when the

supply of calculators increases. If desert is based on value created, that value cannot be estimated without taking account of what others have produced; the notion that the service you render has the same value regardless of what others do is absurd.

(1989, p. 166)

Value should here be understood as market (or equilibrium) price, meaning that we measure desert by 'the value of the resources each person creates, the standard of value we invoke is value in general, not the particular, unique value that an item has for any given customer' (Miller, 1989, p. 164). Because the market price takes into account the actions of a large group of market participants, it seems that economic desert has a strong comparative component also on this view.

But is this conception of economic desert plausible? It is important to see how Miller is making a very controversial claim in this example. We believe that most people would argue that Smith does *not* deserve less simply because the market for pocket calculators becomes saturated. This is one of the reasons why modern societies tend to complement markets with regulations such as wage control and welfare functions such as income insurance. How can we explain this intuition? It seems that we already have access to a robust theoretical answer: According to the responsibility requirement of desert, as noted, the basis of desert must be something that is within one's control. But the increase in pocket calculators on the market was precisely an event outside of Smith's control. There is therefore something problematic with a conception of desert that ultimately appeals to market sentiments.

Our argument here is the same as before, namely, that economic desert cannot be fully divorced from moral concerns. More specifically, morality tells us that someone who in good faith puts in many hours to produce a good that under normal circumstances is socially useful (although its exact usefulness can change with market conditions) does not deserve a sudden and drastic pay cut. Put formally, if our moral assessment of the desert basis (Z) stays the same, it seems inconsistent with desert that what is deserved (Y) should vary enormously. This may be thought of as a non-comparative, or at least market-independent, background to economic desert.

There is also another non-comparative concern to take into account. To bring this to the fore, consider how some people argue that all workers deserve at least a 'living wage'. One interpretation of this is the claim that 'anyone who works for the standard number of hours at a job that is socially useful, and so contributes at least a minimum amount to the social product, should get in return a wage that covers the basic necessities of life' (Miller, 2003, p. 37). We obviously cannot analyse the merits and demerits of this claim in any detail here, but what is interesting for our purposes is its salient non-comparative character. Put formally, the argument seems to hold that as long as a worker's effort or contribution (Z) is at a decent level, he or she also deserves decent pay (Y).

The considerations here indicate that economic desert, just like moral desert, is best understood as a combination of non-comparative and comparative elements. There is a moral dimension lurking in the background that sometimes makes non-comparative desert claims. However, to translate this into actual monetary amounts will certainly require comparisons amongst different workers and different jobs. Moreover, we cannot get around the fact that economic desert claims ultimately are claims on scarce resources, which makes the comparative dimension central. An employee deserves a slice of the cake, and to know how large that slice should be, we need not only know how large the cake is; we also need to know how the employee's performance stands in relation to his or her co-workers' performances so that everyone's slice is proportional to the available cake. In the end, then, a moralising conception of economic desert also has problems with finding a baseline or anchor for economic desert claims. We will return to this issue in the next main section.

Pre-Institutional Versus Institutional

A third and final purported difference between moral and economic desert concerns their relationship to social institutions.[2] It is typically thought that moral desert is a pre-institutional phenomenon or, as Joel Feinberg puts it, a 'natural' notion—'one which is not logically tied to institutions, practices, and rules' (Feinberg, 1970, p. 56). The distinction between institutional and pre-institutional desert can be defined as follows:

> *Institutional Desert*: Desert is an institutional principle if its demands are wholly determined by the rules and purposes of the institutions within which desert claims arise.
> (Olsaretti, 2004, p. 16)

> *Pre-institutional Desert*: Desert is a pre-institutional notion if its demands are not wholly reducible to those created by the rules and purposes of the institutions within which desert claims arise.
> (Olsaretti, 2004, p. 17)

To illustrate this distinction further, we can compare moral desert to entitlement (where we can understand entitlement more as a sociological or empirical concept, giving rise to rights and not desert). Consider a case of two grandchildren who are anticipating an inheritance when their grandfather passes away.[3] One of the grandchildren is virtuous and poor; the other is vicious and rich. The poor grandchild has always taken care of his grandfather, whereas the rich grandchild never put any effort into caring for his grandfather. Suppose that the grandfather decides to leave his fortune to the rich and nasty grandchild. We will now say that the rich grandchild is entitled to the fortune due to the legality of inheritance, but he does not deserve it because he is simply not a good person. The opposite applies to the poor grandchild. He is not entitled to the inheritance, but we would like to say that he deserves it due to his blameless set of virtues.

To say that moral desert is pre-institutional, then, means that it does not flow from the content of certain social institutions; instead it is the other way around—we typically want our social institutions to track moral desert.

Turning to economic desert, some authors argue that the connection to social institutions is much stronger here. For example, a first observation is that the very currency of economic desert (economic input and output) seems to require the existence of social institutions. Owen McLeod writes:

> Consider some typical *objects* of desert [. . .] grades, monetary awards, championships, promotions, and so on. Each of these seems to be an artifact of some social institution. Next, consider some typical *bases* for desert [. . .] excelling on a physics exam, winning the Boston Marathon, closing the big deal with Microsoft, engaging in Medicare fraud or insider trading, and so on. None of these could exist without social institutions.
>
> (1999, p. 187)

The argument is that economic goods cannot exist without there being some institutions around. However, this is a weak argument because we must distinguish between desert and its realisation. Consider cases of the desert of merits; such as the fastest runner, the student who scored highest on the test, or the hockey team who scored the most goals. We could say that these people cannot be deserving of recognition and accolades outside of an institutional setting. However, there is an underlying normative judgement here that has little to do with institutions, namely, that *excellence* should be recognised and awarded. What binds all these people together is that they demonstrate excellence in one way or another. Now, it seems obvious that outside of an institutional setting, these people cannot get what they deserve. But this is consistent with saying that people who display excellence outside of an institutional setting can be deserving, whereas their desert is realised only when the proper institutions are in place (see Lamont, 1994).

A stronger argument in this context would be to say that there is no similar pre-institutional principle that economic desert seeks to track. This argument could be backed up by the observation that economic desert is strongly tied to our current capitalist economic system. Consider Scott Arnold's defence of profits for entrepreneurs. Arnold argues that the desert basis of an institution, such as the market, is logically tied to the goal or the purpose of said institution. The market, according to Arnold, is 'a production-distribution system which allocates, via voluntary exchange, (rights over) scarce goods and resources' (Arnold, 1987, p. 396). The purpose of the market is to meet the wants and needs of the consumers who can be satisfied by scarce and exchangeable goods and services. Entrepreneurs promote this goal and unveil misallocations of resources by exploiting the many profit opportunities that can be found in a complex market economy. The relevant desert basis for entrepreneurs who act in the market, then, is the alertness to a suboptimal allocation of resources.

This institutional account of economic desert is quite elegant but becomes rather implausible as a justification for what goes on in the market if markets themselves lack moral justification. Even Arnold recognises this problem, holding that institutional desert claims are not justified at this fundamental level, but he nevertheless chooses to ignore the importance of this issue (Arnold, 1987, p. 394). This should not, however, be overlooked as it is a central task for market proponents who seek to claim the moral high ground for market outcomes.

In addition to this, we have two main objections to an institutional account of economic desert. The first objection concerns limitations of relevant institutions. If economic desert is truly institutional, then there should be very few limitations to the possible content of the underlying institutions or principles. That is, instead of having the sort of capitalist system and therefore desert bases that we now have, it should be (at least theoretically) possible to have a radically different economic system and therefore very different bases for economic desert. However, when pondering some possible alternative desert bases, this implication is difficult to uphold.

To see this, consider some institutions that fly in the face of the very concept of desert: At Leisure Inc., employees are paid to do as little work as possible; in fact the less work they do, the higher their income. At Random Inc., employees are paid to draw a random number from a hat (once per month); the higher number they draw, the higher their income. Let's say that our Diligent Derek takes up employment at these companies. Does it make sense to say that Derek deserves very little income from Leisure Inc., because he simply does too much work? And does it make sense to say that his work at Random Inc. makes him deserving of a wage that is proportional to the number that he happens to draw from the hat? If either of these things make little sense, then economic desert cannot be fully institutional.

The second objection concerns what kind of explanatory value there is to institutional economic desert. If one's income is due to the details of some background principle or institution, then what is really added by saying that one *deserves* that income? Consider the example of financial executives again. There does not seem to be any added value to the explanation in saying that financial executives *deserve* to be paid for performing the job that they were contracted to do. Rather, it seems as if this interpretation more or less hijacks the concept of desert to have a stamp of normative approval for whatever financial firms hire their employees to do. As noted, we believe it is important to distinguish desert from other concerns that seem relevant with regard to justice in wages. One such concern is the duty to respect the contract between employer and employee, which obviously is an institutional artefact. But nothing is added by also saying that contracts make employees *deserving* of their contracted wage.[4]

Another way to put this point is to say that institutional economic desert comes closer to entitlement rather than desert. As Feinberg notes, entitlement is qualification tied to an institutional rule, where anyone who satisfies said rule can claim the good provided by the institution as his or her right (Feinberg, 1970, p. 57). But in our view, economic desert is something different than mere qualification, and in the next section we will take a closer look at what a moralising economic desert looks like.

In Defence of Moralising Economic Desert

Our argumentation to this point indicates that the non-moralising conception of economic desert is untenable, and we instead favour a moralising version of it. This section will sketch a possible version of moralising economic desert based on two main objections that are usually directed towards such ventures.

A first point of discussion concerns the proper relationship between wages, or instrumental value, and virtue, or final value. Many authors have pointed out the absurdity of moralising economic desert by stating that it is morally repugnant to pay people for acting virtuously (see Olsaretti, 2004; Miller, 1999). Surely it would be silly to abstain from praise and instead simply pay the person who saves a dozen out of a train wreck or to give a hefty bonus to an employee for acting kindly towards his or her colleagues. Feinberg puts this point so eloquently: 'Economic benefits seem to be a highly inappropriate vehicle of recognition partly because they tend to render the recipient suspect and to tarnish the disinterested altruism essential to moral worth' (Feinberg, 1970, p. 91). As far as the argument goes, then, morality should not be taken into consideration when it comes to economic desert.

However, this criticism misses its target when it comes to the conception of economic desert that we defend. A moralising version of economic desert need not imply that virtuous people should be paid. There is a distinction to be made between basing income solely on moral considerations and taking moral considerations into account when determining economic deserts. More specifically, we propose a distinction between *foreground* and *background* conditions of economic desert. The foreground condition is the one outlined, namely, that economic inputs (effort and contribution) should be rewarded or compensated with economic outputs (wages and bonuses). Claims about economic desert should most directly be analysed as claims about the proper balance between these two elements. However, there is also a background relationship to considerations of moral desert that involve elements that have final value. Plausible claims about economic desert must also have an indirect connection to this background condition or at least not be inconsistent with strong intuitions of moral desert.

Our view implies that the only relevant desert bases for economic desert are the economic inputs of effort and contribution. Therefore, we are able to block the conclusion that virtuous people deserve economic benefits. At the same time, we have argued that the instrumental values of effort and contribution must have some link to background final values. For example, one cannot be economically deserving for doing meaningless work, such as counting blades of grass or performing work that is harmful to others. There are different ways of spelling out this background moral condition, depending on one's choice of moral theory. For example, one version is consequentialist or outcome-based. The requirement would then be that one's work is causally connected (at least in typical cases, or on the whole) to the welfare of society in a broad sense. For example, it seems plausible to reward workers for manufacturing products or providing services that satisfy people's needs (or wants) but not for activities that are harmful or hurtful. An alternative version could appeal to virtue. The requirement would then be that one's effort or contribution flow from a virtuous character or, perhaps better, are consistent with the choices that a virtuous worker would have made. Finally, there could also be a deontological version. This view would roughly say that there are certain kinds of work that are consistent with duty, or even mandatory, whereas other kinds are strictly forbidden.

To put our point differently, there are two necessary conditions for economic desert: (i) One has to put in effort and contribute at work, and (ii) one's effort and contribution must have some connection to final value. Both (i) and (ii) are necessary but not sufficient on their own. It is not enough to go to work and do nothing, even if one's job is one that a virtuous person would hold. At the same time, it does not matter how much effort one puts in or how large one's contribution is if one's work lacks a connection to a final value. This is akin to McLeod's idea about *prima facie* economic desert: 'It is the claim that, other things equal, those who work hard deserve success. If other things are not "equal"—for example, if the hard work is directed towards some evil end—then the *prima facie* desert generated by the hard work is outweighed' (McLeod, 1999, p. 193).

A second point of discussion is how to match pay levels (Y) to desert levels (Z). This is a challenge for moralising conceptions of economic desert because they hold, as we have argued, that one's desert does not necessarily correspond to one's market value. The problem is especially relevant when it comes to questions of whether some professionals are overpaid, as Jeffrey Moriarty (2005a) has pointed out:

> [S]uppose contribution is the basis of desert, and suppose the firm's profits increase 20 percent in a year. We might think the CEO deserves a 20 percent raise. But what should his initial salary have been? Without a way of matching desert levels to pay levels, we have no way of answering this question [. . .] if we cannot map desert-creating behavior onto pay, we cannot say for sure exactly how much CEOs deserve to be paid.
>
> (p. 263)

The common response to the CEO case is to say that regardless of what we hold to be the most relevant desert base when it comes to economic desert, American CEOs cannot be 361 times more deserving than the average rank-and-file workers in the United States (AFL-CIO, 2018). But even if the wage gap is unjustified, in the absence of an 'anchor', it is not possible to tell whether the CEOs are overpaid, adequately paid, or even underpaid in absolute terms. This means that we are back to the idea that economic desert is strongly comparative in nature, which makes it difficult to connect to more definite moral conclusions.

Once again, we think that our combination of economic and moral elements can make some headway in this regard. Whereas economic desert most directly concerns the balance between economic inputs and outputs, there is also a background connection to considerations of moral desert. What is helpful about this is that we may be able to import some non-comparative elements from moral desert. Once again, consider the saying that all workers deserve at least a 'living wage'. We analysed this argument as the claim that as long as a worker's effort or contribution (Z) is at a decent level, he or she also deserves a decent pay (Y). This notion of a living wage or decent pay seems to be a non-comparative baseline that can give at least some further guidance on appropriate connections between pay levels and desert levels.

In the end, however, we must acknowledge that the anchoring problem is a significant challenge for our view as well, at least in practical terms. This is so because translating deserts into actual monetary amounts will require a broad range of comparisons, not only amongst different workers and jobs (to measure the input Z) but also to the costs of products and services (to determine the appropriate income Y). Moriarty (2005b), contrasting distributive justice with retributive justice by recognising that the supply of social benefits is scarce, writes: 'Provided that we do not want to let any go to waste, there are fewer places to anchor to benefit scale. In the case of social benefits, then, the crucial question will be who is more or most deserving of them, not whether someone deserves them absolutely' (p. 220). We do not expect ours to be the final words on the anchoring problem in economic desert, but we nevertheless hope that we have indicated some paths forward.

Concluding Remarks

This chapter has sought to develop a more exact understanding of the concept of economic desert, that is, the idea that employees deserve wages and bonuses on the basis of their effort or contribution. There is an attractiveness and intuitive appeal to the concept of desert in the sense that it purportedly spells out simple conditions under which you are morally justified to the fruits of your labour. This is perhaps why it is frequently embraced by both market proponents and market critics. However, any philosophers, political scientists, or economists who dig deeper into the matter will find that desert is a very complex and multifaceted concept that requires serious and delicate consideration. We have not been able to address all aspects related to economic desert in this short chapter, but we hope that we at least have made some good headway on some of the important themes.

With regards to the GFC, there are two important conclusions to take away from this chapter. Firstly, we started off by asking whether the concept of economic desert could be used to justify the pre-crisis remuneration practices of Wall Street. This seems possible if economic desert is something entirely instrumental, comparative, and institutional. However, we noted several major problems for non-moralising conceptions of economic desert—most importantly, that it seems both inconsistent and counterintuitive to completely divorce economic from moral desert. Secondly, the public outcry that followed the crisis consisted of a plethora of intuitions directed towards performance-based pay practices. We argued that our moralising conception of economic desert can help explain and justify these intuitions. Most importantly, the executives of Bear Stearns and Lehman Brothers acted in complete disregard for the moral background conditions of economic desert, namely, that the instrumental value of work must be connected to some final value such as virtue or the public good.

Acknowledgements

We are very grateful to Chris Cowton, Tom Sorell, Huub Brouwer, Bengt Brülde, Richard Endörfer, Jasmine Elliot, Clément Fontan, Nina van Heeswijk, David Rönnegard, and Adrian Walsh for their comments on earlier drafts of this chapter. Our research has been made possible by financial support from the University of Gothenburg, the Knut and Alice Wallenberg Foundation, and the Swedish Foundation for Strategic Environmental Research (Mistra).

Notes

1. We will draw on Miller's (1999, p. 137) distinction between primary desert judgements and secondary desert judgements. Primary desert judgements are judgements concerning the actions and performance of agents. Secondary desert judgements concern the personal qualities and abilities of agents. Secondary desert judgements are parasitic on primary desert judgements '[D]eriving their moral force from others that are primary. Roughly speaking, when we say that a person deserves some benefit on the basis of a quality, we are anticipating a future performance in which that quality is displayed'.
2. By 'social institutions' we follow Arnold in saying that it is a social activity that is governed by rules and that has, as part of its purpose, the distribution of certain benefits and/or costs (Arnold, 1987, p. 390).
3. We borrow this example from Feldman and Skow (2016).
4. Olsaretti (2004) sums up the problem of institutional desert claims eloquently: 'Defences of market rewards that appeal to these ecumenical conceptions of desert—to conceptions of desert on which there are very few limits, if any, on what can count as desert—are easily and commonly formulated, and seem to reach their target without difficulty, but do so at a serious cost. They may coherently affirm that free market rewards are deserved, but the principle of desert in question is not one which confers justification. Rewards could be "deserved" in some sense, but it does not follow that they are *just insofar as they are deserved*, since the principle of desert in question is either parasitic on another, independently defined principle of justice, or purely institutional, and therefore is incapable of justifying the institutions themselves' (p. 24).

References

Admati, A., & Hellwig, M. (2013). *The bankers' new clothes: What's wrong with banking and what to do about it*. Princeton, NJ: Princeton University Press.

AFL-CIO. (2018). *Executive paywatch*. https://aflcio.org/paywatch

Arneson, R. J. (2003). The smart theory of moral responsibility and desert. In S. Olsaretti (Ed.), *Desert and justice* (pp. 233–258). Oxford: Oxford University Press.

Arnold, N. S. (1987). Why profits are deserved. *Ethics*, 97(2), 387–402.

Bebchuk, L. A., Cohen, A., & Spamann, H. (2010). The wages of failure: Executive compensation at Bear Stearns and Lehman 2000–2008. *Yale Journal on Regulation*, 27(2), 257–282.

de Bruin, B. (2015). *Ethics and the global financial crisis: Why incompetence is worse than greed*. Cambridge: Cambridge University Press.

Feinberg, J. (1970). Justice and personal desert. In J. Feinberg (Ed.), *Doing and deserving* (pp. 55–94). Princeton, NJ: Princeton University Press.

Feldman, F. (1995). Desert: Reconsideration of some received wisdom. *Mind*, 104(413), 63–77.

Feldman, F., & Skow, B. (2016). Desert. In E. N. Zalta (Ed.), *Stanford encyclopedia of philosophy* (Winter 2016 ed.). https://plato.stanford.edu/entries/desert/

Freiman, C., & Nichols, S. (2011). Is desert in the details? *Philosophy and Phenomenological Research*, 82(1), 121–133.

Galston, W. (1980). *Justice and the human good*. Chicago, IL: University of Chicago Press.

Goya-Tocchetto, D., Echols, M., & Wright, J. (2016). The lottery of life and moral desert: An empirical investigation. *Philosophical Psychology, 29*(8), 1112–1127.

Hurka, T. (2003). Desert: Individualistic and holistic. In S. Olsaretti (Ed.), *Desert and justice* (pp. 45–68). Oxford: Oxford University Press.

Jenkins, R. (2011). You've earned it! A criticism of Sher's account of desert in wages. *Social Philosophy Today, 27*, 75–86.

Kagan, S. (2012). *The geometry of desert.* Oxford: Oxford University Press.

Kershnar, S. (2005). Giving capitalists their due. *Economics and Philosophy, 21*(1), 65–87.

Kolb, R. W. (2012). *Too much is not enough: Incentives in executive compensation.* New York: Oxford University Press.

Lamont, J. (1994). The concept of desert in distributive justice. *Philosophical Quarterly, 44*(174), 45–64.

Lanchester, J. (2010). *I.O.U.: Why everyone owes everyone and no one can pay.* New York: Simon & Schuster.

Mankiw, G. N. (2013). Defending the one percent. *Journal of Economic Perspectives, 27*(3), 21–34.

McLeod, O. (1996). Desert and wages. *Utilitas, 8*(2), 205–222.

McLeod, O. (1999). Desert and institutions. In L. P. Pojman & O. McLeod (Eds.), *What do we deserve?* (pp. 186–195). Oxford: Oxford University Press.

Miller, D. (1989). *Market, state and community: Theoretical foundations of market socialism.* Oxford: Clarendon Press.

Miller, D. (1992). Distributive justice: What the people think. *Ethics, 102*(3), 555–593.

Miller, D. (1999). *Principles of social justice.* Cambridge, MA: Harvard University Press.

Miller, D. (2003). Comparative and noncomparative desert. In S. Olsaretti (Ed.), *Desert and justice* (pp. 25–44). Oxford: Oxford University Press.

Moriarty, J. (2002). Desert and distributive justice in a theory of justice. *Journal of Social Philosophy, 33*(1), 131–143.

Moriarty, J. (2005a). Do CEOs get paid too much? *Business Ethics Quarterly, 15*(2), 257–281.

Moriarty, J. (2005b). The epistemological argument against desert. *Utilitas, 17*(2), 205–221.

Moriarty, J. (2018). Risky pay and the financial crisis: Who's responsible? *Midwest Studies in Philosophy, 42*(1), 156–173.

Olsaretti, S. (2004). *Liberty, desert, and the market: A philosophical study.* New York: Cambridge University Press.

Rachels, J. (1978). What people deserve. In J. Arthur & W. H. Shaw (Eds.), *Justice and economic distribution* (pp. 150–163). Englewood Cliffs, NJ: Prentice-Hall.

Rawls, J. (1971). *A theory of justice.* Cambridge, MA: Harvard University Press.

Sadurski, W. (1985). *Giving desert its due.* Dordrecht: D. Reidel.

Sinn, H.-W. (2010). *Casino capitalism: How the financial crisis came about and what needs to be done now.* Oxford: Oxford University Press.

Soltan, K. E. (1987). *The causal theory of justice.* Berkeley, CA: University of California Press.

Sternberg, E. (2000). *Just business: Business ethics in action* (2nd ed.). New York: Oxford University Press.

Stiglitz, J. (2010). *Freefall.* New York: W. W. Norton.

Strawson, G. (1994). The impossibility of moral responsibility. *Philosophical Studies, 75*(1), 5–24.

Walen, A. (2016). Retributive justice. In E. N. Zalta (Ed.), *The Stanford encyclopedia of philosophy* (Winter 2016 ed.). https://plato.stanford.edu/entries/justice-retributive/

Wolff, J. (2003). The dilemma of desert. In S. Olsaretti (Ed.), *Desert and justice* (pp. 219–232). Oxford: Oxford University Press.

Index

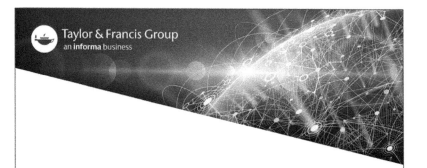

For Product Safety Concerns and Information please contact our EU
representative GPSR@taylorandfrancis.com
Taylor & Francis Verlag GmbH, Kaufingerstraße 24, 80331 München, Germany

www.ingramcontent.com/pod-product-compliance
Ingram Content Group UK Ltd.
Pitfield, Milton Keynes, MK11 3LW, UK
UKHW020944180425
457613UK00019B/510